The Politics of
Child Abuse

THE
POLITICS
OF CHILD
ABUSE

by Paul and Shirley Eberle

LYLE STUART INC.   SECAUCUS, NEW JERSEY

Published by Lyle Stuart, Inc.
120 Enterprise Ave., Secaucus, N.J. 07094
Published simultaneously in Canada by
Musson Book Company,
A division of General Publishing Co. Limited
Don Mills, Ontario

Address queries regarding rights and permissions
to Lyle Stuart, Inc., 120 Enterprise Ave.,
Secaucus, N.J. 07094

Manufactured in the United States of America

Library of Congress Cataloging-in-Publication Data

Eberle, Paul, 1928-
    The politics of child abuse.

    Bibliography: p.
    1.   Child abuse—United States—Case studies.
2.   Child abuse—Law and legislation—United States.
I.   Eberle, Shirley, 1929-   . II.   Title.
HV6626.5.E24   1986   364.1'536   86-14529
ISBN 0-8184-0415-9

Contents

The Politics of
Child Abuse

I

Child Abuse
Goes Public

On a sunny September afternoon, our neighbor's eight-year-old daughter was accosted by a pedophile as she was walking home from school. He pulled his car to the curb, rolled down the window and asked her to touch his penis. He offered her money. The girl laughed, said good bye, went home and told her mother. The next day, her mother met her at the school and walked home with her, and the same car, with the same man in it, was parked at the curb as they passed by. The mother got the license plate number, called the police, and the young man was subsequently arrested.

When the girl's parents brought her to court for the arraignment they were politely told by the police officer that there would be no hearing. The district attorney, he said, would not go forward with a case in which the only witness was an eight-year-old child. He apologized. Most such cases never went to court, he explained, because the courts considered the unsupported testimony of a child unreliable.

That was 1965. In the past two years a multiplicity of widely publicized cases has been sustained entirely on the testimony of child witnesses—many of them less than six years old, telling of events, in some cases, that allegedly occurred when they were only two or three.

"They're taking them younger and younger," a Los Angeles deputy district attorney observed. "In Massachusetts one of the courts installed a little, tiny, child-size witness chair for the kids." In Minnesota a frightened child witness was permitted to testify from under the prosecutor's table. In Los Angeles child witnesses have been videotaped so that the tapes could be shown at the trial.

Until about two years ago stories about sexual molestation of children were not seen in the daily press (editors considered them unsuitable for publication in a respectable, family newspaper) or on television. Now we see accounts of child molestation in newspapers on an almost daily basis with sometimes two or three such stories in a single issue.

Sentences are getting tougher. In the past, persons accused of child molestation were generally able to get the charges reduced to a lesser offense through plea bargaining, and recitation of the correct litany of remorse. That too has changed. Recently, a California man was sentenced to 129 years in state prison for molesting an eleven-year-old girl. Defense attorneys noted that the man could have done less time if he had killed the child. In a recent California case, a woman was sentenced to 405 years, and her co-defendant, a man, also got 405 years. In a 1984 case, Luis Johnson received a term of 527 years.

Child molestation, according to the current literature, has been a well-kept secret. Child victims have been afraid to talk, and the community has been reluctant to listen. Many child abusers have been pillars of the community, men of power and influence, while child witnesses lacked credibility. A number of books have appeared in the past three years, authored by victims and psychologists, telling us that the sexual abuse of children is far more prevalent than most of us suspect, and that most of the victims went through years of adult life without telling anyone.

In a recently published book, *The Assault On Truth*, by Jeffrey M. Masson,* the author, a psychoanalyst, states that Sigmund Freud's theory of the etiology of hysteria postulated that a great deal of mental illness was caused by sexual abuse of children at an early age. In his medical studies in Paris Freud discovered that rape and violent sexual abuse of children was extremely common—

*New York: Farrar Straus and Giroux, 1984.

most of it perpetrated by the victims' fathers or other members of the family, persons in a position to exercise direct authority over the child. Freud stated that the experience "wounded the child in every aspect of his being" because of the imbalance of the relationship, with the adult, "armed with complete authority and the right to punish," imposing his sexual demands on the child who is helpless, prematurely aroused, and terrified by the experience. Freud believed it was one of the major causes of hysteria and other mental illness.

He was not prepared for the reaction of his colleagues. When he read his paper, "The Aetiology of Hysteria," before the Society for Psychiatry and Neurology in Vienna on April 21, 1896, it was received with icy silence, not only by the physicians in the room, but later in the medical journals as well. He was urged never to publish it, and to repudiate it before his reputation was damaged beyond repair. The psychiatrists were not ready to accuse those who paid their fees. Freud's loneliness and ostracism deepened. In 1905 he repudiated the theory.

Jeffrey Masson was fired from his position as Projects Director of the Sigmund Freud Archives in 1981 after suggesting in a lecture that Freud's theory may have been valid after all. "I was challenged," he said, "not on the basis of my evidence but because I had revealed this evidence."

"The time has come," he states, "to cease hiding from what is, after all, one of the great issues of human history."

If it is one of the great issues of human history, it has also been one of the least talked about. What, then, is bringing about the change?

One significant event was the disclosure, on the ABC-Television Five O'Clock News, of the sensational McMartin Pre-School molestation case in southern California in February, 1984. Seven defendants were charged with two hundred nine counts of sexual abuse of forty children. The defendants were teachers at a fashionable, suburban day care center in the town of Manhattan Beach, and authorities said they believed the children were rented out to pedophiles during the day.

What followed was a tidal wave of similar cases reported in newspapers and on television. In Jordan, Minnesota, twenty-four residents, including a police officer and a deputy sheriff, were charged with sexual molestation of forty children amid allegations of bizarre ritual murders of infants.

In Bakersfield, California, seventeen persons were arrested and charged with child molestation. A ten-year-old boy accused his parents, his aunt and uncle, both sets of grandparents, and the therapist, employed by the county, who interviewed him. He also accused a deputy sheriff and a deputy district attorney. Other children told of satanic rituals, cannibalistic murders and drinking of human blood. They said that as many as seventy-seven adults were involved, and as many as twenty-seven infants killed. A number of children were taken from their parents and placed in protective custody in foster homes and institutions, some of them children of parents who had not been charged with any offense.

In California, an Assistant Attorney General was arrested and charged with molesting a nine-year-old girl. A rabbi was charged with child molestation. Both were exonerated. A Catholic priest was sued by the parents of four boys whom he had allegedly molested. The priest had pleaded no contest to three counts of molestation. In New York, a sixty-year-old grandmother was charged with sexually abusing children at a daycare center.

An ultra-conservative Los Angeles City Councilman was accused by his wife of molesting their daughter. The judge concluded that the evidence presented to him during an eight-day hearing substantiated the allegations of abuse by the father, and two physicians concurred. No criminal charges were filed. A high school principal was charged with molesting his students, and a woman who was a special education consultant in San Jose was charged with molesting six teen-age boys.

In Kansas City a respected physician was arrested and charged with "aggravated sodomy" and indecent liberties with a fourteen-year-old girl. He was co-author of a book titled *Child Care for Christian Parents*.

An FBI agent was charged with molesting his eight-year-old son and infant daughter. His trial ended in a hung jury. Three police officers were accused, by parents, of molesting their children.

A deputy district attorney was arrested and charged with sexually abusing his daughter. He was charged with six felonies: two counts of attempted incest and four counts of lewd conduct with a child.

A superintendent of schools was arraigned on seven counts of child molestation. He had served as foreman of the local grand jury.

In Washington, D.C., a woman called Child Protective Services (C.P.S.) and complained that social workers were coming to her apartment and accusing her of abusing her son. The woman who took the call asked her to wait while she checked her files.

"Yes," she said. "I have a complaint that you are abusing your son."

"But my son is fifty-eight years old," she said. "And I'm seventy-seven. And they're going to all my neighbors and asking them if they've seen me molest my son. He's a veteran of World War Two."

In the McMartin case in southern California, a ten-year-old boy on the witness stand identified photographs of the film actor Chuck Norris, a Los Angeles City Attorney, a priest and four nuns as being among the people who had molested children, mutilated animals and participated in weird, satanic rituals at a church. (There is no evidence that the children had ever met Chuck Norris or the politician, or the priest and nuns.) The boy said these people had taken him and other children to a cemetery where the children were forced to dig up dead bodies and watch while teachers hacked them to pieces with knives, and that the bodies bled. Other children told that they were molested in airplanes, in hot air balloons, in a supermarket, and in a car wash—all of which raised serious questions about the competence of child witnesses. Some of the children were only five or six years old and had not been at the McMartin Pre-School since they were two or three.

The newly-elected Los Angeles City Attorney, James Kenneth Hahn, said in a telephone interview, "We have to exercise great care in using photographs as evidence in these cases. Just because Chuck Norris and I are prominent, we have credibility. But what if some other people's pictures are included? Their lives could be ruined . . . . I'm only hopeful there aren't others in the situation wrongly identified." Defense attorneys charged that the case was part of a nationwide witch hunt.

"There has been an explosion in the number of reports of child abuse," California attorney general John K. Van de Kamp told a news conference. He stated that when he first started tracking child abuse cases in Los Angeles County there were fewer than 5,000 logged. Since then, there has been a flood of new cases, with 45,000 logged in 1983.

Since its inception in 1974, the Los Angeles Police Department's Abused Child Unit has seen its annual caseload grow from 927 to 3,346 cases. The chairman of the Los Angeles Commission of Children's Services said, "The caseload is too high and nobody is able to do his job properly."

Capt. John White, commander of the department's juvenile division, stated that ". . . child abuse and sexual exploitation of children are epidemic in proportion. It is a social problem of such enormous proportions as to be beyond the control of any one agency." He said the rise in cases can be attributed to mandatory child abuse reporting laws and media attention.

The National Center on Child Abuse and Neglect estimates that one million children are abused by their parents every year. Of those, as many as 200,000 are physically abused, 60,000 to 100,000 are sexually abused, and the remainder are neglected. In addition, more than 2000 children die in circumstances that suggest abuse or neglect.

A women who went to a group counseling session for child abusers said, "I was waiting for all the men with raincoats and greasy hair to come in. What I saw was your average, middle-class people."

There were 1,835 reports of child abuse filed with the Los Angeles Unified School District in the 1984-85 school year, and the school system has been heavily criticized in the news media for not taking action on these cases. The Associated Press, in a recent newspaper article, states that as many as a million children a year are abused.

A nationwide survey conducted by the *Los Angeles Times* found that about twenty-seven percent of the women who participated, and sixteen percent of the men said they themselves had been sexually molested as children. The survey showed that 41 percent of the molesters were friends and acquaintances of the child and 23 percent were relatives. Only 18 percent of the victims said physical force was used.

Reasons given by children for submitting to molesters were: "I was afraid," and "I felt there was no one I could turn to for help." Fewer than half the victims told someone, a parent or a friend, about being molested, until this survey, because they were afraid or ashamed. Ten percent said they did not think the abuse was serious. Molesters are usually someone the victim knows.

Fifty-five percent of the molestations involved sexual intercourse, one percent involved sodomy, 36 percent involved fondling, and seven percent, exhibitionism. Half of the victims said the molester was someone "in authority." Ninety percent of the victims said they felt that permanent harm was done by sexual abuse, and 83 percent said the greatest damage is emotional. Two percent said child molestation has little permanent effect. Most molestations happened only once, but 39 percent of the victims of intercourse reported multiple incidents, in some cases over a period of more than ten years. One in three victims never told anyone about being molested until this survey. Forty-two percent told somebody within a year of being abused. Only three percent told police or other authorities. Seven out of ten of those who did tell said no effective action was taken. Because some people have difficulty discussing the matter, percentages dealing with victimization may be lower than the actual number.

Social workers and some law enforcement officials have stated that the spectacular increase in complaints has been accompanied also by an increase in unfounded allegations, often made by adults against other adults. After the child abuse charges in the McMartin Pre-School received heavy media coverage, the Los Angeles Police Department was inundated by callers reporting suspicious actions by teachers and child care workers, according to Detective Ralph Bennett, head of the Sexually Abused Child Unit. Most of the reports turned out to be baseless, Bennett said. Another detective in the child abuse unit said that a number of schoolteachers have been fired as a result of charges that police later determined were false. Some were fired, he said, even after police told the school administrators there was no evidence to support the allegations. John Rosenman, a school principal, was suspended from his job after being charged with sexual abuse of a five-year-old girl. The charge was dismissed after it was learned that he had washed the girl after she soiled her underwear.

"I doubt that I'll be able to get another job because of the publicity," he said. "People will say, 'That's the guy who molested the little girl.' They will just remember that I was charged."

Another teacher was accused of sexual molestation by a female high school student who later admitted that she fabricated the story as a way of getting even with the teacher for giving her a poor grade.

Employees at daycare centers all over California, when interviewed by news media, said that they were avoiding any physical contact with children in their care, for fear of being accused of molestation. One woman said that when she wants to compliment a child she no longer pats him on the back. "I tell him, 'Give yourself a pat on the back,' " she said. Dozens of child care professionals said they would avoid touching a child at all costs, after the McMartin and other cases received heavy publicity.

What does it all mean? Has there really been an increase in child molestation, and if not, why has there been such a spectacular increase in reports? And why has there been such a radical change in the handling of child abuse allegations?

We have researched several current cases and interviewed leading experts in the field to find out what is known about child abuse and the extraordinary epidemic of cases now pending. And we got some stunning surprises.

II

McMartin

The prosecution of the McMartin Pre-School in southern California was the first of three spectacular child abuse cases that made headlines all over the world in 1984 and 1985. As I write this, the McMartin preliminary hearing has been in progress for well over a year—the longest preliminary hearing in the history of California and probably the longest ever held anywhere. It is the most interesting case I have ever heard of, and the most frightening. It is bizarre and unreal—so much so, in fact, that jaded, middle-aged, veteran newsmen from major, national news media have left the courtroom rubbing their foreheads in disbelief after a day spent covering the proceedings. Several of the newspeople who have attended the hearing for all these months have complained of chronic nightmares and sleep disturbances. So have the lawyers. So have I.

The media coverage has been superficial, infrequent and not very informative. They apparently do not understand that it may be the best story they will ever get. It is a landmark that will affect every child abuse case in the country. It will affect much more than that. McMartin may well be talked about three hundred years from now.

Seven defendants, six women and one man, sit in a row behind the ten attorneys at the counsel tables. They are: Virginia McMartin, 78; Peggy Buckey, 58, her daughter and director of the school; Peggy Ann Buckey, 29, her granddaughter; Raymond

Buckey, 27, her grandson; and three teachers who were employed at the school: Mary Ann Jackson, Betty Raidor and Babette Spitler. They were pillars of the community. Virginia McMartin was presented with the Rose and Scroll Award by the local Chamber of Commerce, commending her as the "Citizen of the Year." She has received several other, similar community awards. The pre-school they operated was the most prestigious in the affluent South Bay suburb of Los Angeles County, the place you would have sent your child if your wanted to start him on the road to Harvard or U.S.C.

They are charged with 207 counts of child molestation and one count of conspiracy. Children who attended the pre-school testified that they were raped, sodomized, penetrated with objects, forced to perform oral copulation. It gets even more bizarre than that. They also said the teachers engaged in satanic rituals and threatened to kill them if they told anyone, that the teachers butchered and mutilated animals in the children's presence to underscore threats that they too would be killed if they told "the secrets."

The women look surprisingly benign and gentle, when you think about the horrendously odious acts of which they stand accused. Betty Raidor, one of the teachers, looks like a kindly grandmother. She is sixty-five. Babette Spitler, another teacher facing twenty-two counts, looks wistfully pretty and delicate. She is thirty-seven. Peggy Ann, the granddaughter, is an attractive, thin, brown-haired young woman in her twenties. Mary Ann Jackson, the other teacher, is fifty-seven, good looking, almost glamorous. Virginia McMartin is seventy-eight. Her daughter, Peggy is fifty eight. They look, in every way, like your average, white middle-class Americans.

They are charged with what are generally viewed as the most loathsome acts in the entire penal code. There may be crimes of greater magnitude, such as murder and high treason, but none considered quite as detestable. There may be some forms of deviant behavior equally raunchy, but they do not embody the violation of the innocent and defenseless. The acts specified here are not benign pedophilia. What these people are charged with is the forcible rape of infants. The youngest children at the pre-school were two and the oldest were five. The charges of child molestation are only the beginning. According to the prosecutors, children told of sadistic and satanic rituals in which the teachers allegedly involved the children. In this as well as other child abuse cases in other cities, children told of witnessing the sacrifice of animals and the drinking of blood and mass murders of infants. Some of the parents insist that the defendants are part of a nationwide network of devil worshipers who practice sexual abuse of children.

Raymond Buckey sits at the far right, next to his mother, Peggy. Buckey is the key defendant with 170 original counts. Ninety still remain. He is pale from spending a year and a half in jail. He and his mother are still in custody while the others are free on bail. He is a thin young man with brown hair and wears thick glasses. They have been sitting there for over a year, through endless testimony and procedural wrangling by the seven defense attorneys and three prosecutors.

The defense attorneys are a formidable team. Daniel Davis, who represents Ray Buckey, is combative and dominating. He does most of the cross-examining, sometimes spending weeks interrogating a prosecution witness. He was a captain in the military police. He has tried fifteen molestation cases and won them all. He is occasionally pompous and puts extremely long, convoluted questions to the witnesses, but in spite of his verbosity he is an extremely competent, intelligent lawyer and he has been steadfastly loyal and supportive to his client despite Buckey's impoverishment by the marathon proceedings. He is thirty-nine.

Dean Gits is representing Peggy Buckey, Ray's mother. He is an impeccably groomed Beverly Hills attorney, appointed by the court. About forty, he is soft-spoken, austere, greatly respected by other attorneys. Walter Urban, representing Betty Raidor, and Bradley Brunon, representing Virginia McMartin, are experienced, accomplished L.A. lawyers. Forrest Latiner, a senior public defender representing Peggy Ann, is highly articulate and resourceful, passionately committed to his belief in his client's innocence. He is a veteran of twenty-five years in the courtroom.

The prosecution includes Lael Rubin, the chief prosecutor, a short, dark-haired woman, about forty, whose past experience was in prosecuting organized crime cases. She has been a deputy district attorney for only about seven years, but she has risen rapidly in the D.A.'s office and has been getting some big cases. Glenn Stevens, like Rubin, has never prosecuted a child abuse case before this. He had been assigned to the prosecution of L.A. gangs. The only member of the three-person prosecution team who had previous experience in child abuse cases is Christine Johnson, a young woman who looks very much like Lynda Carter of "Wonder Woman" fame.

The judge is Aviva K. Bobb. She is only thirty-nine years old but her short, gray hair and black robes give her the appearance of a much older person. She too has not been involved in a child molestation case prior to this. Her past judicial experience was negligible. She was a traffic judge, one of the last appointments of former governor Jerry Brown. She appears to know the evidence code but frequently finds it necessary to stop and ponder for a long time before ruling on an objection or an offer of proof. In the early months of the hearing she was having difficulty controlling her courtroom. She has cited both the defense and the prosecution for contempt in this chaotic hearing.

The first day I arrived at the McMartin preliminary hearing, most of the reporters came over and introduced themselves. They all knew who I was and why I was there. I had told only one reporter, about a week earlier, but that was all it took. Each of them asked me what side I was on: "What is your point of view?" I told them I didn't know anything about the case.

It is very factional at Division Seventy-two. The defense attorneys and their clients regard Wayne Satz with bitter anger. He is the reporter who broke the story on ABC Television on the five o'clock news. It was a big scoop for Channel 7 at a time when ABC's audience ratings were not particularly impressive. Defense attorneys have denounced him, and his biased reporting of the case, during court proceedings. When I was talking to one of them outside the courtroom, he gestured contemptuously at Satz as he passed by and said, "Look at him! He's made a career out of this!"

I was regarded with hostility and distrust by the prosecutors because they saw me talking to the defendants and their attorneys. When a defense attorney showed me photographs of the McMartin kids, the chief prosecutor, Lael Rubin, asked the judge to admonish him, and ordered the bailiff to search me.

During the lunch recess I saw the defendants sitting together in the cafeteria. I wanted to talk with them, but I had noticed that they coldly turn their backs on reporters who approached them, and I did not want to assault their privacy. The reporters have treated them very badly. Newspapers have reported only the statements of the prosecutors and police, ignoring the defendants and their lawyers. Television stations have presented them in such a way as to make them appear as sinister, diabolical vampires. They don't look like criminals. And they certainly don't look like child molesters. They look like bright, sensitive, intelligent people. I had a feeling there was something seriously wrong with this case.

After lunch, while we were all waiting for the bailiff to unlock the door to the courtroom and let us in, there was a crowd of well-dressed people in their thirties and early forties in the hallway. One of the reporters told me they were the parents of some of the children who attended the McMartin school. He introduced me to one of them, a man in his fifties.

"If I had my way," he said angrily, "we'd just take those people out, one by one, and nobody'd ever see 'em again. There is more to this than just molestation and satanism," he growled. He told me that the defendants were killing babies and secretly cremating them. That the accused women had traveled around the country as consultants to child molesters in other states, to instruct them in child molestation. He told me that it was an international child pornography ring.

An older man joined us and began telling me even more lurid stories of the devil worshipers. One of the reporters elbowed me and whispered, "Don't pay any attention to him. He's cracked. He believes in the Illuminati."

The group of militant parents crowded toward the doors, waiting to be let in. It was almost one-thirty. They were a well dressed, affluent-looking crowd; the women were somewhat overdressed for an afternoon in the courtroom, bedecked with jewelry, and frilly, expensive dresses. One of them came over and started talking to me.

"I hear you're writing a book about McMartin." She was a slender, red-haired woman, about thirty-two.

"Partly about McMartin," I told her.

She told me about the allegations of satanism and said that her children had come home telling her of having witnessed these rituals.

"Have you met the parents?" she asked.

"No."

"Come down to Manhattan Beach. I'll take you to them." She gave me her number.

The next day, when the judge recessed the hearing at noon, a reporter invited me to join him for lunch. We walked across the street to a Greek restaurant where all the attorneys go. As we ordered our sandwiches he told me, "They've only scratched the surface of this thing. Ninety percent of the molesters are still out there. Hundreds of thousands of kids have been victims of mass molestations. And it's still going on! When you look at the prosecution, don't look for some clever, devious plan behind their bungling. Look for incompetence. You'll find it every time."

The hearing had been going on since June, 1984, and it was now September, 1985. Nobody knew when it would end. There were only five child witnesses still slated to testify, but that could take months and then the defense could call its own witnesses in an "affirmative defense." Then, there could be a year or two of defense motions, petitions, demurrers and appeals, if the defendants were bound over for trial, before jury selections began.

Let's go back to the beginning. In August, 1983, according to newspaper reports, the mother of a two-year-old child went to the Manhattan Beach Police and told them that her son had been sexually molested, and that he had accused Raymond Buckey of tying him up and photographing him. Buckey's family and friends said that the child was "non-verbal," that he could not speak coherently enough to say those things. One of his teachers said that he could not speak at all, that he was unintelligible. A policewomen later testified at the preliminary hearing that the child's mother had called her on the telephone and told her that she had observed something in the child's anal area when he was getting out of the bathtub, and asked him if anybody had touched him there, and that the child had given two names, one of which was unintelligible, and another, which she believed to be "Ray." She concluded that this was Ray at the pre-school and called the policewoman and accused Buckey. She then brought the child to be interviewed by officer Jane Hoag, of the Manhattan Beach Police Department.

According to her testimony in the hearing, Hoag interviewed the child, asking him if anyone had touched him in his anal area, and the boy gave two names, one of which sounded like "Ray." There is nothing in the testimony indicating that it was Raymond Buckey at the pre-school. It was not clear whether the child even understood the question.

According to Hoag's testimony, she later showed the child pictures, including a photograph of Buckey, and the child did not pick, or identify, Buckey as his assailant. She also testified that the mother had said that her child had stated that his father had molested him. The mother later suffered a mental breakdown and lost custody of her children.

Officer Hoag began calling parents of other children to find out if they had ever been touched, if their temperature had even been taken rectally. There was a long list of questions asked. Some of the parents said that Hoag called them as many as three times in a single day.

Police searched the school and the homes of Virginia McMartin, Peggy Buckey, and Raymond Buckey. Then they arrested Buckey. He was released the same day and his bail was refunded, and the police admitted to the media that he had been released because of lack of any evidence. He and his family filed a lawsuit against the Manhattan Beach Police charging libel and false arrest.

The next day, the Manhattan Beach Police Department sent a letter to a large number of parents of children enrolled at the school telling them that an investigation into allegations of molestation was underway and that Buckey had been arrested, asking them to question their children. The wording of the letter strongly creates the impression that molestation had occurred, and that Buckey was the culprit. Buckey family members believe, not unreasonably, that Ray was arrested in order to lend credibility to the letter. Many people in the community felt that, because he had been arrested, "something must have happened."

September 8, 1983
    Dear Parent:
    This Department is conducting a criminal investigation involving child molestation (288 P.C.) Ray Buckey, an employee of Virginia McMartin's Pre-School, was arrested September 7, 1983 by this Department.
    The following procedure is obviously an unpleasant one, but to

protect the rights of your children as well as the rights of the accused, this inquiry is necessary for a complete investigation.

Records indicate that your child has been or is currently a student at the pre-school. We are asking your assistance in this continuing investigation. Please question your child to see if he or she has been a witness to any crime or if he or she has been a victim. Our investigation indicates that possible criminal acts include: oral sex, fondling of genitals, buttock or chest area, and sodomy, possibly committed under the pretense of "taking the child's temperature." Also, photos may have been taken of children without their clothing. Any information from your child regarding having ever observed Ray Buckey to leave a classroom alone with a child during any nap period, or if they have ever observed Ray Buckey tie up a child, is important.

Please complete the enclosed information form and return it to this Department in the enclosed stamped return envelope as soon as possible. We will contact you if circumstances dictate same.

We ask you to please keep this investigation strictly confidential because of the nature of the charges and the highly emotional effect it could have on our community. Please do not discuss this investigation with anyone outside your immediate family. Do not contact or discuss the investigation with Raymond Buckey, any member of the accused defendant's family, or employees connected with the McMartin Pre-School.

THERE IS NO EVIDENCE TO INDICATE THAT THE MANAGEMENT OF VIRGINIA MCMARTIN'S PRE-SCHOOL HAD ANY KNOWLEDGE OF THIS SITUATION AND NO DETRIMENTAL INFORMATION CONCERNING THE OPERATION OF THE SCHOOL HAS BEEN DISCOVERED DURING THIS INVESTIGATION. ALSO, NO OTHER EMPLOYEE IN THE SCHOOL IS UNDER INVESTIGATION FOR ANY CRIMINAL ACT.

Your prompt attention to this matter and reply no later than September 16, 1983 will be appreciated.

    HARRY L. KUHLMEYER, JR.
    Chief of Police
    JOHN WEHNER, Captain

One of the parents told Mrs. Buckey that Officer Hoag had called her repeatedly and said, "Your child has been named as a victim. And if you really love your child you'll ask him these questions. . . ." Others gave similar accounts of the telephone calls.

A number of parents complained to the District Attorney's office about Hoag's abrasive calls, and the district attorney's office in November referred the parents to Children's Institute International (C.I.I.) in Los Angeles, a private agency which offers therapy and counseling for abused children.

Naturally, all of this created pandemonium in the small community of Manhattan Beach and the gossip of molestation was rampant. Parents began taking their children to C.I.I. to be interviewed by its director, Kee McFarlane, and her assistants, Shawn Connerly and Sandi Krebs. C.I.I. also began calling the parents. In the ensuing months, six other South Bay area pre-schools were closed, following allegations of child sexual abuse. The nearby Manhattan Ranch Pre-School was closed and an attorney representing the Department of Social Services stated that children were being swapped between that school and McMartin, and molested at both locations. The McMartin school was set afire by an arsonist who left his spray-painted message on the sidewalk: "ONLY THE BEGINNING."

The prosecutors claim that three hundred eighty nine former pupils told interviewers at the Institute that they had been molested, and that examinations by physicians had produced "positive medical evidence" of the alleged molestations.

On February 2, 1984, KACB's Wayne Satz broke the story on Channel 7's five o'clock news. In March, a grand jury began hearings, and the seven defendants were indicted, and arrested. All but two of the defendants were jailed on a no-bail hold, including sixty-five-year-old Betty Raidor, Babette Spitler, Peggy Ann Buckey, Ray Buckey and his mother, Peggy Buckey. Peggy Ann, Babette, and Betty Raidor were released on bail after two months in jail. Ray and his mother were still in custody.

Each of the children initially told their parents and police that they had not been molested. Then, during interviews at C.I.I., they began to tell some remarkable stories.

Several children told that they had been molested in a supermarket in full view of shoppers passing by. Other children said they were molested in other supermarkets, but they were not called as witnesses, and the interviewers did not pursue this line of inquiry, so it is not known in what supermarkets these events purportedly occurred.

One child told that he was molested in a hot air balloon, high above the California coast; another stated that he was molested in a helicopter. Others mentioned molestations in several kinds of aircraft. One child told of parachuting out of an airplane. And there were the children who told of being molested out on the ocean in boats. One of them said there were two boats, "a big boat and a little boat."

Others told of being molested in underground tunnels and chambers beneath the school. The District Attorney's office obtained a search warrant and investigators went to the school with various children who pointed to where the trap door to the underground tunnels was supposed to be. The investigators tore the tiles off the floor, and found that there were no trap doors. Some of the children told the investigators that the trap doors to the underground tunnels were out in the play yard, but the investigators searched the playground and found no trap doors there. They brought high-technology equipment for detecting differences in sound waves from under the ground to detect cavities or material of different densities, equipment which has been used for archaeological excavations. No underground tunnels or caves were found.

A small boy told of being taken to a cemetery where three- and four-year-old children with hoes, pickaxes and shovels unearthed coffins (carrying the soil out in their pockets), raised the coffins up out of the ground, removed the lids, and watched while the teachers removed the bodies and cut them to pieces, as an example of what would happen to them if they ever told the "nasty secrets" of molestation. Some of the bodies, he said, bled. Then, he said, the children put the coffins back into the ground, put the earth back in the hole, and put the turf back on top, so that nobody would know what happened. Another boy told of being taken to a farm, and out into a field, where Ray Buckey, using a baseball bat, had killed a horse.

Several children told of being molested in a Catholic church where priests and nuns were running around, naked. One of them said he saw the priests and nuns at an Episcopal church. Others told that they were molested in Lutheran and Baptist churches. Some told of molestations at churches that have never been discovered and may not exist.

A small girl told of being taken to a home in Palos Verdes where the children were thrown off a cliff, and that the teachers had put up nets to catch them as they were falling. She was not called as a witness for the protection. Children told of molestations in rooms that were found not to exist. Yet, they gave vivid, detailed descriptions of these imaginary rooms, both in the schoolhouse and under the ground. One boy told of going through a trap door, down thirteen circular steps, through a tunnel to two rooms, and described the furniture and decor of the rooms in elaborate detail, as well as the alleged molestations. One child said that the rooms were entered through a cellar door, like the one in *The Wizard of Oz*, and that under the cellar door there was a slide, resembling a swimming pool slide, which would take them to the subterranean rooms, and that they exited through a tunnel that took them to a building on the neighboring lot. Other children told of being taken to mortuaries where they were shown dead bodies in open coffins. One told of "naked movies" being filmed on an airplane. Another said that Ray took the children out on the freeway in a station wagon, and that he stopped the vehicle on the side of the freeway and the children got out and undressed, and Ray photographed them in the nude, on the freeway, and that he drove wildly, bumping the cars on each side.

A nine-year-old girl told that she and other children were taken to a car wash by Ray and molested there in the lavatory, one by one, an act of remarkable stamina. How long a time this took is not clear. One of the children said the little boys and girls were flown in an airplane to far-off, exotic lands where there were wild animals and jungles.

Most of the McMartin kids were at the school for only three hours, from nine to twelve. Some stayed for lunch and were picked up by their parents at one. Another interesting fact is that none of the children remembered anyone else being a part of these adventures. A few said they remembered their closest friend being there, but they didn't remember the things their closest friends had said. For example, Jimmy's closest friend is Richard. Jimmy told of underground tunnels. Richard didn't know anything about underground tunnels. Richard didn't know anything about the farm Jimmy said they had visited. Dan talks about visiting underground tunnels. His best friend, Brad, didn't know anything about underground tunnels. And they're close, inseparable friends.

"It's just fantasy, based on an awful lot of coaching," one of the defense attorneys told me. "And a lot of inculcation by the therapists. If you take it at face value, as the judge does, with total acceptance, then you can believe almost anything. But her job supposedly is to sift out that which, logically, has no credibility."

One of the children who was interviewed by the District Attorney's office and evaluators said, "It's all a big lie." She was not called as a witness by the prosecutors.

Several of the children told that they were forced to drink blood and ingest feces. Two children told of seeing babies murdered. They were dropped as prospective witness by the District Attorney. A five-year-old girl told the evaluators that she was taken on an airplane and flown to a ranch and then later flown back to the school. Months later, on the witness stand, she was asked if she remembered going to the ranch. She said no, and said she just flew around and then landed and returned to school. Some of the children told one story during the original interview, and then told a totally different one at the grand jury hearing, and then a still different one at the preliminary hearing. Some told three stories during the preliminary hearing, one during direct examination and then a different one during cross-examination, and a still different one on the second day of cross-examination. Most of them never told the same story twice. Some told five different stories. One small girl told that Ray had killed birds and rabbits, and then, later, said it was turtles that were killed. One child told three different versions of the "Naked Movie Star" game. One small girl told the District Attorney's investigator that she had been taken to a farm where Ray stabbed a pig. Later, in court, she said she had no recollection of going to a farm or seeing a pig.

Some of the children accused three police officers who interviewed them of molestation. One child said he was molested on the playground at the McMartin School, in full view of cars and pedestrians passing by on a busy street. One small boy said he was taken to a house where there were lions in the basement.

"I don't know how we could have done all those things," said Virginia McMartin. "Those children were only there for three hours."

"Where did they get all those wild stories?" I asked one of the attorneys.

"From the interviewers," he said. "When you keep asking a kid over and over again to tell you about something that never happened, and tell him he's a rotten kid if he doesn't cooperate, he'll tell you almost anything. If you don't believe that, watch the tapes. The cops and the D.A.'s have their favorite child abuse clinics where they send the kids, because they can count on them to always find child sexual abuse, even on the Virgin Mary. Have you seen the videotapes of those interviews? When you see those tapes, and see what was done with those kids, and how they were manipulated, you'll begin to understand what this case is all about, and what a fraud it is.

"The prosecution is saying that about twelve hundred kids were molested at the school, and that it was going on for twenty years. If that were true, wouldn't at least one of them have told somebody? It's inconceivable that some kids wouldn't have said something to somebody, that would have blown this, long ago. It's inconceivable that children would have experienced and witnessed the kinds of animal mutilations and killings and the satanic rituals without having some kind of emotional and psychological disturbance. Instead, they get up and talk about it without any emotion at all. And they don't describe sexual conduct. They describe touching that is totally asexual, although they describe touching the sexual parts. The kids describe oral copulation as though they're being urinated on. They talk about yellow liquid coming out of someone's penis. They're not talking about ejaculation. They're talking about urine. They describe it as yellow, warm liquid. Not sticky. Because they don't know from semen! And it didn't happen.

"Those defendants are totally straight, conservatives," he said. "Church members. They don't even drink. Betty Raidor turned in her own son for smoking marijuana. The McMartin-Buckey family has lived in the community for fifty-eight years! If they were slaughtering animals and raping babies, don't you think someone would have noticed? And even if they were perverts, would they be insane enough to do it on the side of the highway? Give me a break!

"All these people have lost their homes, their savings, their property, everything—including their reputations. They're branded for life."

"How did all this insanity get started?" I asked.

"Well," he said, "Robert Philibosian was the district attorney then, in 1984. He had been appointed to fill out the unexpired term of John Van de Kamp, who was elected Attorney General. And in 1984, Philibosian was up for re-election. Nobody of any consequence filed to run against him, and it looked as though he would easily win re-election to the office of district attorney. The primary election was to be held in June, and the runoff in November, unless one candidate could muster a majority, plus one vote. Philibosian didn't have much to worry about.

"However, starting at the end of 1983 and early 1984, Ira Reiner, the City Attorney, began to make public statements that he was considering entering the race for district attorney. Reiner had always had an uncanny ability to get his name and face into the newspapers and on television. On the other hand, not very much was known about Philibosian, and he had very little name recognition. Reiner is a handsome man with white hair and a crisp, resonant voice, like a television announcer. Philibosian is a rather dull man.

"Philibosian suddenly realized it was going to be a tough race, and he was the underdog. Reiner had always been able to find an issue that would give him a high visibility, and Philibosian had not, even though his office dealt with major felonies, while Reiner's office dealt only with misdemeanors.

"Suddenly, into his lap dropped McMartin! Whether or not he pushed the grand jury to indict the McMartin defendants before they were ready is not known—whether the case was prematurely presented, prior to completing the investigation, because Philibosian wanted the indictment to use as a springboard for his re-election campaign.

"But when the indictment came down, he did use it as a springboard. Philibosian sat there in the courtroom, at the prosecution table, bland, smiling, with a rather paternalistic demeanor while Lael Rubin did the talking. He sat at the counsel table. Ronald George, who was the judge of the master calendar, allowed the media in. And then when the court proceedings were recessed, Philibosian was out in the hallway, holding court before the cameras, making his prepared statement. It was the first time in memory that *the* District Attorney himself sat at the counsel table in a trial or arraignment.

"He stood before the cameras of nearly all the channels, telling that his office had just broken the biggest child pornography case in the world, with links to organized crime, and that his office was investigating and would present the evidence and there wasn't a shadow of a doubt that this was the biggest and most important case of all time. And he used it, pulled out all stops. And it is reasonable to assume that if it were not for the re-election campaign he would not have been in court, nor in the hallway doing his dance before the cameras. It cannot be proven that he precipitated the presentation to the grand jury and rushed it before it was ready to go, but his actions certainly suggest that this was the case. The defense attorneys believe that nobody in the D.A.'s office had even looked at Kee McFarlane's videotapes. But once the indictments came down, he used it to maximum political benefit. He has denied it, but one can hardly argue with what occurred."

One of the defense attorneys stated that the reason the District Attorney's office was holding up the filing of the criminal complaint for the post-indictment preliminary hearing was because they were waiting until the Friday before the Tuesday, June 5, Primary Election, so that Philibosian could again, on the eve of the election, come to court and step before the footlights, and the television cameras. As a result of this statement, the lawyers believe, the District Attorney rushed the filing to a week earlier, and Philibosian stayed out of court, and did not appear before the cameras, because it would have looked bad, after what the defense attorneys had said was picked up by the media.

In any case, Reiner won the primary by a large plurality and did not have to face Philibosian in a runoff. He was the District Attorney elect, and Philibosian was on his way out.

The defense attorneys state that there was no good reason to lock up the defendants on a no-bail hold, except to exaggerate the importance of the case and create the illusion that Philibosian was saving the community from evil monsters. They also believe that the then prosecutor, Jean Matusinka, was removed because she was unwilling to make a media circus of the case, and was replaced by a grade-three prosecutor, Lael Rubin.

Daniel Davis, the attorney representing Ray Buckey, filed a motion to disqualify the district attorney, stating that Philibosian had "publicly exploited the McMartin case, in abuse of his powers as prosecutor, and obligations to insure fair and impartial prosecution, in order to gain political name recognition and advantage." His motion was given short shrift, and he was not allowed to call witnesses in its support.

The defense attorneys also allege that the prosecutors relied on statements from C.I.I. and did not look at videotapes before going forward with the case.

The prosecutors asked the judge to let the children testify over closed circuit television in an adjoining room to spare them the stress of having to appear in front of the defendants who, the prosecutors say, threatened them and terrorized them by butchering animals. On November 9, 1984, a state appeals court ruled in the Hochheiser molestation case that closed circuit testimony cannot be used in a trial. In April, 1985, the California State Legislature passed a bill that gave judges power to allow children under ten years of age to testify from outside the courtroom over television. The bill had been heavily lobbied by the McMartin parents. Under the new law, PC 1347, children were to be allowed to testify on television if the judge found that the alleged victim would be unable to testify in an open courtroom because he was threatened or intimidated. The defense attorneys argued that the new law would deprive defendants of their Sixth Amendment right to confront witnesses. Even supporters of the bill acknowledged that the courts might find the bill unconstitutional. Governor Deukmejian signed the bill into law on May 20, 1985.

Judge Bobb, however, denied a prosecution motion to permit some of the child witnesses to testify on television because, she said, the new law could not be applied retroactively to a case that was already in progress before the new law was enacted. The chief prosecutor, Lael Rubin, then told the judge that the remaining twenty-eight complaining witnesses would not testify, and that the prosecution "conditionally" rested its case after the thirteenth witness. Six of the seven defense attorneys then rested their case and immediately moved for dismissal of the charges against their clients. The judge dismissed 64 counts for which the prosecution had not called any alleged victims. She dismissed twelve molestation counts against Virginia McMartin, thirteen of the fourteen counts against Peggy Ann Buckey, and forty-two of the sixty-seven counts against Peggy McMartin Buckey, and took several counts under submission. At the end of the day she recessed amid protests from defense lawyers demanding that more counts against their clients be dismissed. She told them that more counts would be dismissed the following day.

The prosecutors argued that their case could not move forward without permitting the children to testify on closed circuit television, but Bobb pointed out that thirteen children had already taken the stand and testified to ninety counts of molestation and one count of conspiracy—enough to send Ray Buckey to prison for three hundred years, and his mother, Peggy McMartin Buckey, for forty years. Her decision not to allow the children to testify on television, she told prosecutors, was "hardly fatal to your case."

Prosecutors feared that several of the defendants who faced few changes could go free or get short sentences because of the ruling. Mary Ann Jackson was charged with fifteen counts but accused by only one witness. Deputy District Attorney Lael Rubin told reporters that although forty-one of the alleged victims had been expected to testify, only the first thirteen could do so in open court. The prosecutors had intended to have five other witnesses testify by closed circuit television. Several of the children had been withdrawn by their parents. The prosecutors had already eliminated other child witnesses, who, they said, could not withstand even the protected television situation. It was also alleged by some of the parents that their children had not been called as witnesses because it was feared that their testimony might be so bizarre as to damage the prosecution's credibility.

The defense attorneys rested without calling witnesses. They had announced that they would call former teachers from the school and psychologists to refute the allegations in an "affirmative defense." Judge Bobb did not rule on whether the defendants would be ordered to stand trial. She had first to dispose of the remaining counts for which no evidence was presented, the counts she had taken under submission—and on motions to strike the testimony of several witnesses and hear arguments on the sufficiency of testimony on the remaining counts.

Judge Bobb told the prosecutors that her ruling shouldn't affect the case because thirteen children so far had testified to 90 of the 207 counts of felony child molestation and one count of conspiracy. She said the children also had testified to about ninety other uncharged molestation offenses which the prosecution could file at the conclusion of the preliminary hearing. Rubin's decision to rest her case caught the defense attorneys by surprise.

The next day, June 13, the judge dismissed an additional 145 counts against the defendants for failure on the part of the prosecution to produce any evidence on those counts. She dismissed 80 of 170 counts against Raymond Buckey; 33 of 45 counts against Betty Raidor; 15 of 22 counts against Babette Spitler; 16 of 20 counts against Mary Ann Jackson, and one count against Peggy McMartin Buckey. Of Ray Buckey's original 170 counts, only 90 remained. Of Peggy McMartin Buckey's original 64 counts, only 21 remained; of Peggy Ann Buckey's original 15 counts, only two remained, and Judge Bobb said she would consider requests to dismiss even more of the remaining counts. Defense attorneys said the prosecution's case was now in shambles.

Deputy District Attorney Lael Rubin hotly contradicted them, and said she intended to seek additional counts based on the statements of the thirteen child witnesses who had already testified. At this point the exact number of counts remaining against each defendant was unclear. William Powell, co-counsel for Mary Ann Jackson, said that two of the remaining counts against his client were for the same offense. Even the prosecutors admitted that some but not all of the 115 indictment counts were duplicated in the 208-count complaint. "There's no point in keeping count," Rubin said.

The erosion of nearly two-thirds of the charges left the parents angry. They jammed the courtroom corridor, muttering that the prosecutors had taken "a dive."

"It's just a massive, judicial chess game!" said one of the mothers whose children were raped and sodomized, she said, at the school. Dean Gits, the attorney representing Peggy Buckey predicted that all counts against his client would be dismissed because of the incredible testimony of the child witness.

Courtroom security was tightened because of the anger of the alleged victims' parents who crowded the spectators' section of the courtroom and the corridor displaying bumperstickers, some of which were pasted to the front of their clothing, some held in their hands, that read "I BELIEVE THE CHILDREN." All spectators were searched for weapons, including some of the parents, before they were permitted to enter the courtroom. Armed guards stood at the back of the room. The defendants walked out of the courtroom smiling for the first time since the proceedings began— except for Ray Buckey and Peggy McMartin Buckey, who were still in custody.

"I'm very relieved," Betty Raidor told reporters. "I'm innocent. . . ." Virginia McMartin left the courtroom in her wheelchair, saying, "Father forgive them for they know not what they do." She recited a poem she had composed while the charges were being dismissed.

Rubin, the chief prosecutor, said she planned to appeal the judge's ruling that child witnesses would not be allowed to testify by closed circuit television, in order to reopen the preliminary hearing for testimony by additional children.

The next day, the prosecutors asked the court to add 50 more molestation counts against the seven defendants, based on testimony by the child witnesses during the ten-month hearing. Rubin said state law requires that defendants must answer to any additional counts introduced during the proceedings. One ten-year-old boy who had accused three of the former teachers of six molestation counts later implicated all seven defendants. The defense attorneys requested that all 90 remaining counts be dismissed, arguing that there was insufficient evidence to support some counts and because the defense had been unconstitutionally limited in cross-examination. Prosecution attorneys said they would ask the Superior Court for a stay of the proceedings until they could file an appeal of Bobb's decision on the closed circuit television issue. The hearing was recessed.

That evening, angry parents crowded into the American Martyrs School in Manhattan Beach for a meeting they had demanded with the district attorney's office. A deputy district attorney, head of the sex crimes unit, refused to speak to the parents until reporters were excluded from the room. Parents who left the meeting told the reporters that they had been given no satisfactory answers. One parent wanted to know why children who were willing to testify were dropped. Another wanted to know if the dismissed charges would be refiled, whether the district attorney would pursue the additional charges that had emerged during the hearing. Other parents complained that there had been no communication between the prosecutors and the parents for months. Some of the parents said they had been contacted by the district attorney's office and asked not to attend the parents' meetings.

Four days later, a Manhattan Beach police sergeant was suspended after allegations that he had threatened to do "great bodily harm" to the defendants. He had testified at the preliminary hearing as a parent of one of the child witnesses. He told of symptoms of sexual molestation he had discovered in his child. On the boarded-up windows of the pre-school appeared the words: "RAY MUST DIE" in spray paint, next to a spray-painted drawing of a man hanging from a gallows.

A month later, Superior Court Judge Paul Turner ruled that the five remaining child witnesses should be allowed to testify on closed circuit television. In his ruling he stated that Judge Bobb ". . . is free to order closed circuit questioning in connection with the five child witnesses or to deny the prosecution's request as to one or more of the children." Turner said that use of the new state law pertaining to closed circuit television did not violate state or federal restrictions on retroactive application of laws, because the legislators had intended it to apply to that case. He dismissed the defense contention that it would violate the defendants' right to confront their accusers.

Turner stayed the effect of his ruling for five days to allow defense attorneys time to appeal to a higher court, which they said they would do. The defense attorneys were pessimistic about the probability of any appellate ruling favoring the defendants. "The climate of the times does not favor these defendants," said Bradley Brunon, who represents McMartin. The deputy district attorney, Lael Rubin, called it a "significant victory" for the parents and children. Judge Turner, in his ruling on the appeal, stated that Bobb must determine by a legal test whether each child is too traumatized to testify if required to face the defendants in court. He noted that children had stated that they did not want to testify in the courtroom because of the alleged threats made by Buckey. He said that many children had already told that Buckey butchered animals in front of them and said the same thing would happen to them if they told their parents of the alleged molestations. Turner ordered the preliminary hearing to resume July 22, but defense attorneys filed an appeal with the California Supreme Court. On July 18 the

Supreme Court issued a stay order halting the resumption of the preliminary hearing which was scheduled for the following Monday, stating that it wanted time to review a defense request for reversal of the Superior Court ruling allowing the children to testify on television.

The Supreme Court refused to intervene, and denied Peggy Ann Buckey's request for a hearing on the issue. Only one justice voted for the hearing and Chief Justice Rose Elizabeth Bird took no part in the case. This meant that Judge Bobb would now have to consider whether to allow the five children to testify in a separate room on television.

The preliminary hearing resumed at the end of August with the prosecution attempting to convince the judge, with the testimony of expert witnesses, that the next child slated to testify was qualified under PC 1347, the new "McMartin Law," to testify on television. Dr. Cheryl Kent, a psychologist who had interviewed the child, testified for the prosecution that her patient, a nine-year-old boy, was so traumatized by his experience at the school that he sleeps in a cardboard box, stutters and has difficulty speaking when he talks about having to face the defendants in court. She told of his nightmares and insomnia. The defense attorneys cross-examined her at great length, while Rubin, the prosecutor, hammered them with objections in her shrill voice. Almost every objection was sustained.

I was introduced to another parent in the hallway during a recess. In a harsh, angry tone he told me, "This is more than just pedophilia, pornography and satanism. Those satanic rituals, the same story turned up all over the country. I don't think them kids in Minnesota read the *L. A. Times*. They talk about blood sacrifices, desecration of religious symbols, violation and destruction of innocence." He said that violation of children is a part of the molesters' religion. Most of the parents are Roman Catholics.

The parents of the alleged victims have meetings, picnics and other social gatherings at which they plan to sponsor new legislation to allow the admission of hearsay evidence in molestation cases. They believe the defense attorneys send infiltrators into their meetings to find out what they are planning.

These affairs are not pleasant, relaxed evenings. These parents are angry. They complain that they have been betrayed. They contend that their children were molested and they demand that something be done about it. They are enraged by the legal system. They don't understand that the system must run its course, that the rights of defendants can't be denied without committing reversible error (errors in judge's rulings that could be grounds for appellate court to set aside or reverse the preliminary court's decision). They don't care. They are angry at the school, the community, the legal system, the District Attorney's office, and, most of all, the defendants.

Another interesting question is the behavior of the defendants during the marathon hearing. They have endured the stress of this thing hanging over their heads for almost two years. They know they could spend the rest of their lives in prison. Yet, they show no signs of cracking. In a case where there are several defendants it is not unusual for one of them to accept an offer of immunity in exchange for testifying against the others. The McMartin defendants have flatly refused all such offers. They just sit there, calmly, month after month.

The McMartin defendants also have an organization which meets regularly and disseminates information to the public. It is called "Friends of the McMartin Defendants." They have mounted a newspaper ad campaign with full-page ads in local newspapers drawing a parallel between the McMartin case and the Salem witch trials. There are many similarities. In Salem and elsewhere, it was the testimony of children, coached by adults, which was used to condemn and burn innocent women in the notorious witch trials. The interrogation spun out of control. The children accused dogs of witchcraft, and even animals were executed. These pious folk also stated that they believed the children.

At a recent meeting, a woman who had been employed at one of the now closed pre-schools told her listeners that the police came and searched her home and confiscated a photograph of her granddaughter at a dance recital, wearing a tutu, and called it "child pornography." Another Manhattan Beach resident who babysat for some of the McMartin children told that the police came to his home with a search warrant, confiscated family photograph albums, address books, candles, a vase and clothing.

"They dug up our garden, the strawberry patch and the front lawn," he said. Other residents also complained that the police had dug up their yards looking for pornography.

Dr. Cheryl Kent was on the stand for a week. Then, on Monday, September 23, the prosecution called the mother of the next child witness. She is dark-haired, pretty, fashionably dressed, doll-like. When she was cross-examined, most of the questions were objected to and the objections sustained. She told the court that her son was a shy child and terribly frightened. She said he was afraid to be alone at night, that he bundles up until he breaks out in a sweat. When he learned that the McMartin defendants and their attorneys were trying to get his address, she said, he screamed, "No! No! They'll come and get us!"

"How do you know he can testify on closed circuit television?" Daniel Davis, the defense attorney asks.

"He wishes to do so and we will support him," she answers.

"Have you told him he will be protected if he testifies in open court?"

"The fears instilled in him are still with him."

"What kind of fears?"

"A horrible feeling inside he can't explain. Feelings of sadness."

"Didn't his sister testify in open court?" Davis asks.

"His sister is much stronger than he is," the mother answers. She tells the courts that her son sleeps in a box because he feels the need to be protected. She says she feels he couldn't face Ray Buckey's "stare-downs."

I think about the allegations. I can't imagine Buckey being insane enough to perform an act of sodomy right there in that little schoolhouse with all those people coming and going. The risk would be terrifying. They said he did it with the whole class there, watching. Would anybody be that reckless?

And what about Virginia? She can't walk. How was she able to get up out of her wheelchair and do these things?

The child's mother is still on the stand. She tells the court that her son watched as Ray Buckey took a live rabbit and chopped its ears off, and it died. Her son told her, she testifies, that Buckey showed him a knife and threatened him.

"What did he say?" the lawyer asks.

"That Joe and I would be killed."

Buckey laughed silently as the woman testified. He usually sits there, expressionless, but when he smiles he has an extremely engaging, charming smile. Most of the time he looks bored. He has been sitting there for almost two years.

The questioning goes on, hour after hour. Lael Rubin pounds the defense attorneys shrilly with her objections.

"Objection!"

"Sustained."

"May I ask on what ground, your honor?"

"Asked and answered. Also vague. Assumes facts not in evidence. Also 372 and 451." Most of the questions are thrown out. Hundreds.

On September 24, the prosecution calls Dr. Fiona Leigh, another child psychologist who has interviewed the boy. She states, "It was my opinion that he could not stand stress, that he could not testify in any form."

This is a hearing on the prosecution's motion to allow the next child witness, a nine-year-old boy, to testify over closed circuit television outside the courtroom, under the new law, PC 1347. I am told that this will be the last child witness, if he is allowed to testify on television. What happened to the others? Nobody knows. The prosecution says they were withdrawn by the parents. The parents say they were withdrawn by the prosecutors.

Dr. Fiona Leigh is still on the stand, answering endless questions, most of them objected to and the objections sustained. I'm staying because I want to be there when the last child witness goes on the stand. I don't want to miss that. The lawyers say it could be next week. It could be tomorrow. They say he is a fragile, frightened kid. Will he be able to go through with it?

It is September 24. Tomorrow is Yom Kippur. The judge has announced that the hearing will be recessed for the High Holy Day. Dean Gits moves to have the charges against his client dismissed on the ground that the hearing has not been continuous. "Your motion is denied," she tells him.

September 26: Kee McFarlane is on the stand again. She is the therapist who interviewed many of the McMartin kids when the allegations were first made by the parents. She is blond, thirty-eight years old, stylishly coiffed. She looks distressed.

"Did he testify that he didn't want to testify in open court before the defendants?"

"Yes," she replies, with a look of profound anger at the attorney.

"What was it he told you about not wanting to testify before the defendants?"

"He told us he would not go in there if the defendants were present. We had to assure him that the defendants would not be there. He asked a lot of questions about how closed circuit TV worked. I told him the defendants would be in a separate room. He talked about weapons, things that made him afraid. I have never seen him discuss it without difficulty."

"What kind of difficulty?"

"Anxiety, changing the subject, stuttering, talking in a higher-pitched voice. Nervousness."

"What would happen if he were to testify in open court?"

She paused for a long time. "He might become mute."

"When he told you about the fears and threats, did you ever observe him to cry?"

"Yes."

"Do you recall what he was crying about?"

"Objection. Irrelevant."

"Sustained."

"Do you have any reason to believe that his statements about knives and guns were the result of suggestion by his sister and others?"

"No."

"What did he tell you about guns and knives?"

"There was a threat that he would be shot with a gun. He would be stabbed if he told the secrets. He saw real knives."

"Did he tell you about seeing real lions?"

"We were talking about the things he was threatened with. I don't remember any description of seeing a real lion."

"And was it at the devil house?"

"Yes."

"In the context of talking about the devil house did he say he was frightened?"

"Objection."

"Sustained." McFarlane's facial expression is hostile and sarcastic when she answers the defense attorneys' questions. She looks at Lael Rubin, the prosecutor, with a look of exasperation, rolling her eyes upward.

In the afternoon, Dr. Fiona Leigh is brought back on the stand. Daniel Davis goes on with the questions.

"When you interviewed him, did he appear to be frightened?"

"Yes."

"What did you observe?"

"He was frightened, reluctant to answer questions about the threats."

"Did you see anything that would lead to believe he would not be able to testify in the presence of the defendants?"

"Yes. Many things."

"What did you observe?"

"Primarily and underlying fear. He is not sturdy when he talks about these things. He is emotionally fragile."

"Did he tell you he was at McMartin when animals were mutilated or killed?"

"Yes." It goes on and on into the afternoon. "Objection." "Sustained." "May I be heard, your honor?" "Yes." "Your honor, this witness testified . . ."

At the end of the day, as I leave the courtroom I see Betty Raidor being interviewed by a television news crew in the hallway. The hot, white lights are on her. She smiles sadly. She looks radiant, like a benevolent grandmother in bright sunlight.

"Do you feel that this is unfair to you?" the young man asks.

"Well," she reflects, "my home is gone, my savings are gone. All the things I put away for my old age are gone. And I didn't do anything." They turn the lights off and thank her.

Mary Ann and Virginia were there in the hallway, leaving. As I watched them, they smiled and said hello.

On Monday, September 30, Judge Bobb announced that she would allow the boy to testify over closed circuit television from an adjoining room, over the vigorous protests of the defense attorneys who contended that even the most sophisticated equipment could not accurately simulate the attorney-witness confrontation. She said in her ruling that the boy had met all the conditions, that there had been evidence that the boy believed that he was threatened by the defendants, Ray and his mother, Peggy. Defense attorneys spent most of the day restating arguments against the closed circuit television. They argued that because only Ray and his mother had been accused of threatening the boy, the judge could not justify removing the boy from the presence of all seven defendants.

Tuesday morning, October 1: I arrived early at the courtroom, slightly before ten. The monitors and cameras were in place, three nineteen-inch television screens, two for the boy and one for his "support person," in this case, his mother, who was to take turns with the father. The cameras and monitors were turned on but there was no boy there yet. Just an empty chair and a blue wall behind it.

The place was packed with reporters and television cameras. This is it. Everybody is dressed in their best clothes for television. Even Judge Bobb has put on lipstick. She is in the hallway behind the courtroom. For half an hour the reporters and spectators wait. Then, finally, the judge comes in and the bailiff calls the courtroom to order. The boy walks on camera. He sits, brown hair neatly combed, dressed in a blue and white shirt. The judge states the ground rules to the attorneys. "When making an objection, you are to state only the legal grounds and not argue before the witness. No motion to strike before the witness. All motions can be made during the break in the child's testimony." Daniel Davis asks that the audience be rearranged so that all spectators can be seen on the monitor by the witness. He also insists that Ray Buckey be visible on the child's monitor, citing the statutory right of the accused to a public preliminary hearing.

The boy on the screen is eight years old, and surprisingly small. He puts his hands to his face, nervously, wringing them together as one might do in cold weather. He leans forward over the table.

"Good morning, James," the judge greets him. "Can you hear me?"

"Yes," a tiny voice replies.

"Do you promise that everything you tell will be the truth?"

"Yes."

"Miss Rubin is going to ask you some questions. Can you see me?"

"Yes."

"How old are you today?"

"Eight."

"What grade are you in?"

"Third grade."

"Do you know the difference between telling the truth and a lie?"

"Yes."

"What is the difference?"

"Well . . . telling the truth is telling what happened and telling a lie is telling something that never happened."

"What would happen if you told a lie?"

"The judge would punish me." He puts his hands to his mouth nervously. The judge smiles. He is a charming little boy.

"When we talk about telling the truth . . . tell what you remember. . . . We don't want to know what other people told you happened." His mouth twitches. Lael Rubin begins the direct examination.

"When you were little, did you go to the McMartin School?"

"Yes."

"Did you go in the morning or the afternoon?"

"Morning?"

"Did you ever stay in the afternoon?"

"Yes."

"Who were your teachers at McMartin?"

"Peggy, Ray, Babs, and sometimes Mary Ann."

"Look at the screen. And see if you see a person whom you said was Ray. Can you tell us what he's wearing?"

"He's over in the corner, wearing glasses . . ."

"Objection," one of the attorneys calls out. The boy's hands go to his face, clasped together.

"The person you said was Ray . . . can you tell me who is sitting next to him?"

"Yes, Peggy, sitting next to him in a blue dress with flowers on it."

"Was there anyone else who was at McMartin when you were there that was not a teacher?" "Yes. Ray's friends."

"When you were at McMartin did you play a game called Naked Movie Star?"

"Yes."

"And when you played the Naked Movie Star game did you have to take your clothes off?"

"Yes."

"What other games did you play?"

"The Naked Movie Star Game and the Lookout Game."

"The Lookout Game—was that a game you played inside or outside?"

"Outside."

"Whose classroom did you play Naked Movie Star in?"

"The classroom that was farthest back."

"When you played Naked Movie Star was there anything covering the windows?"

"Yes."

"When you played Naked Movie Star, were there any of the teachers in the room?"

"Yes, Virginia, Peggy, Ray . . ."

"Do you see Virginia in the courtroom?"

"Yes."

"Can you look and see what she's wearing?"

"She's wearing a dark blue dress."

"Where is she in the courtroom?"

"Over to the right side of me, right behind you."

"Were there any other people in the room when you played Naked Movie Star—grownups who were not teachers?"

"Yes."

"Who were they?"

"Ray's friends."

"Were they men, or women, or both?"

"Men."

"Were there children in the room when you played Naked Movie Star?"

"Yes."

"How many? Do you know how many?"

"No."

"Were you in the room?"

"Not always. I was not always in the classroom when they played it."

"Did the kids have to take their clothes off?"

"Objection."

"Overruled"

"What did the kids have to do when they took their clothes off?"

"Objection."

"Overruled."

"May I be heard?"

"No."

Rubin asks the question again. The child answers:

"Ray would say to dance around like you are a movie star."

Dean Gits speaks: "Would the court please mark the last three questions."

"Did you do that?" Rubin asks the boy.

"Yes."

"Did any grownups, during the Naked Movie Star game, photograph the kids?"

"Objection," several attorneys call out.

"Overruled."

"Did any grownups take pictures during the game?"

"Yes."

"Who?"

"Ray's friends. And Ray."

"Objection."

"Overruled."

"Did anyone else besides Ray go into the room?"

"Peggy."

"James, during the Naked Movie Star game did you get touched by anyone?"

"Objection."

"Overruled."

"Yes."

"Who touched you?"

"Ray and Peggy."

"What part of your body did they touch?"

"My bottom and my penis."

"Did Ray put any part of his body inside you?"

"His finger." the boy squirms nervously.

"Did he put any other part of his body inside of you?"

"His penis."

"You said Ray touched you somewhere else beside your bottom?"

"Objection."

"Sustained."

"James, you said Ray touched your penis. What did he touch your penis with?"

"His finger."

What part of your body did Peggy touch?"

"My butt." He appears to be uncomfortable. The judge tells him, "We're going to give you a break, now, James . . ." And the monitor is turned off. There is a multiplicity of objections. Davis enters a motion to strike. "Motion to strike is denied," Bobb answers.

The monitors are turned on again. The judge asks James, "James, are you ready to answer some more questions?" His head jerks. "Yes."

"When we took a break I was asking you where Peggy touched you."

"Objection."

"Overruled."

"Well, she touched me on my bottom and on my penis."

"Did Peggy put part of her body inside your body?"

"Yes."

"What part of her body . . ."

"Her finger."

What part of her body did she touch your penis with?"

"Her hand."

"James, when you were at McMartin did you ever play a game called Lookout?"

"Yes."

"James, would you tell us how you played the lookout game?"

"All of the kids would get undressed and the kid that didn't would get up on the slide, and if he saw a parent coming he would slide down and tell Ray as fast as he could."

"Would you tell us what you did when you were on the slide?"

"I ran down and told Ray when I saw a mother coming."

"Did you go inside the classroom and tell Ray?"

"Yes."

"When you went inside the classroom, did the kids have their clothes on or off?"

"Off."

"Sometimes when the lookout game was played, did you stay inside the classroom?"

"Yes."

"James, when you were at McMartin, did anybody ever tie you up?"

"Yes."

"Who?"

"Ray."

"When Ray tied you up, did you have your clothes on or off?"

"Objection."

"Overruled."

"James, when Ray tied you up, did you have your clothes on or off?"

"Off," the tiny voice answers. He seems stiff and jerky.

"When Ray tied you up, James, did he touch any part of your body?"

"Yes."

"Objection."

"Overruled."

"Where did Ray touch you?"

"On my penis and on my bottom."

"Did he put anything inside your bottom when he tied you up?"

"Yes."

"What?"

"His finger."

"Did you see any animals at the school?"

"Yes."

"What kind?"

"Rabbits."

"James, did you see him hurt animals?"

"Yes."

"Which animals?"

"Rabbits and turtles."

"Tell us what you saw happen to the rabbits."

"Well, Ray would cut his ears off."

"What did Ray use when he cut the rabbit's ears off?"

"A knife."

"Did that scare you?"

"Yes."

"James, at the time you saw Ray cut the rabbit's ears off, did he say anything to you?"

"Yes."

"James, did you say you saw a turtle get killed?"

"Yes."

"Tell us what you saw."

"I remember that the turtles got hurt."

"Do you know what the word 'weapon' means?"

"Yes."

"What does it mean?"

"Something you could hurt with."

"Did any of the teachers have weapons?"

"Yes."

"Which teacher?"

"Ray."

"What weapons?"

"A gun and a knife."

"Did Ray show you the gun?"

"Yes."

"What did Ray tell you?"

"That he would kill us if we told our mom and dad what happened."

"Did Ray say anything about the knife?"

"Yes."

"What did he say?"

"That he would kill our moms and dads if we told."

"What did Ray say to you when he cut the rabbit's ears off?"

"He said he's cut us if we told our moms and dads."

"James, when you were at McMartin, did you ever stay in the afternoon and take a nap?"

"Yes."

"And when you stayed in the afternoon, did anybody ever give you shots?"

"Yes."

"Who gave you the shots?"

"Ray."

"Did they hurt?"

"Yes."

"How did you feel afterwards?"

"Drowsy."

"When Ray gave you the shots did he say anything to you?"

"I don't remember."

"Where in your body did he give you the shots?"

"I don't remember."

"Was it away from the school?"

"Yes."

"Which teacher went with you?"

"Ray."

"When you went away from school with Ray, did you walk or go in a car?"

"In a car."

"Do you know what kind?"

"No."

"Who drove?"

"Ray."

"Did any of the other kids go?"

"Yes."

"Do you remember how many?"

"No."

"Do you remember any of the places you went with Ray?"

"We went to houses . . ."

"Do you know how many houses?"

"No."

"When you played Naked Movie Star, did Ray ever put any part of his body in your mouth?"

"Yes."

"Would you tell us what part of Ray's body he put in your mouth?"

"Yes. His penis."

"We were talking about places you went away from school, some houses. Did you play games at these houses?"

"Yes."

"What games?"

"The Naked Movie Star."

"Who was there?"

"Ray and his friends."

"Ray and his friends were at the house. Had you seen them before?"

"Yes. At the school."

"James, when you played Naked Movie Star, did anyone take any pictures?"

"Ray."

"Was there anything scary at these houses?"

"Yes."

"Tell me what."

"Ray would open this door in the floor and there would be lions."

"What did they do?"

"They would run around and roar."

"What did Ray tell you?"

"That the lions would jump up and get us if we told what happened."

"How was Ray dressed?"

"Well, there was this red . . . Ray was dressed up as the devil and it was real scary."

"Wearing what?"

"A red coat, dressed up like the devil."

"More than one time?"

"Yes."

"At this house, did anybody touch you?"

"Yes."

"Who?"

"Ray and his friends."

"Did Ray put any part of his body inside you?"

"Yes."

"What parts?"

"His penis and his finger."

"Did you go anywhere else with him?"

"I don't remember."

"Do you know what a mortuary is?"

"Yes."

"What is a mortuary?"

"A place where dead people are taken to get ready for . . ." He couldn't find the right word.

"Did you go to a mortuary with anyone from school?"

"Yes."

"Who?"

"Ray."

"Did you go in a car?"

"Yes."

"Was there anyone else?"

"Yes. His friends."

"Would you tell what you saw in the mortuary?"

"Well, he opened up some coffins and we saw some dead bodies."

The boy smiles easily and does not appear to be terrified. What the closed circuit television did accomplish, however, was to create the illusion that the defendants are dangerous maniacs, to be feared, people from whom the children must be protected.

After the direct examination by Lael Rubin ended, the defense attorneys restated their position that the children had been led, coaxed, programmed by the therapists at Children's Institute International to say they had been molested when in fact they had not. In support of their position they pointed to the following facts:

(1) That the children did not complain while they were enrolled in the school, and, in fact, many came back to visit after they left the school.

(2) That none of them accused anyone except Ray, until after they were interviewed by Kee McFarlane and others at the C.I.I.

(3) That Dr. Ronald Summit, the prosecution's chief expert witness, has expounded, and published, his theory that it is *necessary* to coax children in order to get them to tell when they've been sexually molested. The defense attorneys state that Kee McFarlane and the other therapists who interviewed the McMartin kids are adherents to Dr. Summit's theory.

In the corridor, at lunch recess, 78-year-old Virginia McMartin sat down on the bench, leaving her wheelchair nearby. Suddenly she was surrounded by television cameras and lights, questions.

"That little boy used to sit on my lap!" she exclaimed. "Can you believe it? The lies he's telling about my daughter and my grandson! They can't take anything away from me. I'm seventy-eight years old. But the lies he's telling about the others! Father, forgive them for they know not what they do!"

One of the mothers is talking to another television camera crew: "The press report the bizarre testimony of one or two kids, but hundreds of kids have told the same thing all over the country . . ."

The cross-examination begins with Dean Gits asking the questions. The TV monitor comes on. The small boy grins, his elbows are on the table, his chin resting on the palms of his hands. There are endless questions about the "devil house," the airplane ride, and the molestations.

The defense scored heavily on cross-examination. Dean Gits asked the boy why he had told Kee McFarlane, the year before, that when he played the Lookout Game, he waited on a bench by the back door, and now he said he waited at the top of the slide. And why did he tell the grand jury that he did not always tell Ray when a parent arrived, and today told the court that he did?

Bradley Brunon, Virginia's lawyer, asked the boy, "When you talked with Kee McFarlane at the C.I.I., she told you that Ray was a bad guy, 'and we're going to get him,' Didn't she?"

"Yes."

Later, Brunon stood behind Virginia McMartin and asked, "Do you see Miss Virginia?"

"Yes."

"You're not afraid of her, are you?"

"No."

"You don't think she would hurt you, do you?"

"No."

While I was having lunch in the cafeteria, Betty Raidor and Babette Spitler walked over to my table and spoke with me. Both of them have gentle, kindly faces.

"What do you think of this?" Babette asked.

"It's too bizarre for words," I told her.

"What do you think of that kid's story?" she asked.

"I don't know. Lions? Devils? What is that all about?"

"Have you seen the school? It's a very small place. A kid wouldn't have time to run in and tell Ray before a mother got there. You can't even see the street from the slide, if you go down to Manhattan Beach and look at the school, you'll see that all those things would be impossible."

"How have you managed," I asked, "to stand up under the strain of this thing hanging over you for two years?"

"The first six months were the roughest," she said. "After that you get used to it. We were in jail for six months. They took my children away. When they first arrested me I didn't believe it. I said, 'Under arrest for what!' "

"Were you mistreated in jail?" I asked. "Were you threatened and insulted?"

"Oh yes! But the food was so bad at least I lost twenty pounds."

Seventy-eight-year-old Virginia McMartin asked me, "Did you know that one of the counts against Mary Ann Jackson was that the little boy said she molested him in a secret room! Now that judge has been all through that school. She knows there's no secret room. Where would one be? And, you know, those sheriffs dug up our floors looking for trap doors and tunnels, and one little boy said we had slides going down under the road to the other side. Can you imagine the sheriffs being that dumb? Another little girl said that Betty tied her hands behind her back, naked, and put her in a closet. We have no closets! There are no closets in the school. The only thing we had was cupboards with shelves. One little boy told how Ray locked all ten children in the bathroom. You were doing good if you could get two people in the bathroom. There was just enough room for a toilet and a basin.

"And that judge! The attorneys took her down to the school and she climbed up the slide and she could see that from the slide you cannot see the main boulevard. And another kid said that Ray dressed all ten kids in two minutes while the mother was coming. Can you imagine dressing ten kids in two minutes?"

I asked Virginia to tell me about the mother and child involved in the original complaint to the police in September, 1983.

"There was something wrong with that woman," she said. "When she came to the school she told Peggy, my daughter, that she was on the way to the doctor. I did not like the way she acted, and I didn't want to take her, but my daughter said, 'But Mom, she's got this child that needs help, and we should be compassionate . . .'

"I'll tell you what she did. I was working out in the yard and I saw this lady and this strange little boy standing there, and I wondered whom she was waiting for. And then I looked up again and she was gone, and here stood the little boy. She left this little boy! He was two years old, and we didn't know who he was or anything about him, and Peggy called around to all the schools, to find out if there had been a mistake. Well, Babs happened to stay that afternoon and she took care of him. Everything was in his sack, his name and everything. And she had called Peggy to see, and Peggy had told her 'I do not have any openings until June.' And the mother just left him there and didn't tell anybody! Not a soul. Well, that was enough for me. Then she went up to another school. And the school called Peggy and said, 'That child you called about is here.' She only left him there one day. Then she came in on the twenty-second when our term started for summer and that's when I told Peggy, the way she acted, I don't want him.

"So this little boy was at our school for only six or seven weeks, twice a week. He couldn't even talk plain. In fact, he didn't talk hardly at all. He ran around a lot. Then she quit bringing him. And we tried to call her. She owed us money, but we never got to talk to her. She lied. She said she enrolled him in March. And she didn't. I had proof of that, with the checks and all.

"He couldn't even talk. And the police said he told them all these things! Well I don't know how they understood it. We couldn't, and we work with children. *We* couldn't even understand him. Babs said she would call him 'pre-verbal.'

"Peggy Ann was a teacher in Orange County, and during the summer she worked as a ranger in South Dakota at the Wind Caves National Park, and she had sent Ray a ticket to come spend two weeks up there because she thought it would be interesting for him. And on the Thursday before we closed for summer vacation, Peggy called me. She was at the beauty parlor and she said, 'This Mrs. Bell called in and she wants to know what's going on. Somebody turned Ray in for child molesting. Do you know anything about it?' Peggy was so upset! Well this mother called and said, 'What's going on?' She had two children enrolled, and she left them in there—until the institute got hold of her and brainwashed her. Oh! They have done the most awful damage. They should get rid of those therapists. They're not even truthful! I wish you could see those video tapes!

"We tried to find out what was going on. The police, behind our backs, without telling us anything, called all the parents in town and got them all stirred up. So finally we demanded to see them. Well, the chief said he knew nothing about it. He told me I had no rights whatsoever. He would not tell us the name of the child. In less than two hours they came and ransacked my house. They arrested Ray and then sent that dirty, filthy letter out! They made it sound like it was conclusive that Ray had molested a child! The police started the whole thing. They got everybody all stirred up. A lot of people didn't believe it, but do you know that Hoag and the other one kept after our parents, and they said, 'Oh, but the other children said they *saw* your child molested.' It was October before we found out the name of the child. And we hardly knew the child.

"Then that woman deputy district attorney sent all the children to the Children's Institute, to that Kee McFarlane. She has made so much money off of this, and made a big name for herself. And they did all this brainwashing of the children. All of these child therapists, or whatever you call them, are making money off of this! They got this one little girl down there and she said she was never molested, and they said, 'That's very normal for a molested child.' That's Roland Summit's theory. If the child says he was molested he's telling the truth. If he says he wasn't, he's lying; and you have to keep working on him until he says he was molested. That little girl never got to testify.

"But if you could see those tapes, and see how they manipulated those kids, and put ideas into their heads! They only showed the parents short parts of it. They only showed them what they wanted them to see. One of the parents they turned against us . . . she didn't see the parts that show how they manipulated her little boy. And at the end he says, 'Ray did not touch me. Nobody hurt me at all.' They didn't show any of that. But my daughter saw it.

"One little girl, they couldn't do anything with her, couldn't get her to say anything, and they treated her terrible. They told her she was dumb, and stupid, and she said, 'Well maybe I am but I want to go home.' And she never got to testify.

"They got another little girl, and they said, 'Your mother's going to be disappointed because you haven't cooperated.' And the little girl said, 'Well, they were disappointed before when they took me to the other place, and they can be disappointed again.' She didn't get to testify either. But you know what—*those parents still prefer to believe that their kids were molested!*

"But can you believe that prosecutor, Lael Rubin! She went on TV and said that I founded this school for the purpose of pornography! The FBI went all over the United States. I heard they even went to Europe. They went to South Dakota and dug up part of the National Park to see if Ray and Peggy had buried some pornography! And they went to my niece's place in Oregon, looking for pornography. And they never found anything. And that district attorney sat up there on the stand and said that they had never found a single piece of evidence against us. They interviewed all the neighbors, all the businesspeople, and they never found one thing against us. And I spoke right up in court and I said, 'Why you dirty sneaks!' Every time my daughter and grandson were taken to Beverly Hills or to court, they bugged the car, to see if they could get some information out of them. Well, they never got a thing. He said so. And I said, 'Why you dirty sneaks!' And both of them looked embarrassed.

"They planted a sneak, a snitch, in Ray's cell when he was first there. Well Ray's a very quiet person so I guess he didn't talk much, and the snitch couldn't get anything out of him. Well, he was allowed to sit up there and make up a pack of lies. He said that Ray said that he did it and that he'd had sex with his sister when he was growing up and all that, and oh! It was horrible! And that awful Channel Seven got a tape from him, and that Wayne Satz put it on television! All those lies! And when they told all those stories about Ray killing rabbits, that Wayne Satz showed live rabbits on television, cute, little rabbits!

"I want to tell you something about Ray. He loves animals and he's always had pets, and he's so gentle that when he went fishing, he threw the fish back in the water.

"There was a teacher that came in and testified in our behalf and they asked her if the kids ever sat on Ray's lap, and she said yes they did and the kids loved Ray, but there was never anything improper or sexual. I don't see how he's held up like he has. And to think they've done all this to him, and he's done nothing!

"The men's prison is so much nicer than the women's prison. When Ray's dad went in to see him last night they allowed him to stay an hour and a half. Ray's very close to his dad. At the women's prison it doesn't make any difference if there's only one visitor there. Ten or fifteen minutes is all you're allowed. Peggy's husband goes to see her every Saturday and Sunday. He leaves here at nine, and doesn't get back 'till eight or nine at night. It takes all that time, just to get in to see her. He waited all afternoon, and because it was five minutes past the visiting hour, he didn't even get to see her.

"They sent down a Catholic priest from San Francisco, an exorcist, to unwind all that satanism. Can you believe that? And I saw one of those therapists that interviewed the kids, and she takes that Valium, and she's all glassy-eyed. It's no wonder, with the kind of life she leads. But that judge, Bobb, and Lael Rubin, I think they're out of touch with reality. Anybody who could believe that we could bring little children four years old to a cemetery and dig up caskets, and that the mortuary would allow you to come in and view dead bodies, anybody that could believe that stuff, they have got to be cracked! One of those little children said that Ray pulled out a knife and killed a dog, and there was no blood. No blood! And her parents still prefer to believe she was molested.

"You'd be surprised how many people didn't believe a bit of it in the beginning till Kee McFarlane and the police got a hold of them. A lot of them didn't even believe the police. There's something very sinister behind this whole thing. I wish I could find out what it is. That little tiny girl, Linda, came in and testified that Peggy put her vagina inside of her vagina. Can you imagine a large, grown woman putting her vagina inside of a tiny, two-year-old girl's vagina. Really! And every time a kid got stuck in a lie, Judge Bobb would given them a recess. And then the D.A. would take them out and talk to them, and they'd come back in and tell a completely different story. One little girl said that Peggy took a lighted candle and put it up her vagina. And nobody ever heard her scream, and the mother never heard about it or even noticed anything. If that really happened, you'd hear that kid scream for a mile! Now I'd be embarrassed to turn a story like that in, because it would make you look like an imbecile. One little kid said that Ray took him to a Catholic church and the priests and nuns were running around naked, and that Ray made him stand on the altar, naked, and say that there was no God, and that he hated God, and that there wasn't any. Can you believe that?"

Two events occurred the same week that should be mentioned:

(1) *The Torrance Daily Breeze* reported that there had been a meeting in the Los Angeles District Attorney's Office, six months earlier, in March, attended by District Attorney Ira Reiner, his top aides, and the three deputy district attorneys prosecuting the

McMartin case. According to the newspaper story, two of the prosecutors had recommended that charges against five of the defendants be dropped. The newspaper did not say which of the prosecutors had recommended the dismissals but quoted unnamed sources as saying Deputy District Attorneys Glenn Stevens and Christine Johnson disagreed with the chief prosecutor, Lael Rubin, on the legitimacy of the charges against Virginia McMartin, Peggy Ann Buckey, Mary Ann Jackson, Betty Raidor, and Babette Spitler. They did not recommend dropping charges against Ray Buckey and his mother, Peggy Buckey. According to the story, two of the prosecutors questioned whether the child witnesses were improperly influenced by C.I.I. therapists who interviewed them.

(2) Another story appeared five days later in the same paper reporting that the prosecutors, when they filed the 208 counts in the McMartin case in 1984, failed to interview two-thirds of the children named as witnesses. According to the story, the district attorney's office relied on information furnished by unlicensed therapists who interviewed the children, and that the children were not interviewed by police or prosecutors. Parents of the alleged victims said they did not even know their children had been slated as witnesses until the preliminary hearing had already begun. Kee McFarlane, director of the C.I.I.'s Sexual Abuse Diagnostic Center, said the taped interviews were inconclusive for the purpose of prosecution, and were not seen by prosecutors before the charges were filed. Both parents and defense attorneys believe the case was rushed so the media coverage would bolster District Attorney Philibosian's re-election campaign against Ira Reiner.

What all this implies is pretty scary. It suggests that the district attorney's office, with extremely questionable motives, charged the defendants in great haste, on extremely shaky evidence, without sufficient investigation, and now wants to dispatch them to prison, to spare themselves further embarrassment. It is well known that a prison term for a convicted child molester is the equivalent of a death sentence. Convicted child molesters are routinely killed by other inmates. The district attorneys know that. What it suggests is that the prosecutor and her superiors in the D.A.'s office, in order to protect their careers, are willing to send innocent people to their deaths.

Friday, October 4: The cross-examination goes on all day. The little boy looks uncomfortable when defense attorney Bradley Brunon asks about Peggy touching his penis. He moves his fingers across the table.

"Did Peggy touch your penis?"

"Yes."

"Can you tell me how long she touched your penis?"

"I don't remember."

"Did she touch you on the tip of your penis or somewhere else on your penis?"

"I don't remember."

"When she touched you on your penis, did she say anything?"

"I don't remember."

"You said Peggy put her finger in your bottom. Was she standing up when she put her finger in your bottom?"

"No. Squatting."

"Where was she?"

"Behind me."

"So you didn't even know it was Peggy."

"Yes, because she said something."

"Did you cry?"

"Sometimes."

"Did you scream?"

"No." His face twitches again.

Brunon switches to the Children's Institute and Kee McFarlane: "When Ray was arrested and went to jail, you know he was accused of doing bad things to children, didn't you?"

"Yes."

"Now after you had become aware that Ray was accused of doing bad things to children, why didn't you tell your parents?"

"I don't remember."

"When you talked with Kee McFarlane, she told you it was your duty to get Mr. Ray, didn't she?"

"Yes."

"She said, 'We're gonna get Mr. Ray,' didn't she?"

"Yes."

"You know Cheryl Kent wanted to get the teachers didn't you?"

"Yes."

"Did they tell you why you were testifying?"

"So we could put the people in jail."

"Did you know the name of the Lookout Game before you went to C.I.I.?"

"I don't remember."

"Kee told you the name of the game to remind you."

"Yes."

"Can you tell me when you first heard the name, 'Lookout Game'?"

"I don't remember."

"Can you remember having heard it any time before you went to C.I.I.?"

"I don't remember."

That afternoon, the McMartin mothers, after swarming at the district attorney's office with bumperstickers printed with their slogan: "I BELIEVE THE CHILDREN," descended on the courtroom en masse. They are a harsh looking bunch. One of the lawyers told me, "They have all been asked on cross, if they looked at the videotapes of the interviews at C.I.I. None of them had. Not one. They really want to hang on to the belief that their kids were molested."

"Why?" I asked.

"Some of them are just brainwashed by the police and the C.I.I. people. Some of them are doing it out of a desire for self-exhibition. Some are doing it because they want to blame child molestation for all their own inadequacies. And, of course, if those people are convicted, the parents have grounds to sue the insurance company for millions. The school had liability insurance of one million dollars per kid. I'd like to believe they're motivated by something other than greed, but I wouldn't be too sure. They have consistently refused to look at any of the evidence that their kids were *not* molested. There's one woman who always gets up in front of the TV cameras and talks about how her little boy was scarred and ripped. Her kid never said he was molested."

"Why does she do that?" I asked.

"Her husband's running for political office," he explained. "None of those people's kids are complaining witnesses."

The mothers crowded tightly toward the door. There must have been almost thirty of them. The recess was nearly over. I walked over to listen. They were making insulting remarks about the defendants and veiled threats of violence. They refer to the defendants as "The Magnificent Seven."

I talked with Mary Ann Jackson's lawyer, Barbara Aichele. "I'm as offended as anyone by child abuse," she said. "But Mary Ann! If ever there was a couple who exemplified the traditional American dream, Mary Ann and her husband were it. Hard work, saving for the future, church, family . . . And now they're ruined. They've lost everything. Those people are so conservative! If the prosecution wanted to make a case against somebody for child molestation, they certainly picked the wrong people!"

The hearing may go on for months. Davis and Gits, the lawyers representing Ray and his mother, have announced that they intend to put on an "affirmative defense," calling witnesses on behalf of their clients. Attorneys for the other five have asked that their clients be severed from the hearing and brought to trial, sparing them the cost of counsel in the endless preliminary hearing. Walter Urban, Betty's lawyer, said, "The district attorney's office . . . created a monster that developed a life of its own." Forrest Latiner, Peggy Ann's lawyer, commented that "The D.A.'s office doesn't want to take the heat for saying that this case was a mistake." Even the media are beginning to shift. One reporter wrote: "There is a notable change in the prosecution's demeanor. At the outset they touted to television cameras the strength of their case. . . . Now they scurry down the hallway to avoid reporters."

James was on the stand for eight days. Defense attorneys brought up many inconsistencies in his testimony. Bradley Brunon, Virginia's lawyer, got him to say that he remembers the teachers as nice people, that he knew C.I.I. interviewer Kee McFarlane thought they were bad people, and that he did not remember being molested until Kee McFarlane told him the teachers were bad people. Toward the end, the attorneys began asking extremely explicit questions about the purported sexual acts of which he had accused Buckey:

"When Ray put his penis in your behind, James, did it go in the hole?"

"I don't remember."

"What was the color of the fluid that came out of Ray's penis when he put his penis in your mouth?"

"I don't remember."

His father interrupted the questioning and asked that his son be given a short break. He said the boy was too agitated to continue. The judge agreed: "We're going to take a short recess, James." And the monitor went dark. Contrary to what the father had said, the boy appeared to be relaxed and was smiling when his father interrupted the cross-examination. The defense attorneys angrily protested the interference.

Another interesting development: On Friday, November 4, the chief deputy district attorney assured the McMartin parents and media, when the parents visited the district attorney's office, that his office intended to "pursue this case to the very end." The band of parents had gone there to proclaim their support of the prosecution.

However, four days later, *The Los Angeles Times* reported that the Sheriff's Task Force on Child Sexual Abuse, created a year earlier, was being quietly disbanded and that it was extremely unlikely that any more charges would be filed. The team had identified fifty-six suspects, spent more than a million dollars, and did not make a single arrest. Some of the parents told reporters they felt that the district attorney's office had "knifed them in the back." Sources in the investigative organization said that pullouts by parents made prosecution impossible. Parents, on the other hand, said child witnesses were dropped by the prosecutors "because they knew too much."

The contradictions in the boy's testimony were very striking. James had said that Ray Buckey tied him to a chair, in which he was sitting, and then sodomized him.

"Did Ray cut a hole in the back of the chair," Brunon asked.
"No."
"Was there a hole in the bottom of the chair?"
"No."
"Then he really didn't sodomize you, did he?"
"No."

Reports of dissension in the ranks of the district attorney's office continue to surface in the daily press. The Chief Deputy District Attorney, Gil Garcetti, second only to District Attorney Ira Reiner in rank, smilingly told reporters there was no disagreement, but on Tuesday, October 20, Reiner summoned the McMartin prosecution team to his office and directed them to speedily make written assessments of the prosecution's case.

The Los Angeles Times quoted an unnamed prosecutor as saying, "For a long time I believed that all seven (defendants) were animals and should be thrown to the wolves. Until I began to study the evidence."

The parents and the defense attorneys agree on one issue, if nothing else: that the prosecution has bungled the case from beginning to end. On Saturday, October 19, a group of parents held a press conference and asked the state's attorney general to investigate the district attorney's handling of the McMartin case.

The defense attorneys began their affirmative defense. One of the witnesses was a father who admitted that his son never said he was molested until he was interviewed by Kee McFarlane at C.I.I. "Did Dr. Astrid Heger, after she examined him, say he was molested?" The father said no.

I had lunch with Daniel Davis, Ray's lawyer, in the courthouse cafeteria. "Is it true," I asked, "that you've tried fifteen molestation cases and won them all?"

"Yes," he said, "And I'm gonna win this one too."

"What do you think of all the allegations that the kids were touched?" I asked him.

"I think children *should* be hugged and touched," he said.

When I went back into the courtroom at one-thirty, the hearing was already in session. Dean Gits, who is usually soft-spoken and restrained, was saying, "Your honor, my client has been in custody for nineteen months, on charges that were a fraud!"

At the end of the day, after court recessed, I talked with Peggy Ann. She is twenty-nine, tall, thin, soft-spoken. She has an M.A. in special education, from U.S.C. She teaches handicapped children.

Peggy Ann is interesting. She is bright and articulate and she has a remarkably beautiful speaking voice, like a singer's, as pure and unaffected as a child's. There is something about her, a kind of clear-eyed, natural innocence and wholesomeness that cannot be faked.

"You know," she said, "you grow up with all these ideas that the police never would do anything that wasn't right, and all these ideas of how the law works, and you don't understand how things can go wrong. I had heard of Jordan, Minnesota,* and some of the others, but I had no idea it had gone this far.

"The techniques they use, once those techniques are learned, they can get any kid to say anything! Before this I never knew children could be manipulated so easily, that you could get kids to say things that they didn't know anything about, and get them to agree with you. I didn't know they were so easily manipulated. I think some of them actually come to believe that it's true. I've heard of some legitimate cases where the kids cried and the kids really show some emotion because they've been through something terrible, but these kids here, it's like they're reciting from a little script. They show no emotion. It's scary, because it could happen to anyone in the world."

I asked Peggy Ann, "Is it true that you only taught at the school for five weeks, about seven years ago? How did you get pulled into this thing?"

"You know why I think they pulled me into it is . . . they showed the kids the pictures, the group pictures, and during the five weeks I was there happened to be the time when they took the class pictures. So, the Institute, they didn't even find out who was there, or when they were there. They didn't even find that out. And I think they just assumed I was there the entire year. And so they would point at my picture and say 'How about her?' And they brought me in that way. If I hadn't been in that picture, I never would have been brought into it. Because the teacher who was there before me, that I replaced, she wasn't in the picture, and she was there far longer than I was. She's been named by a couple of kids, but they never charged her. She came to testify and said that during the time she was there she never saw anything. The only kids that accused me were the two that told the wildest stories. Rooms that don't exist, doors that don't exist, cemeteries and dead bodies, and the nuns. Drinking blood at the church, on the altar, and all the animals were killed on the altar and just left there.

"But its very hard when you sit in a chair . . . because I remember the first kids that came up on the stand, and they'd say this happened, and that happened . . . But when that kid says your name! It's just like someone hitting you right in the face.

*See Chapter VI.

"But they've gone to such extremes, they've searched so many houses, they've dug up so many yards, they stepped on some feet that weren't the right feet to step on. I think now they've sort of backed off from doing that. They came to the school and dug all the tiles up, because the kids said there were all the underground tunnels, so they actually pulled up all the tiles, and then underneath, it's just a cement slab. So they couldn't go any farther. But they brought in those machines that can see if there's anything under the ground—something like sonar—they brought all that in and they tore the whole place up! Trying to find the tunnels. You could almost make a comedy out of it if it wasn't so awful. These kids should get A's in creative writing. I mean, their imaginations are great.

"But you sit there and you just wonder, why are they doing this to me? And Raymond, everything comes down on him because he's a male. It's surprising how well he's holding up. Sometimes I think he's holding up better than me. They searched my car enough times. I said, this is ridiculous! Can you believe this? They went up to the Wind Caves National Park in South Dakota. They dug it up because I had worked there. And the lady who was my boss there told me they actually went up there and dug up the park! They dug up quite a bit. They dug up, like, in back of this housing for the people who work there, and they dug up at the entrance of the cave. And then they wanted to go into the cave and dig it up and the lady said, 'That's ridiculous!' And she put her foot down and she said, 'Nobody could have buried anything inside the cave.' And so they stopped at that point.

"But when they first sent out that letter, and we sued, a lot of people said that was a mistake because the police are very vindictive, but you can't go back. My mom called Hoag a couple of times and talked to her, and she wouldn't back down and she said, 'This is a bunch of baloney! What are you doing?' And Hoag was like, 'Well, this is my business and I'm running things.' And Hoag didn't like my mom doing that, speaking up to her. And people have said that Hoag was—even before this case—was the type of person that even if a bicycle was stolen she made a huge case out of it and acted like it was a Supreme Court case. She made a big ordeal out of everything. And that's what they kept telling my parents through this whole case. I remember sitting here and all these people were being called and everybody was saying, 'Oh, don't worry. Jane Hoag just makes a big deal out of everything. Don't worry.' And they didn't know. And if you've never been involved in a case like this, you don't know who to go to . . . . So we went to a lawyer who was recommended and he turned out to cause more problems than he solved. We tried to show malice—that there were many other people they could have arrested. And they didn't. There's probably a hundred people. In the discovery that came in, you wouldn't believe some of the people that have been named in the community. The kid that was the first complaint, he was pointing out people in ads in the paper. They showed him a picture of Raymond and he didn't know who it was. But he started pointing out everybody, including his father.

"Jane Hoag kept calling people up and saying, 'We have information that your child was a victim. Another child has named your child. Will you please go ask your child . . .' And then they'd say, 'Please bring your child down to the police station and let us ask him questions.' And they still came up with nothing, even with that technique. Can you imagine? You're a parent and the police call you and say, 'Your child has been named.' And they came up with a big zero. All they had was this one kid, and he wasn't saying it. It was just his mother saying it. I think Jane Hoag has that philosophy of Roland Summit, that there are molesters everywhere.

"Then, the parents complained about Jane Hoag. They didn't like her technique, of what she was doing, so they called in Kee McFarlane. It wasn't the police who called her in. Like, Hoag is more straight-forward. I don't like her, but . . . Kee McFarlane is so devious! It was the D.A. She didn't have a case, and some parents asked her, 'How come charges aren't being filed?' And the police gave the case to the D.A. And there wasn't any case, so they brought in Kee McFarlane to interview the children, instead of Hoag doing it. And there's some connection between the D.A.'s office and Kee McFarlane.

"So Kee McFarlane did most of the interviewing. At first, she did all of it. But when it was time to go on TV, and she went flying all over the country, being on TV, then she handed it over to Sandi, and they hired Shawn Connerly, and another lady too, but she didn't get their technique down so every kid she interviewed, she came up with the kid saying nothing happened. So none of

those children are testifying. But the first ones, Kee did all of
them. Some of the kids didn't even go there until after everyone
was arrested, to the Institute. And then Kee wasn't doing any of
them. And you wouldn't believe how many times those kids were
interviewed. First, some of the parents said they questioned them
every day. Then they were interviewed by the police. Then Kee at
the C.I.I., then they were talked to multiple times before they
testified. What they do at C.I.I., at first they play these memory
games, and they always let the child win. It's the same technique
they all use. They play some kind of game where they let the kid
win. And they tell him, 'Oh, you're so smart! You have a wonderful
memory.' Then they have the kid draw a picture, and they tell
him, no matter how lousy it is, what a wonderful picture it is. So
they build him up the whole time. 'You're wonderful! You're wonderful!' Then what they do is they say, 'I'm going to draw a picture
now, and I'm a terrible artist.' So they draw a picture of a person
and they have the child name all the parts. And if a child can't
name a part, then they tell him. So then the kid gets this lesson in
anatomy. And if it's Shawn Connerly, she tells them all the smutty
names! You know? All the things you'd never want your kid to
hear, she tells them all those things! So they name all the parts of
the body. Then they bring out all the photographs and they have
the class pictures that are taken every year.

"And can you believe this? Kee McFarlane, when she's doing
these interviews, she wears a clown costume, with stripes, like
Ronald McDonald! And if the kid says nothing happened, she tells
him he's dumb.

"They use dolls and puppets, and the one they used to represent
Raymond looked like a vulture! And she tells the kid that the
teachers at McMartin are sick people and that the police are
watching Raymond and following him. And the kids said over and
over again that they were not molested, and you see Kee
McFarlane saying, 'I don't want to hear any more no's.' And she
tells the kid that all the other kids said it happened, which wasn't
true. And if a child says nothing happened, she tells him he's
dumb, and stupid, and makes him feel isolated, like an outcast.
And it goes on for hours!

"First they said it was pornography, and they didn't have any, so
they had to come up with a new theory, so then it was satanism.

Every one of their little theories falls by the wayside, so they come up with something new.

"And these medical examinations. Some of the kids are nine years old and they went to the school when they were two. They had been examined by pediatricians and there was nothing. Then, six years later, they take them to Dr. Heger at C.I.I. and they find something. With Dr. Heger it doesn't matter what's there anyway. She says 'Oh yes, there are signs of molestation.' No matter what.

"We're not talking about, like in the Ruby case, patting them on the bottom. . . . In this case they have made it rape! And they're saying that a three-year-old child can be raped, walk out of the school, no one notices it. That's absurd in the first place. And they're going to have a hymen that's one millimeter different? That's absurd. That child would be ripped to shreds. There would have been blood, and the parents would have known immediately that something was wrong. I have a friend who's a doctor and he's seen legitimate cases, and he says, those children are not walking in. They're being carried in! And they have stitches. They are ripped! They forget how little a child is. And when they talk about a hymen being a millimeter off, I sit there and I say, 'Are you kidding?' I can't believe that people, like the D.A. and the judge, don't apply a little logic and think. They're saying 'raped' and 'sodomized' at the same time! Day after day! And the child just skips out of the school, and goes home. If you put logic into this thing it falls apart.

"And if a kid was taken up in an airplane, wouldn't he go home and say something. You couldn't terrify all those kids and not have one of them say anything. Speedboats, and airplanes! And digging up the cemetery! Do you know how long it takes to dig up a grave? It takes grown men all day to do it. I asked a guy who works in a cemetery. Well, we were good. We had four-year-old children who could do it in ten minutes. And then we lifted it up. Four hundred pounds. Maybe more than that. And they cut up the corpses and they bled. And we have grown people believing it! 'I believe the children.' That's their slogan.

"We had dead babies too. Not in the testimony but on discovery. You see, it depends on what therapist they went to. If one therapist is real gung ho on one idea, then all the children coming out of that therapy come out with that idea. And this one lady, every child that she has had in therapy has underground tunnels, secret passages out of a school, just like in the movies. You lift the carpet up and there's the hidden door, and you go down underneath. All the kids she deals with all have that, and there are dead babies with her kids. And they didn't bring those children to the stand. You can imagine what would have happened. It was the same ideas they had in the Minnesota case. The kids said dead babies were killed right in front of them.

"And there was the kid that said he was taken to a Catholic church and the priests and nuns were running around naked. You see, most of the kids are Catholic, so they didn't name their own church. They named other churches. This child wasn't Catholic, so he named the Catholic church. That same kid also picked out a picture of nuns that was taken forty years ago. I felt like saying 'Are you going to arrest James Kenneth Hahn and Chuck Norris? Are you going to arrest those nuns? Because that child has charges against me. And if I'm charged, then those people should be named too. I mean, if you're going to believe it.'

"This is another thing they do in the interviews at C.I.I. When the child won't say anything, the interviewer says, 'I'll point, and you say yes or no whether you got touched. And then when you come back to see me, we will check you out and do the doctor stuff and we'll know what to check out on you, and then you won't have to worry about it. We'll check out on what happened to you when your vagina was all red. What went inside you when your vagina got red? Was it a finger?' The child says no. And so she points on the dolls, and she'll say 'How about a penis? Was it a penis that went inside?' And the child says no. That's the other thing they'll do. They'll just point to the doll and say, 'Do you think it was this?' And so it isn't even a child pointing. It's *them* pointing. And they just nod their head, yes or no. And then she says, 'Are you sure? That's what some of the other girls told me. Did that happen to you too?' And she says no. And the interviewer says, 'How about a finger? Some of the girls thought it was a finger that went inside. Is that true?' The kid says no, and then she says, 'Oh! A finger went inside Sarah?' She says no. So she says, 'Why don't you come and show me. Show me with the Ray and Sarah dolls. I need you to come help me right now because we're running out of time, and we need to have your help.' The thing is, the kid doesn't even have to point. They point and the kid'll just nod her head, one way or another.

"*This is Dr. Heger talking.** She says, 'It happened to everybody in the school. Every little boy and every little girl in the whole school got touched.' So the kids didn't have to say anything. The interviewer just led them, and if they said no, it just went on anyway. And if they kept saying no all the way through, they still said the kid was molested. They claimed they had four hundred kids and all they were able to bring in were fourteen. And out of those fourteen every one of them had something that was just wacko. Cemeteries, secret rooms, airplane rides, naked nuns . . . Every single one had something that you knew it was just fantasy.

"And then another thing. If you look at the testimony, when they describe it, it's with no emotion. They were asked, 'Tell me to describe how you got touched.' First of all, the judge wouldn't let those questions in. And this is supposedly a sex case! And the judge wouldn't let the questions in because she thought they were too embarrassing! But then, when the questions finally got in, the child said one of two things. He either said, 'I don't remember,' because they couldn't describe anything because they never experienced it. Or—one or two of the boys said things that were just physically impossible.

"Not one child that came to that stand could describe any sexual act. Not one. And that's the part that he would remember. And that judge acted like it was fact. A lot of kids testified that they were molested going through the car wash. There were at least three or four. One of them was a child who took everything back on the stand. She recanted everything. But then Lael Rubin said that was because she was afraid.

"The first child that testified was a sweet little boy who just goes along with everything. So he gets up there on the stand. I don't know why they had him go first. And everything they'd ask him, he'd say, 'I don't remember.' And so Glenn Stevens, the prosecutor, said, 'He needs a break.' So they take a break, and then Glenn Stevens would come back with the child, and the child would say, 'It was Raymond that did it.' And then, when one of our attorneys would say, 'Did Mr. Stevens tell you to say that?' And he said yes!

*Dr. Heger is a physician on the staff of C.I.I.

"And Mr. Brunon got up to cross-examine, after the direct. He said 'This is a story that everybody wants you to tell. Everybody says, "Walter, just tell the story and we'll be happy." Isn't that right?' And the kid says yes. And Brunon says, 'And this didn't happen, did it? This is just a story that your parents want you to tell . . .' And the kid said, 'Yeah, that's right. They just want me to tell the story.'

"But that happened back when the press was so against us that they just played it down. They could have made a big story out of it but they just let it slide. When this thing started I thought, no one's going to believe this. Nobody's going to believe that someone like my grandmother who can barely walk is going to rape a baby. But I couldn't believe from the day this started how easily people can be conned into believing things. It shocked me. Wayne Satz, the KABC-TV newsman, caused a lot of this because the way he presented it, it made us look like monsters. He would come on television and say, 'This is how they say the games were played.' One kid testified that he would watch Wayne Satz and he'd sit there and think 'Wow, did that happen to me?' And if he could imagine it in his head, then he adopted what Wayne Satz was saying. That's what he said on cross-examination! But he did! Wayne Satz caused a lot of this. And he came out in January with the big story and showed Raymond's picture and said things that made it look like he was guilty and no questions asked. This whole thing of 'innocent until proven guilty.' That's a bunch of baloney.

"I think if they, somehow, could get out of this case they would. If they, somehow, could throw it off on somebody else, they would, but, you know, they've spent four million dollars and they can't say, 'Oh. Sorry, we made a huge mistake. We're really sorry.' They can't do that. And no one will admit that they're wrong. No one will say, 'I made a mistake.' I've talked to a lot of lawyers and they all say judges just don't throw cases out in a preliminary hearing. I think if we'd gone to trial right away last year, it would have been good-bye. But people are starting to realize there's something wrong. And all the schools that have been closed down in the South Bay . . . What's the number they're saying? They're saying twelve hundred children have been molested? And not one child ever said anything? I mean, the odds against that have got to be astronomical! It's unbelievable. And when all this happened and

I'm sitting in jail there, and I couldn't believe it. And I kept hearing this about threats and everything and I'm thinking to myself—because I took a number of child development classes, and I'm thinking, children don't understand death. They really don't understand that. So when I got out I went and I read all the research on death, and what children understand about death, and there's some new research out on children's understanding about death, and if you were going to threaten a child, that would not be the way to do it. Because all the research shows that to a child, death is like at night when you go to sleep. When Aunt Martha died, she just went to live somewhere else. They don't understand it as a final thing. It's not until they're older that they understand that it's a final thing. You don't get up and walk away.

"And I read all the literature on pedophiles. I didn't even know what one was. It wasn't a common word that you saw everywhere. And I looked it up in the dictionary and I said, 'Oh my gosh!' Because I had never heard about those things. You know—they take pictures and all that stuff. And this is what they're saying that I did? And I was just shocked. Because I had never been exposed to anything like that. Now it's like, everybody knows what it is, but then it wasn't a subject that people talked about. It wasn't a big issue, and I never really thought about it. And I had never known anyone that anything like that happened to, not even any friends of mine.

"It took years for therapists to get to the point where people began to respect them, and believe in them, and now, these people have torn it all down. I would never take a child to a therapist! I thought it was just in the South Bay, but it's everywhere. These little child therapy clinics are making so much money! They get seventy-five dollars an hour. And they're nobodies! They don't have any wisdom to give you.

"They took Babette's kids to C.I.I. and they drilled them, trying to get them to say something about Babs, and every time I see Kee McFarlane and that group I think about all the pain and the suffering they have caused, and it wasn't ever needed. It's sad, and it's tragic. And here they are getting all these grants, and all this money. And they're so wrong in what they do! The cruelty. And so many families have been put through so much, and it's so unnecessary.

"My mother, before all this happened, she was very friendly, almost naive. And she has kept that, in the jail. She says hi, she talks to the sheriff's people in there, and she tries to find something good about all of them. I was just the opposite. I just said, 'Don't say a word to me. I'm not talking to anyone.' And she tries to help out the other inmates in there and she'll tell you, 'Oh, she's had such a bad life . . .' And even with all the evil around her she still tries to find the good in everybody. And she'll tell me, 'That sheriff isn't as bad as he seems. He just having a bad day.' And I'm saying, 'Mom! That's a bad person. He's just bad!' But she keeps this friendly attitude. She's real religious. And I was brought up that way, you know, there's good in everybody. And I have since changed that belief. But she really believes that. When I was a child and we went to the grocery store, if they gave her a dollar too much, we would drive all the way back and give it back to them. And when we had the school, if we bought groceries for the school, I said, why don't we get dog food too, and just write it off, and she said, 'Oh, no. We won't do that.' I used to get mad at her. Here's everyone else in the world writing off things. And she wouldn't even write off a can of dog food off her taxes. And she's so honest, and so good. And they've got her in the high-power tank, with murderers.

"In that county jail—the women's part—most of the women in there are there for prostitution, and some for drug problems, not real crimes, like murder. And I always thought the idea of jail was to make people come out better. And if anything I can see why everyone returns. It makes you worse in there! And everyone in there treats you like dirt. I mean, they're not hardened criminals. Somebody who's in there for drugs, they need help. They don't need someone who treats you like dirt and insults you. I mean, you wouldn't believe how those sheriffs treat the people in there! And they scream and yell at you. I couldn't believe it! And that's what my mother goes through every day. They scream at her, and say they're going to kill her. She takes medication, and the way the jail's set up, the hospital's on the top floor, and a lot of the girls in there are taking medication, and they all go up to get their medication. So, instead of bringing the medication to my mother each day, they make my mother walk, handcuffed. No one else in the jail is handcuffed. My mother is handcuffed, with her hands behind her back. They make her walk through all those people! And they scream, and they yell at her. And it doesn't get any easier. People say, 'We're gonna kill you! You molest children!' And every foul word you can think of. And the sheriffs don't do anything about it. And she goes through that every single day.

"When we were on the bus . . . we got in the bus. . . When we first started going over there, Lael Rubin had this keep-away order. None of us could talk to each other. We couldn't see each other or anything. And when we were brought over to the jail we couldn't sit on the same bus, which meant that, every single time, I was put on the men's bus. I was handcuffed and put on a men's bus, the only woman on the entire bus, and I had to sit there and listen to all their comments. They didn't know who I was, but it doesn't matter. Here you are the only woman on a men's bus, handcuffed, you can imagine the things they'd say. And so that's how it was for a long time. We would go on these separate buses.

"And then, they took away this keep-away order and they let us all go on the same bus. We were getting on the bus, and one of the sheriffs talks to all the girls that are getting on, and he says, 'These are the child molesters! That's the latest thing to do now!' And he laughed. Well, there were about half a dozen in back of us and they started screaming and yelling and threatening. And one girl had matches and we were in this locked-in little thing, with our hands handcuffed. And she took matches, and she was throwing them, trying to catch our hair on fire.

"And the sheriff just sat there. He'd started the whole thing. And he just sat there. There were two sheriffs in the bus, and I yelled to the other guy. And he told them all to sit down, and to quit it. But they threw six matches in, trying to set our hair on fire, and we were handcuffed! And it was all because of this stupid sheriff. He started the whole thing.

"And after that, I said, 'Excuse me, could you tell me your name?' And he says, 'No. What for?' And I said, 'I'd just like to have your name, please.' And he said, 'I didn't do anything.' So I went and asked the other guy, I said, 'Could you tell me his name?' And he said, 'No. He can tell you, if he wants to.' And the other guy said, 'I didn't do anything. It's all her fault.'

"And, the next day, Forrest got up in court and told what had happened, and after that they ordered a car to take us over there. But I'm sure nothing happened to that guy. And he laughed about the whole thing. But the mentality of the cops! I just couldn't believe it. They enjoy cruelty. And the women are worse than the men. They are far worse than the men. Some of the men are okay. But the women! It's like they're women coming into a men's field that used to be men only. And it's like they have to prove themselves. They scream and they yell and they act real tough. It's like they're trying to prove they can be tough and mean in a man's field. My mom has gone through far more than my brother has gone through. She'll be reading some religious book, and they'll take it away from her, and say, 'You can't have this.' Or a card that a friend or relative has sent to her, and they'll take it from her. And Ray doesn't go through any of that. They'll go into her cell, and everything will be thrown all over the floor. Ray doesn't go through that. It's not easy for him, but he doesn't have those people trying to prove they're tough. They call him names and threaten him. But he's not in with the main population. He's over in the hospital part, where they put the police officers and informers, political people, people that they think can't go in with the general population. He's in there. Lael Rubin had him put down in the general population, and when they found out who he was, they threw cups of urine and feces on him. She's the one who was responsible for the keep-away order, that no one could be with anyone else. And I know the reason why they did that, because they thought they could break people. They put Babs* in with all the people who were crazy. They put me in with the people coming off drugs. They put you in little, cement cells. There's just enough room for a mattress. They don't let you have books or anything. That's where they put me. There was no reason for that. Except Lael Rubin wanted to be mean. I'd ask, 'May I have a book, please?' And they said, 'No, you're not allowed to have anything.' But I sat! I sat for two weeks in this little cell. Nothing to read. Nothing but the walls. I didn't get to go outside. I didn't get to do anything. It's probably six feet by ten feet. And everyone around me . . . here's all these people coming off drugs, screaming, yelling, all night long. And they have what they call 'four point,' where they put the girls. They take off all her clothes and they tie her down with leather straps. And they say it's for their own safety. I don't believe that. There is no reason to do

*Babette Spitler, another defendant

that, but to humiliate them and degrade them. And I'm listening to that all night.

"Forrest put in a complaint. When I got Forrest I told him what was happening, and he put in a complaint, and then they moved me over to another wing of the hospital, and all of a sudden they're saying, 'Oh, well we didn't know you wanted anything to read!' Then they let me have books and things. I was in the hospital part almost the entire time I was there. And I'd hear the doctor, and he'd go in and say, 'What's wrong with you?' And the girl would say, 'My stomach hurts.' And he'd say, 'Well why is that?' And she'd say, 'I don't know.' And he'd say, 'Well I don't know either.' And he'd leave. And I'd hear that every single day. And he didn't do anything. If you were in there with something seriously wrong with you, that would be the end of you. And I know there are some people who are dangerous, but they're not the majority there, but they treat everyone like they're that way. But, I mean, you don't know what it's like in those jails until you go in there. And I can see why people come out worse than they were before—because you get to really dislike law enforcement. You become really anti-law enforcement. And then, they don't have anything for those people to do. And they're just sitting there, idle. They don't have anything to do. And it's filthy. It's just filthy. And they have this big work force there, doing nothing. And they could be doing constructive things. I saw old ladies in there. And an awful lot of people were in there for drugs. And it's not going to help them. And I saw young girls that were fourteen, fifteen years old! And in the jail they have a natural loathing for a child molester, and I can understand that, because it is repulsive, and I thought to myself, if they're going to falsely accuse me of something, please, let it be anything but that! People can relate to murder, because everyone's wanted to kill somebody, but this, it's so far removed from what most people can understand. I can't comprehend it. And I know, for the rest of my life, I will have that following me around. Even if I get married and have a different name. And there will be people who will say, 'There must have been something.'

"And I will never again work with children. Never. And friends of mine who were teachers with me have been very supportive, and I have a real good friend that I team taught with, and he'll call me up and he'll say, 'I still have all your stuff here.' And he has the kids write me letters, and he says, you know, 'We're expecting you to come back.' And I say, 'Chuck, I'm not coming back.' And he says, 'Yeah, you'll come back. When this is all over, everyone's expecting you to come back.' And I said, 'No, I'm not coming back.' And everyone I know who teaches, they say, 'Well why not? Why aren't you coming back?' But I can't live with that behind me, saying . . . like, if I touched some kid on the shoulder, and he got mad at me, I cannot live with that fear that he will go home and say, 'You know what she did? She touched me.' Because I cannot live with that. And I could not go through this again. And people say, 'Oh, it could never happen again.' And I always say, 'Well, how did it happen the first time?' It could happen again—especially since now I have this little label on me. And I teach handicapped children, and their parents first of all, are fearful to begin with, because they have a handicapped child. Most parents have a lot of guilt when they have a handicapped child. And it's not their fault, but they have guilt. And then to have a teacher coming in who was in a big case like this . . . You know? I couldn't deal with it. And there's too many other jobs I can go into where I won't have to deal with this.

"Can you believe this? Babette Spitler worked at a child abuse center with Dr. Summit. And she says, 'I want him to come into court and look me in the face and say that, all those years, I could have been fooling him.' Because she worked right with him! And she said that his big thing was, every day, he'd say, 'Give everybody a hug . . .' And she said, 'I want so much to go up to him and say, "What is this 'Give everybody a hug' stuff?" ' He is someone who worked for years in the field of incest. And he got absolutely no publicity and no notoriety. And he sort of dedicated his life to this. And she said, then, when this came along, this was his chance to become somebody. And he just latched right on to it, and made a big name for himself. He was known, but not outside of his little group. Now, he makes all this big money, consulting.

"When Babs was there, child sexual molestation wasn't the big thing. And it was mostly cases where children were physically abused. Beaten. They said they were going to bring Summit in as a witness for the prosecution but I don't think they're going to now.

"I used to trust everybody. I was brought up in a small community. And everybody knew everybody. And, through this thing,

I've just put a wall up, and I don't talk to anybody, and I don't trust anybody. And then when *you* first started coming to the hearing I saw you talking to Wayne Satz and those other reporters and I said, 'Well, that's another one I can just write off.' "

"But you know," I said, "when I first started coming to the hearing I looked at you and Babette, and Betty Raidor and Virginia and I said, 'Am I supposed to believe that those people are child molesters? Give me a break!' And all those reporters reacted with anger when I said that."

"Yeah," she said, "but Raymond said, the other day, 'God! Look at this picture of me in the paper! No wonder everyone thinks I'm guilty! If I looked at this picture, I'd say, "Yeah, that person's guilty." ' I'm sure there are people in cases like this who look a little bit odd, and act a little bit odd, who haven't done anything, but just because they are a little odd, everyone thinks they're guilty. Just because they're accused.

"You know, if some of the kids had gone home and said that somebody did something, I could believe that maybe something happened, but we've got hundreds of kids, and none of them said they were molested—in fact they all said they were not molested, until some therapist tricked them into saying something. And they're asking us to believe that twelve hundred kids were molested, taken up in airplanes, taken to a church with naked priests and nuns running around, and digging up cemeteries, and none of them ever said anything!

"Hoag came to my house, and she came with four other police officers. This is a two-bedroom little house, at the beach. And they had men all staked outside my house. And I was leaving to go to school. And they came to my house and they said they had this search warrant. And so they made me sit. And at that time I didn't know that you had the right to go with them when they look through your stuff, so that they can't plant things. And so they told me to sit down there, to sit in the front room and not move, and to call my work and tell them I wasn't coming in. So I called and I said, 'I'll be a little late.' And you know, you're teaching and you have your entire class sitting there. But I called in.

"And they were at my house from seven in the morning until like, three in the afternoon. This is a two-bedroom, little house. And they went through everything. And they took everything. And my roommate was a newspaper reporter. And suppose this really was some big conspiracy. Would I have a newspaper reporter as my roommate? Well, they went through everything, and they took everything! They took my family albums, they took out everything they could walk out with! They took out seventy-two things out of my house! And some of them, like all the photo albums, are included as one item. And I had a friend from the east coast. He's an ice climber. He was going on an expedition to Colombia, and he was storing his belongings at my house. So they go through all of his stuff. And he's a writer too, and they took all his slides. They took all his stuff. And he was there that day. He happened to be at my house that day that they came to search. And he said, 'I don't live here. I'm only storing my stuff here. This is how I make my living.' And they still took everything of his. And it wasn't until a year and a half later when Forrest said, 'This is ridiculous. You haven't used these things.' And finally they gave him his stuff back. But for a year and a half they kept all his stuff, and that's how he made his living.

"And they still have my stuff. And Forrest asked the other day, if I could have it back. And what I want is, I want my photo albums. I had a camera. They took my camera. I don't care about that. But a family album! I can't replace those! I can't replace that stuff, and they say, 'Well, we may use it at trial.' They're not going to use it at trial! Forrest said they haven't even looked through my stuff.

"But Hoag, she would look under the piano, and look under every little thing. And the other police would go through a room, and she would go through it again. They go through your drawers and they pull everything out, and they just leave it on the floor! And you have to come back and put your whole house back together—what's left that they didn't walk out with.

"At the school they came up with nothing. They scraped the paint off the walls. And friends of my brother's, they went and searched their homes too. They searched my parents' house four times. You'd think once would be enough, but they did it four times. I don't know how many houses they searched, but there's a lot. And my brother's best friend, they searched his house. And that's a scary thing, to have your house be searched, and you're sure you're going to be the next person arrested, and dragged into the thing.

"And the grocery store guy, they searched his house, and they went down to the church, because that one child said that animals were killed there, and they did the blood tests there.

"And that's the thing too—why would you do that? Why would you have underground passages, or why would you go to a grocery store. Why would you go to a public place to molest a child? Why would you go to a car wash? That's just absurd! And that car wash— it's the most popular car wash in the area, and it's on the two busiest streets in town. In the first place, you can't stay in the car while it's being washed. But then, they have glass, and you can watch your car go through it. And that's where the kids said they were molested—going through the car wash!

"But it's so hard on my grandmother. It's her whole life. I mean, if you would have seen her at the school. There are people who just do their job, but she dedicated her life to that. And then to turn it around and make it such a terrible thing! And then to have her daughter in jail. And she was always so idealistic about the judicial system. And just to have everything come crashing down on you. And to be her age, too. Seventy-eight!

"But I don't care if they gave me three million dollars or what- ever, it's not worth it. I mean, all the pain and everything . . . When this is over I want to just leave. I don't want to deal with this anymore. Once you're accused of something like this, the accusa- tion is always there.

"And Raymond! They've tried to make him out to be such a mon- ster! And it's so opposite to his character. Slaughtering animals! Why would he have animals for pets? He's the one they've come down the hardest on. If he wasn't a male he would probably just be . . . not even in it. But people will believe it, because he's a male.

"But I can't work. I can't even get unemployment because I wasn't fired. I was put on leave by my school district. I can't get anything. And I asked Forrest, 'What do they expect me to do?' And he said, 'They don't worry about that. They just figure you can fend for yourself.' For the first year I lived with friends of mine, but you can only ask your friends for so long . . . to put you up and to pay for your food. And so I stay with my dad, now. But if I was by myself and didn't have my dad, working, who will support me, what would I do? And, you know, my parents lost everything. They weren't rich, but they lived comfortably. They lost two homes. They lost their school. They lost their savings. They lost bonds, stocks . . . They lost everything they had. And that dumb judge, she won't pay Danny, because she doesn't like him. She was against us from the day we walked in there. Could she have really believed all that stuff? I think she just blocked it out. I think she should have stayed in traffic court.

"But I'll never be a teacher again. I'm not going to be a teacher. If they can haul you into something like this, I'd be the easiest person in the world. You should see the paranoia in the teaching profession! They go to extremes. No one wants to be in the classroom alone with the kids. And they go to seminars where they tell you, 'Don't be alone with the kids. And even if you have another teacher in there with you, they'll drag him into it too.'

"By the way, please don't tell anybody where we live. We've had to move five times. Every time we moved, the sheriffs came over and told all the neighbors who we were, and told them all the juicy details of what we were accused of, and we were getting death threats and people calling us up and saying, 'You're gonna die.' And people coming by and saying things like that to my parents and my grandmother. I don't know why the cops did that."

The preliminary goes on and on. In December, Shawn Connerly, one of the C.I.I. interviewers, was called as a witness. She admitted that she had lied when she stated on her application for employment there that she had a M.A. Then she wept.

After the holidays, in January, three physicians who were reputed to be experts in the detection of child sexual abuse were called as witnesses by the defense. They were shown four photographs: two anuses and two vaginas. Their answers were equivocal, and they did not agree with each other. One said he could not say whether there was evidence of molestation without seeing the history of the child.

At the end of the day, after the court recessed, I spoke with one of the defense attorneys. I asked him to explain the medical testimony.

"The older kids, after having been out of McMartin two, three, four years, never said one word about molestation," he told me. "Those older kids never said they had been molested until they were put through the process, with the cops, interviews, evaluators. The younger kids, the ones who were still in the pre-school at the time they arrested Ray, no way! None of them ever said he was molested. Now that is subject to protective orders, but, essentially that's true. But you're not going to quote me on that, right? But if there had been a spontaneous disclosure, we would have known about it a long time ago."

"Several people have told me," I said, "that not one of the kids said anything about the Naked Movie Star game until they were interviewed by the evaluators. Is that correct?"

"That, actually, is a jingle that school kids pass around, like when we were kids it was 'Liar, liar, pants on fire.' Same kind of thing. And apparently the new version is 'What you see is what you are, you're a naked movie star.' That, and a lot of other things, were part of the script that was developed in the process with the interviewers over a period of time. But none of the kids said, 'Oh yeah, we played the Naked Movie Star game and it went like this . . .' None of them said that spontaneously, okay? The therapists are all leading the kids into their programmed approach."

"The militant parents who come and swarm down here," I said, "they all are full of stories about satanic rituals and international child pornography rings. Where did all that come from?"

"It came from the therapeutic community. You know, you shouldn't put all the heat on Kee McFarlane. There were the follow-up therapists too. They're the ones who are sitting on their confidentiality. But I'd like to know the nature of the conversations the kids are going through with these so-called therapists. They're trying to reinforce what went on previously at the institute.

"They're saying that 1,200 kids were molested there, and that it went on for twenty years. You would think that at least one of the kids would have said something, or that someone would have seen this and dialed 911 and had everybody over there.

"They say they have 'solid medical evidence' and that the medical evidence corroborates the children's stories, but they've discovered that the medical evidence does not corroborate what the children are saying because, essentially, the simplest way to put it, the children said that they were repeatedly raped, and sodomized, and the medical evidence does not support the allegation that the kids were penetrated. All the girls' hymens were intact. The medical evidence does not exist. It's a fraud.

"When the case was filed and broke in the news, and as the hearing unfolded and the kids are saying all these crazy things, the D.A. kept saying, 'Well that may be, but we have medical evidence. We have medical evidence.' Well when you look at the medical evidence you find out that the medical evidence does not exist. The medical evidence is baloney. There's nothing there. There is no case."

"But then, why are those people in court every day for two years?"

"Most of those kids told five different stories. One to the cops, another to the evaluators, another one to the Grand Jury, and another in the preliminary hearing, and they told still another story on cross-examination and still another story the next day! If you look at four days of testimony you'll see three different stories from one kid, even in court, not to mention what preceded that.

"What happened was we discovered that the therapists and the D.A.'s and the investigators got the kids in and they played court with them! They had them actually play court! They rehearsed it over and over again. That's how they get the kids to come in and be consistent. And it breaks down on cross-examination, of course.

"They're all trying to hide behind confidentiality, too, which is a very dirty play. Everybody's using these little kids as a shield. They say, 'It's privileged, and what I'm doing is needed for the kids, and you have no right to this information. You're trying to harass the kids.' Everybody on the prosecution side is doing it. And we're accused of hiding behind the Fifth Amendment by remaining silent and forcing the government to prove the case against us. We said, 'Screw the Fifth Amendment! What do you want to know? We've got nothing to hide. Now! You show us what you've got! You're the government and you're putting the case on and you're supposed to have something. Let's see what you've got. Why, are you afraid to let us go to trial?'

"We had to fight them on a day-to-day basis to get them to turn over documents, and material that is normally given to defense attorneys on discovery. They sat on material and held up reports, one of which is the continuing investigation, and that turned out to be nonsense. They were afraid to let us know the extent of the investigation that they had gone into without having turned up anything! And if they had turned over everything in the beginning, like they were supposed to do, they would have had to admit they didn't have anything. So they just dragged the thing out and then finally said, 'Well, okay, you've got everything now.' Of course, it's a year and a half later. But where are the dead bodies, where are the pictures, the pornography? What happened to the porno theory? The D.A., Philibosian, and one of the top aides, said that the school was founded for the purpose of child pornography, and it was repeatedly stated by Lael Rubin that the school existed for one purpose only, and that was to produce and distribute kiddy pornography on an international market. We have a lot of that stuff on tape. And they never came up with a single piece of pornography. Not even one, or any evidence that it ever existed. None. We sat in court and demanded, from the very beginning, we demanded, 'Show us the pictures. We want the pictures. We want to see the pictures.'

"And they kept saying, 'Judge, we want to talk about these video tapes. We don't think the defense should see the videotapes.' And the reason they didn't want us to see the videotapes is because they realized that once they got in our hands they were defense evidence. I'm talking about the videotapes at Children's Institute."

Later, we sat in Forrest Latiner's office and we talked. He is Peggy Ann's lawyer.

"You know," he said. "I've been a public defender for twenty-five years, I've defended some bad people, and I've defended some good people who did bad things. But this case is unlike any other case I've ever seen. I am absolutely one hundred percent certain that these people are innocent. Totally innocent! They didn't molest anybody. This reminds me of what happened to the Japanese Americans in World War Two. They just got caught up in something that wasn't of their making, and they got locked up. Innocent people do go to prison.

"Paul, when I first met Peggy Ann, she was locked up without bail! She was locked up for over sixty days! She was remanded on April sixth, and I wasn't able to get her out on bail 'till June ninth. And when I first met her it was April twentieth. She was in lockup.

"And I looked at her! I've represented many a woman—young girls, even, in custody on a variety of things. And I took one look at Peggy Ann and I said, 'There's something wrong here! This young lady doesn't belong in this lockup, much less in this case!' And I said, 'What are you doing here?' She's the all-American girl. She's better than that. She's real class!

"To give you an example of how deep the prosecution tried to dig to get dirt, they interviewed former classmates by the score, of both Ray and Peggy Ann, hoping that they could come up with, somehow, some way, some perversion associated with the Buckey family, and of course none said anything of the sort, but some really complimented the Buckey's for being such wonderful people. There was one in particular who said, 'Peggy Ann is so modest that she was the only one of the girls who wore her T-shirt when playing volleyball on the beach. And all the other girls would want to flaunt their attributes, and they would wear their skimpy bikinis while playing volleyball. But Peggy always wore a T-shirt.' When I asked Peggy about that, her response was, 'Yeah, it's because once when I was playing without it and my strap broke. Never again!' She's articulate and bright! She's sensitive and sensible. The only irrational thing she does is climb mountains. She goes up the face of cliffs! I sure as hell wouldn't go with her when she does that!

"Of the kid witnesses that testified, not one said he was molested before he was interviewed by Kee McFarlane. More than that— they all *denied* that they had been molested, before they were interviewed at C.I.I. So it's not just that they didn't say anything. And some of them had been asked numerous times, over and over and over again, by parents, the police, interviewers at C.I.I., the D.A.'s, and the Manhattan Beach Police sent out a letter to the parents asking them to ask their kids, and these kids all said they did nothing. And the parents all sent back their responses. And the parents kept asking them. Finally, they began hearing stories about their friends going to C.I.I., and these kids talked among themselves. It's a small community. And the interviewers said, 'We don't want any dummies here. We only want to talk to the smart ones. You're smart, aren't you. Your friends have all told us something. I don't want to hear you say no. If you say no you're a dummy.' Gross! Even if you accept Kee McFarlane's present explanation that she had a social worker purpose in mind, that her purpose was to get kids who had been molested into therapy, and you can't get a kid into therapy unless the kid owns up to the incident occurring. Therefore you've got to use all sorts of pressure tactics to get the kid to own up. That's Roland Summit's theory.

Even if you accept that at face vallue, it taints the stories you're
receiving for prosecution purposes. It's debatable whether that's a
viable approach even for a social worker, but I don't think there's
any question that for prosecutorial purposes that information
you've got in that manner, with those methods, is now totally
worthless. Fortunately, that's what we have. Those videotapes are
our best weapon in this case.

"I'm not going to argue with the social worker or the therapist
about their discipline, but for God's sake, don't use what you've
manipulated the kid into saying to prosecute someone. In
California we have the decision in the Shirley case, that if you hypnotize somebody that may be well and good for whatever purposes
you have in mind, but you can't use that information in a trial. It
can't be admitted because it's unreliable.

"But when you look at the so-called medical evidence, it doesn't
exist. There is no corroborating evidence. There is no case!

"As an attorney there are some things I can do and some things I
can't do. I work within a system that I know has its limitations.
That doesn't mean I have to like it but I have to recognize it.

"But I have never seen the system become as distorted, and as
unjust as it's been in this case. The no-bail holds were the products
of bogus and sham, and I criticize strongly the presiding judge in
the master calendar for allowing it to happen. I have known him for
years and I have a very high regard for that man. But I know he is
extremely ambitious. I know he is seeking appellate appointment,
and I have a deep, nagging suspicion that somewhere in the back of
his mind, he believed that being of some help to Philibosian would
stand him in good stead with the governor.

"But there was never a reason to lock these people up without
bail. Matusinka wouldn't have done it. I know that. She told me.
The evidence that was presented never showed that there would
be any danger of physical harm to the kids or their parents if the
defendants were at liberty. The evidence that was presented in
those terrible form letters merely indicated that the kids were fearful, or would be emotionally upset. And that doesn't even come
within the purview of the constitutional provision, out of Section
Twelve.

"The McMartin family were conservative Republicans and they
voted for all those conservative, law-and-order initiatives, and they

never in their wildest dreams suspected it would ever come back and haunt them. It's a sad lesson in life. I've always had the attitude, and I guess it's why I'm a defense counsel: . . . That the rights of the best of us in our society, are protected only to the extent that the rights of the least of us are. If they can do that to them, they can do it to us. That's why I try to keep the wolf of the government away from the door, from Manuel Gonzales's door and Willie Jones's door. Because if I don't, they are going to be knocking at my door."

I asked him, "In all of these wild, bizarre cases all over the country, with allegations of not only mass orgies of molestation, but satanic rituals and murdered babies, do you think the prosecutors really believe that stuff?"

"No," he said. "I think they are amoral."

On January ninth, after twenty months of testimony, 60,000 pages of transcript, and four million dollars spent, the preliminary hearing finally came to an end. The courtroom was packed with reporters and the angry mob of parents. All the television stations had their camera crews there. The judge walked in and the bailiff called the court to order.

Before Judge Bobb announced her rulings, Dean Gits, Peggy Buckey's attorney addressed the court and asked that his client's bail be reduced. She has been held on one million dollars bail for nearly two years. He said, "For all this time, she has not been able to touch the hand of her long-time husband of many years, nor to speak with him except over a telephone. And communication with members of her family has been prohibited. Since the time she has been in there, her life has been continually threatened, and is, on a continuous basis. She has been assaulted. Inmates have tried to set her on fire. Since then, she's been kept in isolation for her own safety. She has endured all of this better than I could." The judge said she would take the matter under submission.

Mary Ann Jackson's attorney, William Powell, asked that his client be allowed to make a brief statement. The judge said she would allow it if the prosecutors and other counsel had no objection. No one objected. Mary Ann stood and read her prepared statement:

"Each morning, as your Honor enters the courtroom, everyone is asked to rise, face the flag, and recognize the principles for which it stands. Upon hearing these words the first few times, I felt I could safely rely on these principles. I now find, that these long cherished values have been bent and twisted beyond recognition.

"I was brought up to believe that my country and its laws were designed to assist and protect the innocent. Many members of my family have staunchly supported and defended these laws. My great, great, great Uncle Abraham Baldwin was a signer of our constitution. My great, great grandfather fought in the Civil War. My own father fought in the trenches in France during the first World War. My husband served on a submarine in the South Pacific during World War II, and our son was in the Marine Corps helicopters in Vietnam.

"What I have witnessed, through these many months of court procedure has not been a search for truth and justice, but a continuous, theatrical display.

"I have been accused, persecuted, prosecuted, maligned, threatened, badgered, harassed, tried and found guilty due to media-hype.

"We, the defendants, have been pushed to the limits of our endurance, and in this extremity we have learned what few people ever face—that of our very survival. Several of us have read books and diaries of concentration camp survivors which have given us courage and hope in dealing, *not* with an equal situation, but nevertheless a desperate one.

"The truly heroic figures in this tragic marathon are the defendants and time will someday declare this to be true.

"I have seen no political courage . . . little judicial courage . . . and only the beginnings of media courage. What I have come to trust in are the simple acts of daily human kindness. I want to thank you, your Honor for some of these: this courthouse, where we could park in the basement; a good cafeteria, a closed courtroom for the most part, which I used as my own sanctuary, with some measure of peace. And, for excusing those defendants who wished to leave at 4:00 p.m. even though it did interrupt slightly, the proceedings. I do condemn and abhor the hypocrisy, injustice and blatantly vindictive assault upon me and my family regarding this case, and I now admit with great disappointment and sadness that it is easier, in this country, to be guilty than to be innocent."

The parents made derisive remarks as she spoke. One of them laughed, a mean, forced laugh.

Then, Judge Bobb asked each of the defendants to stand up, one by one, as she read off the counts. She bound all of them over for trial. She held Ray Buckey on fifty existing counts and thirty-one additional new counts. She handed down eight existing, and fifteen new counts, against his mother, Peggy; two existing counts and one new count against Babette Spitler; two existing and seven new against Betty Raidor; one existing count and seven new against Peggy Ann Buckey; two existing, and three new, against Mary Ann Jackson. She let stand one count of conspiracy against Virginia McMartin and each of the others. The defendants looked weary and depressed. Virginia slumped against the wall.

"This court is adjourned," the judge announced. As she read the counts to each of the defendants, she smiled. It was weirdly inappropriate. She looked like a woman greeting guests at a garden party.

"This is the biggest pack of lies I have ever seen," Virginia told the reporters. "This is exactly like a Nazi prison camp. I don't think there's such a thing as a truthful judge. There is no justice or honesty. The day I stepped into this court I knew the judge was against us. The D.A. came in here and lied and lied!" A young reporter asked Virginia, "You're seventy-eight years old. Do you think you'll survive this?"

"I'll survive it!" she said. "I'm tougher than they are."

Out in the hallway Lael Rubin, flushed with victory, faced a battery of television cameras and lights, telling the reporters it was "a victory for the children and the parents." She was smiling, but it was a harsh, mean smile. Kee McFarlane was there in the crowd, grinning broadly. The television cameras converged on her too.

I went back into the courtroom. Virginia was standing next to her wheelchair, leaning on her crutches. She grabbed my hand and squeezed it, and neither of us said anything for a long time. Then she shrugged and said, "Well, I guess I'll keep on taking care of Peggy's dog and Ray's cat."

A week later, I called Dean Gits, to get more details on the testimony in the hearing. He said, "Paul, could you call me back later? I've just been told that the D.A. is dropping the charges on all but two of the defendants. I have to go down to the courthouse."

Within minutes it was on all the television and radio stations. In the afternoon there were banner headlines on all the newspapers.

Even foreign language periodicals had the word "McMartin" on their front pages. On the five o'clock news, television stations showed the angry parents snarling about "child molesters going scot free." Ira Reiner, the district attorney, said, "The evidence against those defendants was so flimsy it was almost non-existent." Then, there was Peggy Ann, on Channel Two, saying, "If there's no evidence against me, there's no evidence against my mother and my brother, because it's the same kids telling the same stories." Then, there was the *former* district attorney, Philibosian, being asked if the case was filed for political reasons. "Absolutely not," he said. "There was no politics involved."

Then, on Channel Four, there was Danny Davis, saying, "There is no difference in the evidence against those defendants who were dismissed out, and the evidence against the remaining two."

I changed channels, and there was Walter Urban, Betty's attorney, saying, "They had no case. There is no case. There never was."

III

The Defense Doctor

Lee Coleman, M.D.

Lee Coleman, M.D., is a psychiatrist based in Berkeley, California. He is founder and director of the Center for the Study of Psychiatric Testimony. His book is titled, *Reign of Error,** a pun on Robespierre's Reign of Terror in the French Revolution. In this book, he asserts that psychiatrists are no more able to determine guilt or motivation than any other person—yet they are asked to come into the courts and pronounce defendants guilty or innocent. The questions courts ask psychiatrists to answer are not scientific or medical, but political, he says. He calls for the courts to stop transferring their responsibility onto psychiatrists and make their decisions based on the evidence.

Coleman is the author of a 34-page paper titled "False Allegations of Child Sexual Abuse: Have the Experts Been Caught with Their Pants Down?" In his paper he blames Dr. Roland Summit's Accommodation Syndrome theory for an avalanche of false accusations of child sexual molestation. He states that therapists and po-

*Boston: Beacon Press, 1984.

92

lice across the country are indoctrinating children into believing that they have been molested without any evidence to support it:

"A child is given a play doll and told to pretend. If the child says something happened, it's taken as reality. If he says nothing happened, he's not believed. He's told he'll feel better when the secret is out, that all the other kids say it happened. Finally, to please the adult, the child says what the adult wants to hear."

Psychiatrists, he says, do not have special tools to tell if a child has been molested, nor do they have special tools to identify child molesters. "We expect psychiatrists to tell us whether a child has been abused and by whom . . . and we are regularly judging innocent persons guilty."

As for Summit's assertion that children don't lie about sexual abuse, Coleman states that it has led to a wave of false allegations flooding the police and the courts, who rely on "experts" who tend to assume that accused persons are guilty. "With or without proof, the experts are thus telling us that if a child makes statements indicating sexual abuse, such statements must be true. . . . Worse yet, these experts are training cadres of police, protective social workers, and rank and file mental health professionals to assume that statements of a child, with few exceptions, are to be taken at face value."

These professionals, he says, are anxious to absorb the latest word and are taught that our former tendency to disbelieve a child's statements should be replaced by total belief. "It has led to spectacular accusations against child care professionals like teachers and pre-school workers. . . ."

He concludes his paper by stating that this trend ". . . will lead us down the path of abandonment of due process legal protections for accused persons."

We spoke with Dr. Coleman on two occasions. This was our conversation:

Question: I understand that Dr. Roland Summit's theory that children never lie about molestation is now the accepted belief among the psychologists and child abuse experts. Is he correct?

Coleman: Dr. Summit is the theoretician of this whole movement. And his theory is total baloney. Absolute baloney. You can quote me. And he hasn't studied the issue of false allegations. He has only studied cases where people have acknowledged they were molested. His whole experience goes back to groups like Parents United, where it was not even contested, and the families go in and work on it. And his whole theory is based on an intact family where the mother is coming to the rescue of the father, at the expense of the daughter. His whole experience is with incest cases, and all the baloney about how kids wouldn't make these things up comes from incest cases in intact families. Most of the cases going on right now are not incest cases and that's why my article is entitled "False Allegations of Child Sex Abuse—Have the Experts Been Caught with Their Pants Down?" They have been caught with their pants down because while they're so busy looking at incest cases they have not realized that something new is happening.

Q.: In the McMartin case, it's been reported that even some of the prosecutors are questioning the legitimacy of the testimony against the defendants.

Coleman: Well, you say you've been following the McMartin case. Did you watch any of the videotapes that were shown?

Q.: Not yet.

Coleman: Well, you see, that's what you have missed. You missed the heart of the case. The heart of all these cases is what they're doing with the children. Now all you have to do is look at one videotape of what they are doing with the children in the McMartin case, and you will see what a total fraud is going on here. And even Kee McFarlane is now starting to say, "Oh, well I didn't do those interviews for legal purposes." To which I would like to ask her, "Well, Miss McFarlane, if you didn't do them for legal purposes, for what purpose did you do them? What reason would you have to try to train children to believe that they've been molested? Is that for therapeutic purposes? Is that good for a child—to be trained to believe they've been molested when you have no evidence that they have been?" This is a total farce!

Q.: In the McMartin case, it looks like Ray Buckey and his mother are in deep trouble, but . . .

Coleman: Ray Buckey and his mother are not in deep trouble, because of all those child witnesses in the hearing, there is not a single child that has accused them. They have not told the interviewers that they have been molested. It's the interviewers that have been telling *them* that they have been molested. Now if you don't believe that—and there's no reason why you should—watch the videotapes.

Q.: Some of the child witnesses retracted statements that they were molested.

Coleman: Well, all right, but you know what the prosecution is trying to claim—that that's part of the syndrome—that they will retract it. So the real meat of the thing is, Why would they say it in the first place? And in order to understand that you have to look and see what they did with the children.

Q.: What was your testimony in the Ruby trial in Torrance?

Coleman: Basically, I testified that what little evidence the prosecution and the investigators allowed to surface indicated that these children were being put through the same kind of manipulative, suggestive and leading techniques. But, you see, the limitation there is: the investigators shredded their notes. That's what I've been told by Mr. McCabe, the defense attorney. The police investigators did not videotape their interviews. The therapists they sent them to did not videotape any of their interviews. So all we have is their word for what was supposed to have been said. And all we have is their word that they didn't lead or manipulate the children.

Q.: What about the question of kids, five years old, testifying about things that allegedly happened when they were two?

Coleman: Well, you see, Ray Buckey and his mother, in the long run, are not in trouble. I do not have any doubt in my mind that there will not be a single conviction in the McMartin case. Also I do not have any doubt in my mind that there are going to be massive lawsuits against Los Angeles. And there are going to be massive investigations of the Los Angeles District Attorney's office, the Manhattan Beach Police Department, and everybody who's involved in this hoax is going to pay in the long run. I haven't any question in my mind about it. All you have to do is look at one interview at the Children's Institute International. That organization is being funded by the United Way, among others. That is where our money is going—to pay people to train children to believe they've been molested, in the most manipulative, outrageous way that I have have ever seen. I've seen interviews in these cases all over the country and this is the worst! *This* is child abuse.

Q.: Did you testify as an expert in the Miami case?

(AUTHORS' NOTE: Miami has nothing to do with the McMartin case. It is just one of about 200 cases in which Coleman has testified as an expert witness. Miami is discussed at length in Chapter Five.)

Coleman: Yes.

Q.: What happened there?

Coleman: There was a guy who's been convicted, and given six consecutive life sentences, and there was no evidence that he molested any children. All the evidence there is is based on videotaped interviews, and statements that the parents said the kids made. The only factual evidence in the case is that the man's son was molested by somebody, because he had gonorrhea of the throat. So there we have medical evidence that he was molested. They checked the father out at the time they discovered this. They found no evidence that he had gonorrhea. Now, I don't say that that proves that he couldn't have done it, because maybe he was treated secretly. But the bulk of their case was the interviews that were done with seven or eight children, in which you have the same techniques being used.

Q.: In McMartin and several other cases, the prosecution claims they have solid medical evidence, scarred rectums and vaginas. Could those have been caused by something other than molestation?

Coleman: Absolutely. There is no medical evidence. I've looked at the opinions of the doctors who have claimed they found medical evidence, and there is not any medical evidence. First of all, do you know what they write down as their two common findings? They write, one, "History of sexual abuse." Well that's obviously begging the question, isn't it? In medicine, if you say ". . . history of epilepsy," it means the person is known to have had epileptic seizures even if he's not having a seizure right in front of you. So if they say "history of sexual abuse," it sounds like they have proven sexual abuse. The next thing they say is, "Physical exam consistent with sexual abuse." Well, that's meaningless, because you could have a normal exam and that would be consistent with sexual abuse. You could have any finding that they are finding that is also consistent with any of a dozen other causes. They are coming up with findings which are ludicrous. They're saying, "The hymen is thickened," There's not a single controlled study [that has] ever been done which shows that a person can take a child and not be told whether they're suspicious of being molested, and pick out which ones have been molested and which ones haven't been, by how thick the hymen is. And the same thing goes for finding anal winks and all those other things. There is no legitimate medical evidence that they are finding in these kids.

Q.: Were these medical examinations done at the same place as the videotaped interviews?

Coleman: I don't know how many were, but the ones I've seen were. Like in this Ruby case,* there's a small core of people that the county has learned to send the kids to. These people all sit around and talk to each other and have convinced each other that they have a way to tell if a child has been molested that an ordinary pediatrician can't see.

Q.: Are McFarlane and the other therapists at C.I.I. followers of Dr. Summit's Accommodation Theory?

Coleman: Absolutely. All so-called experts in child sexual abuse in this country—with no exceptions that I have yet seen—are followers of Summit's theory. There's no question about it. They've got a "Catch-22" which says, *"If the child says it happened, it happened. And if the child says it didn't happen, it happened."*

Q.: You said in the Ruby case that the children were rewarded for saying they were molested.

Coleman: In the Ruby case, because they did not videotape any interviews, and all we have is the notes that the police decided to write down, they don't show us what their method is. So what I testified to is that in the interviews that I have seen, this is what is being done everywhere. The children are rewarded for giving answers that they have been molested, and they are given disbelieving responses and negative responses if they say nothing happened. They are told, "Mommy will be proud of you. We are so pleased that you are really giving us a big hand . . ." when they say something happened. And when they say it didn't happen, they say, "Is that one of the secrets? Are you afraid to tell that one? Mommy will be so proud if you talk about it. It's okay. Maybe next time I see you you'll tell me about it." And then they set up another interview. Actually, the people who are the most vicious,

*See Chapter IX.

and the most clever of all—worse than the police—are the mental health professionals. All I'm telling you is just the tip of the iceberg. If you just watch the interviews, you won't even need me. If you read my article on Summit, you'll get to something that's even more basic than that, because sooner or later you are going to have to tell your leaders the answer to a very basic question, and that is, well, if Coleman is right, before I'm going to believe Coleman, or if I'm going to believe anybody who's saying this, why would mental health professionals whose business is to try to help children—why would they do such a thing as this? They're not bad people. If you read my article, and you read Summit's article, you will see that Summit and people like him are training mental health professionals to believe that if you don't see the evidence that the child was molested, and you don't get the child to tell you that he was molested, it's an indication that you are not very competent, not very caring, and you're not capable of really going in there and representing the child and rescuing the child from disbelieving adults. If you do get the evidence that they have been molested it shows that you really care about children, you understand how difficult it is for them to talk about it, you understand that if maybe the other people won't believe the child but you will, and you are the best, you are the finest, the good guy. You care enough and you are intelligent enough that you'll get the evidence whereas the lesser trained people won't get it.

Q.: Where are they getting all the stories about satanic rituals and devil worship and drinking blood?

Coleman: I'll tell you where they're getting it. When you start a child fantasizing by repeated questions . . . when you tell a child, in so many words, that he's been molested—which is what these interviewers are doing, and a child comes to pretty soon believe that he has, he's in a position where he has to say something happened but in fact he can't pull it out of his memory because it didn't happen. Okay, once you get them going, filling in like that, then the sky's the limit. Now this is where these interviewers end up taking it in the rear, because the interviewers and the police don't want the children to talk about murders and satanic cults because they can't prove those things. And they would begin to look ridiculous. But once you get the child started, you can't stop him. They start fantasizing beyond the sexual stuff and—and I see it over and over again. I've got, in my notes of the cases that I've reviewed, I've got more murders, more ridiculous stories . . . In the Ruby case Michael Ruby was said to be sucking on his own cock . . . I've got people making up capsules and slicing them up and giving them to the kids . . . pouring red and white slime on the kids . . . flying off to places a thousand miles away . . . hot air balloons. One of the witnesses in the Ruby case has them going down in a sewer to the ocean, giving them all air tanks and going scuba diving . . .

Q.: The same kind of stories turned up in Bakersfield and Jordan, Minnesota. Did you hear that in Miami?

Coleman: Oh, yes. All kinds of bizarre, crazy stories. Some kids would say that their dad was there, taking part in the molestation.

Q.: The news media are telling us now that some of the prosecutors in the McMartin case doubt the legitimacy of the case and want to dismiss four or five of the defendants. But the chief prosecutor and the higher brass in the district attorney's office want to go ahead with the prosecution.

Coleman: I'm sure it's purely a political decision. I don't think they have the courage to face up to what they've done.

Q.: Some of the attorneys are predicting that this thing is going to blow sky high, and the district attorney's office is going to take a lot of heat for it.

Coleman: You'd better believe it. And if I have anything to do with it they're going to take as much heat as possible. And it isn't just the people who will go to prison and the people who have already been in jail. But they are also willing to abuse children and parents, by having them believe that they've been molested, something which can have an impact. The belief, and all the ramifications of that, can affect these kids for years, and perhaps forever.

Q.: There was a recent case in L.A. in which a man's mother-in-law hated him and told the police he was molesting his kids. The kids were taken away, and examined, and showed no evidence of molestation, but later, after they had been in custody, they came out saying they had.

Coleman: That wouldn't be surprising. That's the way the interviews are done.

Q.: Of all the cases you've been involved in, and all the cases you've read about, which do you think is the most shocking?

Coleman: I think this McMartin case is as shocking as any I know of, because after having seen the tapes . . . *All* the interview methods are bad. I have not seen a single case yet where these interview techniques are not leading and manipulative. But of all the ones that I've seen, the McMartin interviews by Kee McFarlane and Sandra Krebs and Shawn Connerly, these are the worst, and, I would say, the most shocking thing I have seen is the fact that the state of California and United Way are funding that group. I understand that the state of California has given them $300,000 more money—to people who are, essentially, indoctrinating children into the belief that they've been molested. And then the district attorney's office would be so corrupt, or so incompetent—or both—that they either would not look at the tapes to see what was going on, would just go blindly on their way, or, that they would look at the tapes and would not have the intelligence or the courage—or both—to just stop dead in their tracks, which is what they should have done, after the very first tape was viewed.

Q.: One of the defense attorneys said, "Nobody wants to take the heat for admitting that this case has been a mistake."

Coleman: Well it's not a mistake. It's a hoax. It's an utter hoax. And if they carry on with the prosecution, it's because they think they can just sneak out of it.

Q.: When you were testifying in the Torrance trial,* you used the phrase "cross germination." What does that mean?

Coleman: That means that, when you talk to somebody, and try to get at the truth, you don't contaminate their answers by telling them what someone else says, by telling them, "This is what the other kids said," or, there are other ways they can do it. You can take what a young child says, at three or four years old, and then see him again a few weeks later and remind him of something that he told you, only twist it a little bit and feed it back to him, and the kid's not old enough or developed enough to remember clearly and fight it. And he will then accept it back as his own statement. There is also cross-germination going on between the parents. The parents talk to each other and then the parents take what they get from these various sources, and *they* feed it back to the kid. I'll give you an example of just how vicious it is, and it's a kind of cross-

*See Chapter IX.

germination. One of the children that they interviewed became the supposed source of this idea that the children were tied up. When you actually watch the videotapes the child said, "Well, my mom told me that they were tying kids up." Now, later on in the interview, what the interviewer says to this child is, "Well, you told me how they were tying kids up. Show me how they would do it." But, you see, the child didn't say that. She said, "My mommy told me that."

Q.: Is that on the video?

Coleman: Absolutely. It's on the video. If I found out that the media would be able to watch those videos—you know, they're not allowed to show any of them—and if I found out that something had changed, in terms of the media being able to see them, that would make a very big difference in what I would do. Because I would immediately get on all the media's back, and say, "Listen, if you're not watching these tapes, and commenting on what you see, then you're as bad as the district attorney's office, and all the rest.

Q.: Who is Gale Goodwin?

Coleman: Gale Goodwin is a psychologist at the University of Denver who has done some studies which are not really on target as far as this subject goes, and yet is being used in cases to try to show that even though the child says a lot of wild things, you should still believe anything they say, particularly about sexual material, because, while they may be a little off as far as the periphery, but they'll be on target as far as the sexual event. They may lie about the other things but what they say about the sexual event is true—which is total baloney, and it's particularly troubling because there's a lot of material available to study on how the kids are being manipulated, and she hasn't even looked at it.

Q.: When you were testifying at the Ruby trial, I understand the prosecutor tried to smear you with the fact that an article you wrote was published in *Hustler* magazine . . .

Coleman: They just tried to make it look like I'm not really credible because I would publish an article in *Hustler* magazine. A lot of very respectable people have been published in these magazines. The Archbishop of Canterbury was published in *Penthouse.* But I think the point is, that is very demeaning to the jury and the judge because it assumes that they are too stupid not to realize that when you get into these peripheral, personal attacks and you can't attack the substance of my testimony . . . in other words, they don't have the ability to refute my testimony so they try to attack me in other ways. And I think the people can see that. My article in *Hustler* was about lithium. I told the attorneys that these are the things you can expect them to bring up. They won't have any way to deal with my testimony. They will have to attack me in some personal way, and, I said, it'll either be about this article in *Hustler* magazine— and, actually I have two more articles in similar type magazines. But these articles are on basically scientific topics. One is about lithium. One is about the insanity defense, and another is about involuntary psychiatric treatment. And so they asked me all these questions.

Q.: There have been a number of books published in the past three years, written by radical feminists on child abuse—mostly incestuous—that are long, strident diatribes of hatred of the male.

Coleman: Well, there's no question that this whole thing is mixed in with an anti-male bias. There's no question about it. But you see, that's where Summit and all these people have gotten their experience—in incest cases. That is their experience. And when you read my article, you should understand from that why the issue of incest is the false issue that it is, and why these people are taking the conclusions from incest cases, which have some merit—I mean, there is the anti-male bias, but there's nothing wrong with being pissed off at a man if he's molesting his daughter —right? That's legitimate. But then they take something which has legitimacy in its proper place, and transfer it into an improper place. These people have literally been caught with their pants down, in the sense that they were unprepared for anything differ- ent than incest.

Q.: There's an article in one of the Law Reviews that says this national epidemic of child abuse hysteria was instigated by ultrarightist, law-and-order people. Do you believe that?

Coleman: No. I think that's too simple. I think the liberals are a very powerful element in this thing. Senator H. L. Richardson from Orange County is about as conservative as you can get. Well, he and his assistant, Gordon Browning, are very upset about this issue, and are trying to do some very important work, and are bringing me into it, and we're going to be working together. It doesn't follow the usual partisan lines. And I think it's a big mistake for people to get caught up in that either way. Do you think these radical feminists are conservatives? Many of them are on the left.

Q.: Many of these radical feminists, like McKinnon and Dworkin, have formed an alliance with the Moral Majority to eradicate pornography.

Coleman: That's a different story.

Q.: But are these people seriously asking us to believe that children never lie?

Coleman: But the point that I think is more important—and I said it in the Ruby trial—is that it terribly misses the point to decide, "Is it a lie or isn't it a lie." If a child talks about Santa Claus, is he lying? And if the child isn't lying, does that mean *we* believe in Santa Claus? I think that's the point—it's none of the above. The child can be led to believe something. They're not lying. But that doesn't mean that, like a bunch of idiots, we should assume that it's true.

Q.: You would think that the D.A.'s office would have looked at those interviews with some measure of skepticism.

Coleman: They should have looked at the tapes, and once they saw the way these children were being indoctrinated, they should have called it to a halt immediately. Instead, they didn't even study the tapes, and react appropriately, the way they should have. It's not just in this case. This is a tragedy that I have seen that is going on all over the country. And what is happening is that the interviewers are overzealous, and are going into these interviews, not to try to find out if the child has been molested. That is the ostensible reason,, and maybe they have convinced themselves that that is what they are doing, but their behavior shows that they believed the child has been molested before the interview even starts. And what they do then is interview the child in such a way that the child gets a strong, positive feedback if he will say that something happened, and negative feedback if they don't say something happened. So let's say, for example, that a child says nothing happened. Then the interviewer might say, "Is that one of the yucky secrets? Is that a scary secret? We'll be so proud of you if you tell us what happened." Now I'm not talking about just McMartin. I've seen this all over the country. This is the way the children are being manipulated. And, basically, the interviewers don't take "no" for an answer.

No responsible person can condone, in any way, child sexual abuse. It is an abuse, morally, ethically, and legally, in any way that you could look at it, because children, by definition, do not have the power to give consent. We must condemn it. We must punish those who are guilty. I hope that's perfectly clear. But, the methods that are being used, because of the witch hunt, and the hysteria that has been created—and I'm sad to say that certain elements of psychiatry and mental health are responsible for this—these methods are not protecting our children. They are not going to advance the cause of catching and punishing child molesters. What is going to happen, first of all, is that we are overburdening the system with so many false allegations that we don't have the time and energy left to do a good job with the cases where there's real evidence. We are scarring a lot of children terribly by actually training them to believe that something has happened, in such a way that the child can't tell whether anything has happened or not! We are ruining the lives of people who are falsely accused. And we neither promote the adequate prosecution of those who are actually guilty, nor protect the falsely accused, nor protect the children.

There is no question that there are political overtones. We have a child sexual abuse growth industry. It's pumping money into various kinds of agencies in the mental health field. The Children's Institute International, in Los Angeles, which conducted the interviews which I've been speaking of, is receiving large amounts of money, which is tied in with the way these children have been interviewed. I think the public has a right to check it out. So there definitely are political ramifications. We've had a flood of legislation all over the country which, in my opinion, is a grievous threat to the civil rights of people accused of crimes, the protections that the Constitution is supposed to guarantee, like the right of confronting your accuser. We have legislation which is undermining those civil rights and protections in what I consider the most serious threat in years. And legislators feel that, "My God, I can't say no to anything which purports to protect children." Now, that's the surface rationale for it. But I don't think it is protecting children. I think it is undermining the rights of people who are accused.

IV

The Prosecution Doctor

Roland Summit, M.D.

Dr. Roland Summit, a Los Angeles psychiatrist, is ranked as the nation's leading expert on child sexual abuse, and his theories are the most generally accepted by mental health professionals. Like Dr. Lee Coleman he frequently testifies as an expert witness at child molestation trials; unlike Coleman, he testifies for the prosecution. His paper, titled "The Child Sexual Abuse Accommodation Syndrome," is widely embraced by professionals in the field of child sexual abuse. It proposes five steps in the child's reaction to molestation: (1) Secrecy, (2) Helplessness, (3) Entrapment and accommodation, (4) Delayed, conflicted and unconvincing disclosure, and (5) Retraction. In this paper he makes the rather startling assertion that ". . . children *do not* fabricate the kinds of explicit manipulations they divulge in complaints or interrogations," and, "Very few children, no more than two or three per thousand, have ever been found to exaggerate or to invent claims of sexual molestation." I called Dr. Summit to ask for an interview and he graciously invited me to his office at Harbor General Hospital. This was our conversation:

Question: I've just read your paper titled "The Child Sexual Abuse Accommodation Syndrome." . . .

Summit: I need to remember what it is you're writing, who it is . . .

Q.: I've been assigned to do a book on the current controversy about child abuse, and I understand that you are considered to be the leading expert on the subject.

Summit: I would like to know what their interest is. What kind of a book they imagine this is going to be. . . .

Q.: My assignment was to do an objective, impartial journalistic report on the child abuse controversy.

Summit: I wonder what their assumption is, of what's happening with that, and how is it they think this is a salable book at this point.

Q.: At this point there is no assumption. They just want me to go out, like a good journalist, and find out what's happening . . .

Summit: Okay, I'll keep asking you, what is the assumption of what is going on? There's got to be a story here somewhere. And a question. And what has aroused that question, do you suppose?

Q.: In general, my instructions were to get the story and avoid taking sides or identifying with either side in any controversy that might exist.

Summit: I've got that. That isn't even what I'm asking. Something more basic. What's the question? You say you're supposed to stay in the middle of partisan opinions. Opinions about what?

Q.: My assumption is that, on the one side, there are a lot of people who say the big wave of child abuse cases is baseless hysteria, and on the other side, there are people who are saying that it's not baseless.

Summit: I agree with that. Now is it child abuse you're talking about?

Q.: Child sexual abuse.

Summit: Criminal sexual abuse? There's so many things that are controversial right now.

Q.: Sexual molestation of children. There have been several heavily publicized cases, McMartin, Minnesota, Bakersfield . . .

Summit: You're looking at the more lurid and controversial aspects, Criminal cases and mass allegations.

Q.: Okay . . . your theory has five parts to it, or five steps: (1)

Secrecy, (2) Helplessness, (3) Entrapment and accommodation, (4) Delayed, conflicted and unconvincing disclosure, and (5) Retraction. Starting with the first step,, secrecy, does that mean that children are reluctant to talk about it when they've been molested? And what does it take to get them to tell about it?

Summit: Either some impulse on their own to tell, which is very rare, or they may find some way to hint to some trusted person, whoever is safe. There may be hints that we can read, but there are rarely flat-out complaints. What it usually takes is a suspicion—some reason to suspect that the child has been victimized, and then a very careful evaluation, a set of questioning, to focus the child's attention on what's going on, and to give permission to talk about it, and to give time for the child to resolve the fears or the shame or whatever else is keeping it from telling. There are a lot of reasons why the children don't tell. There are very few reasons why they would. In the balance of the child's options, telling is the least likely.

Q.: The second stage . . .

Summit: When you read the Accommodation Syndrome you can learn essentially what I believe about those things, so maybe, rather than going through, rather than recapitulating what I've already written, why don't you stick more to what interests you, confuses you, and what you're looking for.

Q.: Okay. Is pedophilia curable, or is it an irreversible defect?

Summit: Well, there's no such thing as a pedophile. There's not one person who perfectly fits that name, so there's a broad spectrum of what you can put through rehabilitation. If you have somebody who has never molested a child . . . if he was dead drunk and somehow ran into an extraordinary experience where a child was available and eager, or something like that, or somebody would frequent a prostitute once in a while, that would be a different problem than someone who has spent his entire life seeking out exclusively little kids and nobody else, so when you look at the far end of the scale with an exclusive focus on little kids and an active and successful style of being able to find and engage with little kids, I don't look for a cure in such a person. Treatment may help in connection with close supervision, but that's not a person who should ever be allowed to be alone with kids.

Q.: If such a person came to you for treatment would you undertake to treat him or would you consider it hopeless?

Summit: I'm not somebody who provides that treatment. I don't even treat children. I consult to programs and try to maintain . . . I try to maintain a middle position too. But I would not recommend . . . I would take a dim view of anyone who would promise to cure such an individual. I would welcome attempts to treat him, or her, as long as we were sure that there is a probational status, a law-enforcement hook, that would insure that he has no legal right to be alone with kids. That's the problem.

Q.: The seventh pre-school in the South Bay was closed yesterday in the wake of allegations of child molestation. I understand also that the state was very lax in oversight and inspection and licensing of these nurseries. Would better surveillance have helped prevent molestation?

Summit: I don't think so. Whatever's going on in these suspect pre-schools is the sort of thing that would . . . is the sort of thing that can be hidden, even from parents who drop in even at intervals. Whatever systems of abuse there might be, they would not show up to random inspections. . . . I have to speak obliquely because I don't know what's going on in there. It's very mysterious and usually misleading. But if there's anything going on at all, it's so well planned that it would confuse state inspectors even more than the parents and the children. I would like to see us understand what's going on in there before we make sweeping plans on how to protect against it.

Q.: Some of the parents have alleged that there are organized communities of pedophiles that are molesting their kids.

Summit: I'd like to split—I'd like to drop the term, pedophile. Because that's misleading. We don't know what these people are, with the pre-school epidemic situation. But it is always supposed they are pedophiles. Children report being molested, and mistreated in a whole lot of weird ways. And there may be connections with other people that do that. I don't know. But there are certainly connections among people who sexually molest children, and they are called, generally, pedophiles, and there should be no secret and no mystery about that. They are well organized, they have membership lists, they have their own journals and photographic magazines. They have advertisements, they have pen pal clubs and they have exchanges of cassettes. They are well organized. I mean, it may be spontaneously organized, as a network of like-minded people seeking contact. But it achieves a purpose of active communication and sharing of ideas.

Q.: I read in the *Times* that there have been over one hundred bills in the legislature this year, over one hundred proposed new laws pertaining to child molestation. If you were asked to review all of this and make recommendations, what would you recommend?

Summit: Well I haven't reviewed all of it so I can't guess what's in there, but in my sense of what's most needed, in the judicial area, I would look at the rules of testimony as they pertain to cases where children are victims. I would radically alter the restrictions on hearsay, and I would alter the circumstances under which children testify on cross-examination. Little kids don't belong in a courtroom, as it is now. They don't have a chance to tell even a straight story, let alone one that's difficult to believe. If we really want to know what's happening with kids, we'd be relying more on their out-of-court statements than in-court statements. At least we would have a way to admit and consider those things that they have said to other people, closer to the time of the offense because once you spend a couple of years brewing in the criminal courts process and bring the kids in to tell you what happened under the restrictions of confrontation and questions and answers and cross-examination, you just don't get a meaningful story.

Q.: Hearsay has always been inadmissible.

Summit: Except under certain circumstances. If you have a dead child, you deal entirely with hearsay and circumstantial evidence. If the child is unable to testify, for reasons of illness or if the child is mute or mentally disabled, then you have reasons to admit out-of-court statements. If the child can qualify as a witness and say "boo" then all of a sudden the only thing that would count is what the child says in the courtroom or what the child takes back in the confusion of cross-examination. With little kids it doesn't make sense to rely solely on their verbal productions in the courtroom.

Q.: Many of the kid witnesses in McMartin have retracted statements that they were molested, and the defense attorneys take this as evidence that it didn't happen.

Summit: Well, of course, that may be. More often, when children retract, it's out of humiliation or distrust or in giving up, or trying to do the right thing by undoing the problems they've caused by telling. So retraction gets crucial in the discussion of the Accommodation Syndrome. Retraction doesn't necessarily mean that the child wasn't molested. Nor does the lack of retraction mean that the child was molested. You can't tell, from any one of those things. You have to look at the credibility of the positive information that you can find somewhere. Because you know it's going to change. The defense attorneys and skeptical people in general will throw a child's statements away if they're not the same every time. The only time I see a child's statements the same every time is when a child has been coached to recite something, because when you're looking at the child's normal behavior disclosure you get gross inconsistency varying from initial and a certain amount of deliberate lying in order to maintain the secret, into a very grudging acknowledgment under pressure—sometimes you really have to push—to overcome all that. All that denial. And then you get a little bit of acknowledgment, and then it may spill out into all kinds of details, and then it may get exaggerated into all details. About the time you say, "I don't believe that stuff," the child may say, "It didn't happen. I made it up." And you have a retraction. So out of all that stuff, there may be a core in there that indicates the child was molested. And if the child was molested then it's important to pay attention to that, even though it's contradicted by previous denial or later retraction.

Q.: I think the question everyone wants the answer to is "What can I do to protect my kid from molestation. When I was a kid in New York the subways were crawling with perverts but my parents had the foresight to brief me fully on what to look out for, and so I just stayed out of reach.

Summit: That question is hard to integrate into the kind of article or book that you're doing although it can be another chapter. There are two messages that I would wish that they could understand. One is that things like we're talking about are happening. The molestation of children is pretty common. It really is happening. And realistic protection means a change in laws and a change in policies so that it's less likely that dangerous people have access to kids. And it's less likely they'll continue to have access if they are apprehended and charged. So, on the other hand, there has to be a public arousal to make it possible to arrest and prosecute people who molest kids. And within that philosophy, people should know that right now there are no laws that protect children if they are under five or six—that they could be molested and the individuals could be charged and well identified and never brought to trial and never convicted, and that the parents who sought protection under those circumstances will suffer retaliation in a court process that will try and make them into neglectful parents or vengeful liars. The process of protecting children doesn't include the right to belief or to justice on behalf of the children, the right to be safe from continuing contact with people who are accused, for instance. School-teachers who are accused of molesting children, will be returned to their jobs again and again—unless there's a criminal conviction, and a criminal conviction requires, testimony by these same little kids beyond a reasonable doubt. So you keep running in a circle and you never really stop it. As long as that is true, there's no way of guaranteeing, for instance, that schools are safe, even from known previous suspects let alone from all the people who have never been suspected. So in that sense there is not even the beginning of protection. Neither is there the beginning of protection when you are screening the friends you have that you entrust your kids to, whether they're driving the kids to school in a carpool or whether they're babysitting, or whether they're taking them off for a trip to the beach or whatever. We trust one another as neighbors and friends that in our normalcy we don't have to worry that our cherished friends would be dangerous to our kids, or our relatives, and yet the vast majority of molestations are done by people we trust, including our own family members. So in that sense, until we become aware of what the risks are, until we are willing to see that there are risks, then what happens is that parents—even parents that hear from their children that they have been molested, even kids who have managed to tell their parents, that they were molested—would tend to get suppressed and punished for the bad news. They won't be believed.

With that aside for a minute then, to address your question directly, what can parents do to protect their kids, if the laws were in place and if this were a regular world like other worlds, then there's a lot you could do to help acquaint your child with the risks without frightening him and encourage your child to be self-protective and self-assertive, and that would be fine and most people will not molest a child in the face of resistance and sophistication on the child's part. If it doesn't work, however, and the child brings home a report that he was molested, because of this . . . you've done your assertiveness training and the child is free now to try to protect himself or tell us . . . if he tells you, under present circumstances, you're gonna wish he hadn't, because the fallout will be so punishing most people won't be able to handle it.

Q.: Traditionally, we've always taught children that they must give blind obedience to an adult. Isn't that going to have to be scrapped?

Summit: Yes. And most people resent that. Most people are fearful of that because they want their children to be responsive to authority, that's one thing; but they also want children to be affectionate on demand. They want to be able to parade the kids out to the company and run them around in a circle hugging and kissing everybody. And kids usually don't like to do that. If we're going to give kids the power and the awareness to say no to unwanted touching, it'll include just the automatic resistance to ordinary pawing.

Q.: It's common knowledge—so much so that it's almost a cliché—that summer camps and elementary schools do attract molesters. And yet they're there. Isn't that an indication of incompetence on the part of the people who run schools?"

Summit: I don't think so. Well . . . yes . . . almost any of your questions I have to answer in two or three ways. . . .

Q.: At the summer camp I went to everybody warned me: "Look out for Bedford, the riding instructor."

Summit: But how many kids reported it to the superintendent of the camp that he was employed by?

Q.: Nobody. They all liked Bedford. He was funny. They just kept out of reach.

Summit: Okay. Now. If you succeeded in getting kids to report that sort of thing to the parents or to the authorities, if the parents would carry these reports to the proper place, then if the institution refuses to acknowledge that, if the institution won't listen to those kinds of complaints, and insists on employing people who are under that kind of suspicion, then, of course, you can blame the institution for being lax. But for the most part, the administrators of institutions are not aware of the complaints, or if the complaints are forwarded, the traditions are such that they really believe these are false charges and troublemaking kids, and so they sincerely think they are acting in everybody's best interest by protecting their employees against these scurrilous charges. So even in a world where people might believe, there would be lots of child-molesting people who would be able to molest kids, and keep it a secret, unless we have fairly deliberate protective policies, fingerprinting, blanket policies of suspending people from their job any time there is a complaint being investigated. At the present time the complaining individual is usually put on the defensive, to prove it, and there may be a big rally around the accused individual.

Q.: What are the consequences for the victim, of molestation, in childhood, in adolescence, in adulthood? What does it do to the victim?

Summit: It's very complicated. Nobody really knows because nobody really knows how many kids are molested, or how many of them sustain that experience without damage. You are saying that you had lots of times in your childhood when you were exposed to molesting behavior, and you just sort of floated through it without getting entrapped into victimization. So, for you, the effects are probably minor, or educational. For you the effects were to build some strength against getting assaulted. So, for you, the results were beneficial. Disillusioning perhaps, but they better prepared you to deal with the real world. On the other hand, somebody who is entrapped, and caught, then feels just as helpless as you may have felt capable of dealing with it, because if they are entrapped they tend to feel it was their fault, that they are doing something wrong, even if they are being taught by their molester that this is a beautiful love affair, even if that feels good and is a friendship that is unique, that they've never experienced before, because it's so close, and they're palsy, and even if the sex feels good, they're still being led into a position of being a freak in a secret that they can't share, and they tend to feel more and more isolated and guilty. They can't share it with their parents. They begin to feel that their parents don't care, or they may, depending on their relationship with the other person, they may develop a prejudice against the parents. One way or another they become orphans from family traditions and values. Most of them begin to feel that there's something wrong with them and their self-esteem moves from positive to negative. They hate themselves. They think there's something wrong, something wrong with their body. And they think that there's something about them that makes people do things like that. So it increases the helplessness, so if they're approached by anybody else, they're quite sure that it's their fault. They don't develop self-caring or self-assertiveness. They don't become very decisive. They tend not to trust the value of their own opinions because what they learn on the outside world is not useful to them, but what they have to do on the inside world to get along in this continuing molestation—I'm assuming within this discussion that they're molested again and again in a continuous relationship. We're not talking about a one-time incident. Self-hate tends to move into areas of self-mutilation or suicidal behavior to destroy themselves as the only way out, or assaulting or exploiting people or moving into prostitution as a way of getting a sense of power over the situation. You don't get out of the sexual victimization, you try to turn the tables to feel better about it. If it runs its entire course then eventually you might get out of it because your partner loses interest in you or you're big enough to make it stop now. But you don't get away from the sense of being damaged by it. And you don't trust the motivations and intentions of other people. You don't have trust in your own ability to build decent relationships. It's an entirely victimized relationship. Sometimes, one of the reactions of kids who are caught up in long-time exploitation is to learn to be proud of their seductive powers and to be proud that their body is worth a lot of money and to be proud that they can take any respectable citizen and seduce him, and they get a feel of power in that. They get addicted to life in the streets and they may feel they're very happy with that, but, of course, again, they're social outcasts and, eventually, they're gonna run out of that kind of lifestyle.

Q.: Is there any evidence that the molested child grows up to pattern himself after the molester as a role model, and become a molester himself?

Summit: Yes. There is. Very clearly. But we don't know how often that happens, but it's easy to see that most people that molest children were molested, themselves, as kids and it's easy to follow that pattern up as a cause-and-effect relationship. But because we don't know how many kids are molested or what the normal reactions are there's no way of predicting how often that appears. Maybe it's one in a hundred kids that are molested who will become socially dangerous themselves. That's all it would take. Maybe one in a thousand, because there are so many thousand kids molested. Most of them could have no effects at all, and we'd still be seeing a large amount of pain on the one hand . . . people who are disabled . . . and social kinds of pain on the other hand.

Q.: In the McMartin preliminary hearing, the defense attorneys are making the assertion that if a child has been interviewed by a therapist who coached, or coaxed him, or urged him to say he was molested, then that evidence is tainted. Is there any substance to that?

Summit: I don't think so. If there is, that's not where the arguments came from. The arguments are purely contrived in order to look for another explanation for what the children are saying. There is all kinds of evidence that children can be led into agreeing with adults if you ask leading questions with the answers brought in, a lot of kids will agree with you. The charges that that's what's happening really don't look at the techniques that are really used, and don't explain how it is that if the kids make those responses for the reasons of agreeing with their interviewer, how is it that they behave in ways characteristic of kids that have been grossly terrorized, in this case, and how is it that they maintain and develop more and more disclosures apart from that individual or apart from any clinical person. Most of the disclosures, if you added them up, have been made between the children and their parents, once the secrecy is broken. They're not being manipulated by some clever or powerful psychiatrist type of person. Remember that the forty-one witnesses that were selected, that was an arbitrary selection out of several hundred children that were interviewed. And the charges which you name are those which correspond with certain, presumably, things that more than one child is talking about. Many people believe that those charges were grossly . . . over-made, and that it makes for a terribly complicated trial. Another strategy is to charge a minimum number of charges.

Q.: Florence Rush and other feminist writers make the charge that sexual molestation is perpetuated almost exclusively by males against female victims. But in McMartin, Bakersfield and Jordan,

Minnesota, more than half of the defendants are women. Was Florence Rush mistaken?

Summit: Probably. Florence Rush's book was published . . . how long ago? Four years ago? It was written six to eight years ago. Her research has spanned that period of time.

Q.: Is there an anti-male bias in those books by radical feminists on child abuse?

Summit: Well, there is a female victim bias, and there is a historical bias that is authentic, and most of our reported information indicates male offenders and most of it identifies female victims. Male offenders have been identified over many years, in small numbers. The classic child molester is virtually always a male, so it's easy to assume and to study that as a paradigm. In controlled studies so far, it is hard to find more than one in twenty offenders that is a female. But you can. You can get a five percent female offender rate in those surveys. But that's not the person that needs to be looked at. Florence's work, and all of the feminist and most of the child abuse work prior to 1980 was based on the assumption that there were very few women perpetrators. Now, that's changing with the different relevant experiencing. That needs to be updated. The other thing is, when you look at Jordan, Minnesota, or South Bay or Bakersfield, you've got allegations that are descriptions of behavior that have nothing to do with traditional child molesting, and have nothing to do, basically, with a sexual preference for children. They are atrocities, sadism, rituals, and if those things are happening, you have to look to a different set of motivations, and a different profile for what kind of person is likely to do that.

Q.: What is the link between sexual molestation and all these reports of satanism and devil worship and drinking of blood that seem to be coming up everywhere?

Summit: I don't know. It does seem to be coming up everywhere. And that's a question that somebody ought to be looking at.

Q.: In the McMartin case, about two hundred eighty-nine kids were given medical examinations by physicians, and the physicians testified that about eighty per-cent had scarring of the rectum or vagina, or thickening of the hymen. Is there any possibility that those symptoms could have been caused by something else?

Summit: No. None of this we're talking about is so agreeable that you can prove anything by it. It's a disagreeable subject. Nobody warms to this subject, and reaches agreement easily because everybody would like to find a reassuring explanation, so there's a lot of controversy, even against fairly strong findings. A few years ago, the kinds of findings that are being made now weren't even known or described in the literature. Doctors didn't find these things, partly because they weren't looking that closely, and physical exams used to be based on whether or not there was a hymen present, or whether the opening was grossly enlarged. Issues of thickening, small scarring, distortion, have never really been evaluated so what we're looking at now is medical findings that have been developed as significant only in the last three or four years of evaluation of larger numbers of molested kids. Remember, before five years ago you weren't seeing any numbers of molested kids. Nobody thought it was a problem, so most everything that you have to go on now is new information, and new observations, and it's controversial. The doctors who do these exams find that it's conclusive and that you don't see these injuries in any other kind of condition, and they will argue theoretically and empirically that falling on the bar of your bicycle or masturbation or falling on the monkey bars won't produce those injuries, that nothing would produce them, other than penetrating kinds of trauma. The doctors who do them are sure that that's true. The doctors who were brought in to contest those findings are either sure it's not true or . . . They don't have to be sure it's not true; they just say you can't be sure it's true, and it could be a lot of other things that could do it. They bring in the reasonable doubt.

Q.: In the face of all this, why did they abandon the Sheriff's Special Task Force on Child Abuse last week? It's being disbanded.

Summit: They didn't abandon it. You've got to avoid sort of comprehensive judgments about complicated systems. You better ask the sheriffs, because I don't have any idea why that decision was made.

Q.: They said it was because the parents withdrew their kids as witnesses.

Summit: That's one of several simplistic explanations. There were plenty of parents who could have cooperated, but the testimony of little kids is, itself, not a reliable index of . . . In the justice system the testimony of little kids, or at least the plaintive, hesitant testimony of little kids, in a police investigation isn't the same thing as going into court with sworn testimony. And, again, I get back to what we said earlier, about what can parents do to protect their kids: nobody wants to accept the simple explanation that you can't prosecute criminal charges on the testimony of five-year-old kids. You just can't do it. So while the sheriffs interviewed lots of kids, they believed they were molested. When they took the charges to the district attorney's office, the district attorney's office felt they were not strong enough to merit prosecution. If cops can't come up with prosecutable charges, they're not doing the work which cops are paid for. The responsibility of the police was to come up with charges. They did not come up with charges that would . . . It's not that they didn't have suspects they felt should be arrested, but in the present climate of skepticism, the D.A.'s office didn't feel they . had cases that would . . . that were sure enough to prosecute in view of the cost to the children if the cases wash out. If you prosecute a case and you mobilize all these kids to testify, and they go through all the trauma you're looking at in the McMartin trial, and it ends up with a hung jury, then it's worse for the children and more demoralizing to the community than if those charges had never been made.

Q.: I can't think of anything more unattractive and grotesque than copulating with an infant. Does anybody know what makes some people want to do that? Is it arrested development?

Summit: That's again too simple. The explanations of arrested development, for what they're worth, apply to people who seek out young people, older children, whatever else. Anybody who needs to have sex with an infant has a lot of other stuff going in terms of confusion. I don't know what to say, because none of these people that I know has ever confessed or explained what's going on. It's characteristic in the allegations involving young children that the people who are accused maintain their innocence through any accusations or any treatment process. They just say it didn't happen. And so we have no idea what's going on. There is one clue, for what it's worth, with the Country Walk case, which is the one you know least about—that's the one in Florida. And people were pretty skeptical about that case, and the people who were asking questions of the kids were accused of putting those stories in their heads, and nobody wanted to believe that these kids were eating shit, and drinking urine and being drugged in the course of a day with the babysitter. Certainly no one would believe—and they stated they wouldn't believe—that the defendant was forcing the kids to put pennies in his ass. But in that case the co-defendant pleaded guilty and testified to her version of what was going on there. And she described that he had a fetish for feces and for infant functions—talk about regression! His thing was really infantile. Among other things, he wanted to be dressed in diapers, and soiled, and make a big mess, and to do that he would have the kids put suppositories in his rectum, and those were copper-wrapped discs, and that's what the kids were calling pennies. So, on the one hand, what the kids are saying paints an unlikely picture; when you get what's probably the real answer you'll get somebody who's grotesquely perverted, but who passes for normal, and there's no way outside of recognizing this man as a grossly abnormal person.

Q.: Isn't that a fairly common fetish—people who want to dress up in baby clothes? I've heard that it is.

Summit: . . . and the preoccupation with enemas and soiling and shitting and all that kind of stuff. And yet, while that may be shown to be fairly common, in any given situation where a child complains that he was forced to eat shit, that kind of complaint is thrown away as something that couldn't have happened because that's just a child's fantasy. We don't want to believe that there are grownups who would make kids do that.

Q.: Do you believe that the sexual abuse of children could be totally eradicated in the future?

Summit: Not any more than murder or robbery could be totally eradicated. But I think it wouldn't hurt to make it against the law.

Q.: Is there any danger, in child sexual abuse cases, based on the testimony of small children, that the wrong person will go to prison?

Summit: Yes. There's an even greater danger . . . It's an increasing risk as people get more dogmatic about what they believe in. If you believe that children never lie, and that anything a child says is God's truth, and if you put people in prison on that premise, then certainly a lot of people would be run off to prison for the wrong reasons. That kind of belief is being applied sometimes to at least the child protective action. Once a child seems to be molested, let's say they have a physical exam or a venereal disease. They take the child into placement on the assumption that the father is molesting them, and sometimes the father would be implicated with no reason whatever, no statements from the child, no evidence; and that kind of thing, I think, is an expression of the danger of going too far in developing too quickly new ways to identify molested children without any way of telling for sure who's been molested.

Q.: The kid in the Miami case had gonorrhea in the mouth, didn't he?

Summit: One did.

Q.: How many alleged victims were there?

Summit: I don't know. There were some fifteen kids who were selected as index children and witnesses.

V

V.O.C.A.L.

Victims of Child Abuse Laws

V.O.C.A.L. is an organization for people falsely accused of child molestation and abuse, with over one hundred chapters and several thousand members in the United States. Nobody knows how many. They are constantly flooded with new memberships. We have spoken with many of them. All of them have the most frightful stories of harassment and ruin as a result of false allegations of child abuse.

At one of their meetings we met Michael, an extraordinarily bright young man who was conductor and director of The Children's Orchestra. You have almost certainly heard Michael and his orchestra. They recorded the sound track of one of the most noted movies made in the past five years. They have played on many prime-time television shows. They have played most of the great concert halls with the leading opera and ballet companies. Music critics raved with unrestrained enthusiasm about Michael and what he had accomplished with these children. He was—and still is— greatly admired by the great conductors, composers and performers of our time. He achieved an international reputation. He is forty-one.

Michael started playing piano at age four. He also studied the French horn and the violin. After a year in Viet Nam he formed

The Children's Orchestra as a project for his M.A. After he got the M.A. he was so enthusiastic about the orchestra that he continued with it. Soon, he had many contracts, a big, New York artists' management company as his agent, and a busy schedule of concerts to play. A non-profit corporation was formed and Michael was its salaried director. For seventeen years, Michael and the orchestra performed all over the world.

Then, one afternoon in August 1983, he was arrested and charged with child molestation.

He was never accused of having engaged in any sexual act. Not one person accused him of any sexual actions involving nudity or genital contact. He was accused of hugging and kissing a child! "We did things like that," he said. "Especially when the younger kids feel insecure away from home. When we'd go on tour, we were sometimes out of town for six or eight weeks. Kids get homesick. I might put an arm around one, or express affection when I said good night. When we deal with breathing techniques, the teacher might touch the kid's body to indicate where the muscular support should come from."

Incredible as it sounds, he was found guilty. The sentence? Eight years.

These high crimes allegedly occurred while the children were at a summer training camp under Michael's leadership. Three boys accused him of sexual molestation. "One of them," Michael said, "his family had just gone through bankruptcy. His mother was the Parents' Association President for the orchestra. She had access to our files. She knew we had liability insurance. We had a million dollars liability coverage per child. And, sure enough, she filed a lawsuit for twenty-five million against me and the orchestra, as soon as I was convicted.

"Everybody involved in the case had something to gain, politically or materially. The judge that sentenced me was a liberal judge, but he was in a redneck district, and he had to run for reelection. This judge had just recently tried another case. It was a man who was accused of molesting his daughter. His daughter got up on the stand and gave extremely convincing testimony against him. The case against him was very solid. And he walked!

"He got off! Acquitted! How? I found out that he had a very prominent position in the city government. He was a solid citizen.

He belonged to the same country club as the judge, and the jury foreman! They were friends! And he walked. After that, the judge had to come down hard on me so he wouldn't be called 'soft on child molesters.' The cop who arrested and prosecuted me got a promotion because of my case. The prosecutor scored big points toward the advancement of his career.

"The lawyer who represented me in the trial was a very good lawyer, a very good man, but not a specialist at defending in child abuse cases. He was in over his head. We lost. But he did a good job of making objections in a timely manner, which gives me a chance on appeal, but it's twenty-six months past the original allegations. And it's tough putting bread on the table and a roof over my head.

"When I was in jail, when I was first arrested, I was put in a cell with a man who had just killed a cop, and he was using everybody in the cell for a punching bag, just for fun. In the next cell were six murderers who were asking him, 'Hey, is that orchestra director in there?' He actually protected me and said no. They were going to get me in the day room, and that would have been the end of me. My arrest was on all the television stations and they knew I was in there. I was front page every day.

"I had a musical watch that played a musical tune every hour, kind of a neat thing for a musician. The cops broke it, because they couldn't get it to turn off. They smashed it. When I got it back, it was all smashed up, and the parts were rattling around inside. They could have asked me how to hit the right button to turn it off, but they didn't want to do that.

"The judge let very prejudicial information into the trial that had nothing to do with what was alleged. He allowed in an 'expert witness' who was a cop, who didn't even have a degree. He had taken a forty-hour course in child maltreatment, and that made him an expert. And he came in and talked to the jury about pedophiles and his homophobia, and none of these issues were even relevant. Nobody had accused me of being a homosexual. But it was just hinted to the jury that this was the case. The jury foreman said, after the trial, that the expert witness was one of the key factors against me.

"This cop went on the stand and said that even though I hadn't done anything but hug a child, there's always an escalation of activity in the seduction of children by a pedophile, they usually start with buying gifts then maybe hugging, and then rubbing backs, and then on to even greater crimes. Not one of the kids said that I even rubbed his back. But what he told the jury was that if I hadn't been arrested I might have gone on to perpetrate all kinds of heinous crimes on these kids.

"I've never been a pedophile or a homosexual, but the cop who was testifying as the 'expert witness' insinuated to the jury that this was the underlying truth of the case, and the judge let him do it. My lawyer objected but we were overruled. All through the trial, the prosecutor subtly implied that there was something more to this case than what was being said in the courtroom. After the trial was over, the jurors all ran over to the D.A. and asked him about that. They all asked him, 'Was there something more that we weren't told about?' and he smiled smugly and said, 'Yes,' as though he were in possession of some unmentionable secret. They implied this all through the trial, and they made a point of telling the jurors that I was an unmarried man directing a bunch of kids. They didn't mention the fact that I directed that orchestra for seventeen years and there was never any evidence of any misconduct.

"The kids who were witnesses against me told completely different stories at the trial, from what they told at the preliminary hearing. One of them told three different stories. The lawmakers have decided that children can change their stories and that the prosecutors can take their pick, and you can be prosecuted on whichever story they decide to use. And unlike any other crime, where, if you can prove that you were in some other place at the time the crime occurred, you're not guilty, but in this case they say that because you're dealing with children, they can say, '. . . on or about,' and it can be between July 1 and August 30. They give them wide margins. A sixty-day period. We now have a completely different justice system for alleged crimes against children. One of the kids 'remembered' all kinds of things in the trial that he didn't remember in the preliminary. On the cross-examination my lawyer asked him, 'Do you remember more after you talked with the police?' and he agreed that was so. How does your memory improve— unless the cops said, 'Look, Billy, your story isn't strong enough. You're gonna hafta beef it up a little, make it juicier, so you can get money out of this.' Those kids acted very much like they had been rehearsed.

"My lawyer told me when this thing first started, he said, 'You have been dropped into a meat grinder. My job is to reach down into the meat grinder and pull you out—or pull out as much of you as I can.' The prosecution interviewed seven hundred kids to find one that would testify against me. Over seven hundred character witnesses came to speak on my behalf. The judge cut it off because, he said, he had tickets to the ballgame, and wanted to leave. The judge, the cop, the prosecutor, the mother, all of them had something to gain. They all needed my conviction. And since I wasn't a resident of the area and had no family or connections there, they had nothing to fear. If this had happened in New York or L.A. it probably wouldn't have gone to trial."

Michael is waiting to hear from the Court of Appeals. He may spend several years in a prison cell, if he's lucky enough not to get stabbed. He was only charged with hugging a child, but who knows what that can lead to?

Even if he wins, the orchestra, and the career of a gifted musician and dedicated educator is finished. "I don't think I will ever teach children again," he told me.

A woman told me that her five-year-old daughter developed an infection in her vagina and began scratching it. She took her to a hospital where the girl was examined five times over a period of two weeks. The instruments the doctors used to examine her left marks on her vagina and legs. The mother took the child to another hospital, and there the doctor gravely announced: "Your daughter has been molested. There's the proof." The "proof" he pointed to was the marks left by the other doctor and his instruments. The child was taken away from her parents and placed in a foster home. She has not yet been returned.

Donald J., who lives in a suburb of Los Angeles, told me: "Six cops came to the door with their hands on their guns and told me, 'We're gonna take your kids. You've been accused of child molestation and there's nothing you can do about it.' I asked them if they had a warrant or court order. He said, 'There's nothing you can do about it.' I shouted, 'You are *not* taking my children!' He repeated,

'There is nothing you can do about it.' I shouted, 'You are not taking our baby away from his mother.' He said, 'There is nothing you can do about it.' For three hours I was held in my own home with two officers with their hands on their guns while they searched my house. They would not tell us where our children were being held, or when they would be returned. My attorney went to the police station and the police indicated to him that charges would be filed against me. A custody hearing was scheduled. The next afternoon the children's protective services called and told my wife that the children would be returned to us. A day after that, our attorney came to our house to discuss the case with us. He strongly advised us against filing charges against the police because, he said, the police in that city were notorious for retaliating against citizens who made complaints against them. When the kids were returned I discovered that the cops, or somebody, had programmed them to believe they had been molested. One of the kids, the older one, wouldn't talk about it much. The younger one didn't even understand it. I finally learned who made the complaint. It was one of our neighbors. She had had a big fight with my wife and she was really mad at her. This was her revenge."

Another V.O.C.A.L. member, a woman, told me that on several occasions, strangers arrived at her home around midnight and demanded entry into her home and forced their way in, and demanded to see her children. "I have two pre-school children," she said. "My children were awakened and dragged from their beds." These intruders stripped the children naked, stared at them, and ordered the mother to leave the room. These people, technically, were not criminals or neighborhood hoodlums, although they behaved very much like criminals. They were social workers and police. They stated that they were engaged in "child protection." These raids were prompted by anonymous telephone calls to a child abuse hotline, alleging that the mother was sexually abusing her children. All of the reports were false. The woman believes that the calls were made, maliciously, by a relative who bore her a long-standing grudge, but there's no way to prove it. And the anonymous caller can do it again and start the whole process over again at any time.

"My ex-husband decided he wanted custody of my younger daughter," Eileen told me. "We've been divorced for three and a half years. He found out the only way he could get it was to accuse us of child abuse and molestation. I had sent my younger daughter up to visit him because I wanted her to get to know her dad. When I went up to bring her back, she was gone. I was not told where she was. I went to the police department, and I was told that my husband and I had been accused of molesting my two-and-a-half-year-old. I couldn't believe it. He and his lawyer were down here filing charges against me while he knew I was up there going to bring my daughter home. I was not allowed to see my children or have any contact with them. And then in April they gave me four hours Saturday and four hours Sunday—one weekend a month, supervised by my parents. We went in for a custody evaluation. There was no evidence of molestation. My daughter told them nothing like that happened but said they won't believe her. And the psychologists they were interviewed by believe her father's story—that she was molested. My daughter says that they told her she'll be punished if she doesn't say she was molested. She said, 'If I tell the truth they'll punish me.'

"If the child says he was molested, he's telling the truth. If he says he wasn't, he's lying. That's one of the strangest theories I've ever heard. Right now, my kids are with my parents. It's going to be another four months before I'll be able to get them back. I was never arrested or charged. The D.P.S.S. got the report and closed the case for lack of evidence and said it was unfounded. The D.A. wouldn't touch it. The police wouldn't touch it. But I still can't get my children back. You should read the accusations. They're incredible. 'Daily sodomy. Daily intercourse.' With my two-year-old! All because my ex-husband wants custody of my kids. You'd think they would approach this with some skepticism, but McMartinmania has hit, and they're not allowed to give people the benefit of a doubt. You can't believe the evidence any more. The commissioner from the court has been very fair. She doesn't believe the accusations against me. But she hasn't given my kids back, because of the fear that is in everybody's mind."

There has been a torrent of custody cases in which one parent has accused the other of child abuse to get custody of the children. All it takes is a telephone call. Anyone can call a child abuse hot line and make an anonymous call, and have total immunity.

There have been over one hundred bills introduced in the legislature this year, proposing new, tougher laws on child abuse, the V.O.C.A.L. members told me. Every politician in the state has jumped on the bandwagon. Some of them are extremely dangerous and involve the abolition of the rights of the accused.

"There is a whole 'child abuse growth industry' now," one man told me. "There are these 'anatomically correct' dolls, that the psychologists and social workers use to get the child to reenact the alleged molestation. Have you ever seen these dolls? Well, they are not 'anatomically correct.' They have great oversized genitals, way out of proportion to the size of the doll. Not only that, but there is a huge amount of pubic hair—far out of proportion. I've seen the order form. You can buy grandfather dolls, grandmother dolls, black dolls, white dolls. . . . I don't know if you can buy Arabs or Mexicans. But these dolls are not cheap. These are over a hundred dollars. If you want to buy one of each, you are going to need more than your charge card.

"And they have weekend conventions, just like any other industry. You can come and view these dolls, and they're usually held at Holiday Inns, and their tables are out on display for the prospective buyer. These are put on display by the manufacturer for the child abuse industry, and anyone who wants to be a part of that.

"And they have these little booklets that you can read to your kid, and he'll never be molested. They have whole catalogs of them and they send them out to their mailing lists.

"Child abuse is a big windfall for the psychologists and the cops and prosecutors. If they send an innocent human being to prison, they don't care. It's great for their careers. America has a passion for locking people up in prison. All you have to do is be in the wrong place at the wrong time, and if you don't have world-class lawyers, you're a goner.

"And then there are the social workers. I think most people agree on one thing—that the lower level social worker is one of the worst problems, because they have very little training and no education to recognize child abuse, but they are given the authority of the State to go out and identify and say, 'Yes. This is child abuse.' And they have the power to take your children away, just on suspicion, or an anonymous call. And they are drunk with power. If you challenge their authority they get very hostile."

Another speaker told us about Elaine Humlen. She has a nine-year-old boy who is in love with baseball. On May 6, 1985, in the afternoon, he was practicing pitching and catching in front of his house with two other boys. They were using a tennis ball. During the game he missed the ball and was struck in the nose. It left a red mark on his nose and on the side of one eye. It was not painful and the boy continued playing.

The next day, the boy was forty minutes late coming home from school. His aunt went to look for him and took along his sister, an infant only sixteen months old. They went to the school looking for the boy. There, the aunt was met by police, and the boy, who was frightened and crying. The police ripped the baby from the woman's arms and told her they were taking the children for child abuse, and that the mother could not see them. The aunt came home in a state of hysteria.

The police took the children to a hospital to be examined for child abuse. They found no signs of abuse on the baby, but she was placed in a county facility where she sustained numerous bruises all over her body. The boy was placed in a foster home which already had two children sleeping on the floor, and where the children played, unsupervised and unprotected, in a vacant lot. The boy told his teachers, school nurse, and the police and D.P.S.S. workers that the red mark on his face was caused by a baseball accident, but they would not listen, or telephone his mother. There was a dependency hearing where the judge ordered the children detained until the trial, which was set for July 22.

After four days, the mother was allowed to visit her baby in the county facility, and found her sick, dirty, and covered with bruises. The following Wednesday she went before a judge who released the children to her until trial.

The woman has won her case, but she is broke, has lost her job, and has two frightened children. There may be a happy ending. She has sued the county to recover damages.

Another lady told us of a twelve-year-old boy who, because authorities thought he might have been molested, was placed in the county's juvenile facility at McLaren Hall for "protective custody." There, he was raped by older inmates. She said there had been at least thirty-seven complaints of similar incidents at the facility.

"Molestationmania has hit us, full force," she said. "One of the big, daily newspapers in this state recently announced a contest with prizes for the reader who could turn in the most child molesters. If you turned in enough molesters, you could win a hair dryer."

After attending several meetings, we were invited to V.O.-C.A.L.'s National Conference in Minneapolis. At Los Angeles International Airport, we boarded the red-eye flight which Eastern Airlines euphemistically calls it "Moonlight Flight." We arrived, red-eyed, at 7:30 a.m. in Minneapolis. It was cold! We jumped into a cab.

There was a reception and social hour in the hotel's pool area where wine and coffee were served. Robin, an attractive thirty-year-old secretary from California, told me, "My daughter had vaginitis and I called her pediatrician. We went to his office and he took a culture from her genital area, and then reported to the county Child Protective Services that he was suspicious that a molest had occurred. He made the call to C.P.S. before he had the results of the culture. C.P.S. began their investigation immediately. A few days later, I was told by the investigator that the case would be dropped, and that the anatomical doll session with my daughter had proved negative. Then, I took her to another gynecologist who performed a very thorough sexual abuse exam. He was totally disgusted with the allegations.

"The next morning I woke up and saw police cars surrounding my home! The cops knocked on my windows. When I refused to open the door they called me on the phone and told me if I did not let them in they would break down my door. They arrested me with my daughter clutching to my neck, and they took her and they all ran out the door. They had no warrant, and I was told, later, that none was required for them to do that. Since, then, my daughter has been examined by four physicians, one who's an expert at Children's Hospital, and there was no evidence of sexual abuse. The doctor said that the bacteria which showed up in the culture was present in sixty-eight percent of all women. He said she probably got it by wiping her nose and then touching her vagina. All this information was forwarded to C.P.S. but they would not close my case. In fact, they would not even look at my evidence. An overzealous investigator, backed up by a doctor who refuses to admit he made a mistake, tried to destroy my family. This investigator was so determined to prove that my daughter had been molested that she subjected her to endless sessions with her anatomical dolls and two different psychologists in order to get her to say she was molested. All the psychological tests on my daughter and my family came back in our favor—that she had not been molested. What happened to the Constitution and Bill of Rights? According to C.P.S. we had no rights and were guilty until proven innocent.

"I want something done to stop this witch hunt. My family is not an isolated case. Since this has happened I've talked to a lot of other people who've been through the same thing. The C.P.S. and the prosecutor tried to get a guilty verdict, knowing that we were innocent. At no time were any allegations made that the supposed molestation took place in our home. Yet, they tore her away from us and removed her from her safe and stable environment. And my daughter—suddenly she is wise beyond her years in sexual matters, and in the workings of a police state! She is constantly fearful that she will be torn away again. Fortunately we won in court. The charges were dismissed. But the hearing in juvenile court lasted an entire month! The expense of defending against those allegations was astronomical. It cost us more than twenty thousand dollars, and the foreclosure of our home. They can enter your home and take your children away on the basis of an anonymous phone call!

"My case was different from most, in that when I saw all the cop cars, fortunately I had all of the doors locked, and I was able to hold them off for forty-five minutes, and I was able to be on the phone contacting doctors, attorneys, my husband and a psychologist who got right over to the house and was my main witness. She testified in court that when they came into my house nobody would call the doctors who examined my daughter, to verify that there was no sexual abuse."

Robin's daughter was only four years old. She was removed from her home, and another woman was given legal custody of the child. Another doctor who examined the child said, "I would never have reported such a case and would certainly not have removed the child from her home. . . ." The little girl was interviewed and given anatomical doll sessions by sheriff's detectives.

The ending of the story was a rare one, their attorney said. They won, but the price of victory was not cheap. They still owe $20,000 in attorney and medical fees.

Rebecca Barkman, an extremely pretty, thirty-year-old, blond-haired woman was there. Her husband was not. I had read newspaper accounts of her case, and I asked her to tell me the whole story. "In April of 1984," she said, "I filed a complaint for suspected child abuse against a family. We had a little girl enrolled at the pre-school, the Small World Pre-school and Day Care Center in Niles, Michigan. I was the director. It's a non-profit corporation. It's been in existence since 1968. I had been the director there for four years. My husband had been a teacher there for five. I filed the complaint in April. The Department of Social Services started what was supposed to be an investigation. In August, that family then went to the D.S.S. and stated that they thought their child had been sexually abused while she attended Small World Pre-school, by my husband. The day after the allegation I was sitting in a hospital room with my newborn daughter who had pneumonia, and I was told by a nurse that there were two police officers and two other people downstairs who wanted to talk to me. I went down into the lobby, and they said to me, 'Your husband sexually molested a child at Small World Pre-school.' I almost died! I said, 'Who said such a thing! You're crazy!' And the police officer said, 'No, we're not saying someone said it—we're saying he did it.' And they had two social workers and a nurse. The nurse who had taken me down from the pediatrics ward said to me, 'Let me find you someplace quiet to talk.' So we went into the room, and they started yelling at me: 'Haven't you read the newspapers? Don't you know about the McMartin case in California? Don't you know about Jordan, Minnesota? What's wrong with you? Why would you have a man with you at a day-care center? Men do these things!' They wouldn't tell me who it was. They kept up this barrage. They gave me all their disgusting little details of what, supposedly, he did. I almost fainted. I almost threw up. They said 'We have to talk to your daughter.' I have a seven-year-old daughter. I said, 'Fine, she's at my mother's house. Lets go now.' So the two state police officers . . . I called my husband. My husband also coached football for the high school. I called the school and told one of the girls to go down to the football field and tell my husband to go to the police station. She said, 'Why?' I said, 'Because they're accusing him of sexual abuse.' She started laughing. She thought I was joking. I said, 'I'm serious.'

"So the two state policemen started to go to the police station to talk to him, and the C.P.S. worker went to my mother's house with me to talk to my daughter. She interviewed my daughter in a very disgusting manner. She told my daughter that there were parts of her body that were dirty and no one should ever touch them, and really tried to get her to say that someone had done this. She was very confused by the whole thing. I had never taught my daughter that any part of the body was dirty. Plus—my daughter knows the proper names for the body parts. The woman looked at me and said, 'What's wrong with you? Haven't you had any sex education with this child?' And I said, 'Well if you'd talk to her, using proper terms, she might understand what you're talking about.'

"While she was doing that, I looked at her file. I'm not stupid. I wanted to know who said this. So I found out who the complaining witness was. I said, 'Oh! My word! Aren't you aware of the fact that in April I reported these people for suspected abuse?' She looked at me and said, 'No.' She got very uptight and she said, 'Well I can see there's no problem here,' and she left. In the meantime my husband was being questioned by the state police. They did tell him who the accuser was, and he said, 'Are you aware of the fact that my wife reported that family as being possibly abusive?' 'No,' they didn't know that. So they were caught with their pants down. We contacted an attorney, and the attorney told us not to talk to the news media, and a lot of things which they tell you, and now I would never follow that advice. And the next day the police called me and said, 'Well, one of these ladies' friends came in. She was the best friend of the mother who made the complaint. She came in and said that her daughter saw you see this happen. And you can be arrested for failure to report suspected child abuse, and we can prosecute you too unless you'll talk to us about what your husband did.' And I said, 'If you want to talk to me, you'll have to talk to me with my attorney present.' 'We don't want to do that,' they said. So all through this they kept approaching me when I was alone. 'We want talk to you by yourself.' They never wanted to talk to me with an attorney or anyone else present. Now that's really strange, isn't it? Why would they have such an objection to this?

"So the Department of Social Services came in and said that I could not be at the school. And I could not be at the school, and since I was a director, the school has to be closed, because it cannot be open, according to Michigan law, if the director is not present. So they couldn't close the school, because they had no grounds to close it on, but they could require that my presence not be there, because they had someone to say that I was witness to this. So therefore they could close the school. This was done amidst a huge media barrage. And my husband wasn't arrested until October twenty-third, but we were in the media almost every day. They released statements like, 'It is believed that there is a belief that there is more than one child involved.' These are the kind of things that were in the news media. The police then sent the letter out, just like they did in the McMartin case. We had a huge support group that said, 'No way did this happen! We've talked to our kids . . .' They held rallies. They did all kinds of things in our support. The police would contact parents and said, 'What if we told you that someone came in and said they had witnessed that this happened to your child?' Always, 'What if we told you . . .' The parent doesn't hear 'What if we told you?' They hear, 'Your child was molested.' 'What if we told you there were pictures?' 'What if we told you there were videos?' None of this was true, but the parents don't hear that part. They hear 'the videos,' the 'pictures,' 'Oh my God, something did happen.'

"So my husband was arrested, on October twenty-third and charged with four children. Interestingly enough, two of these children, I did not know who they were. They had been there so infrequently and such a long time ago that we could not remember who they were. I did not recognize them when they walked into the courtroom for the prelims. And if we had been put into a lineup, those kids would never have known who we were. And they had only been there just a few times. The prelims were really bad. The kids said their mothers were there. All the crazy stories that come out. I was arrested for failure to report, and the whole thing had started because I had *filed* a report. But my charges, even though they were a misdemeanor, were put in the newspaper every time my husband's were. The media coverage continued. We were always in the news. Sometimes every day, sometimes once a week, but it never stopped. We were constantly in the news. Well, the first four kids bombed out, so they started working on some more kids. They got five more kids. They had more prelims. Well, those kids bombed out too. They recanted stories. They said the prosecutor told them what to say.

"Finally, the last prelim we had, that child, basically, didn't say much of anything. He had three catch phrases he'd say. The catch phrases were, like, 'Pedie in my butt,' and 'Pedie in my mouth,' and 'Touch my pedie.' And the child could not accurately describe what this meant, what he was really saying. He had been taught those phrases, and he'd use those. That's the kid they decided to try him on.

"So the media coverage went on and on. Mine was a misdemeanor charge and it should have been tried within ninety days. They kept putting stays on mine, because they were getting ready for Richard's trial. They didn't have time to do mine. They always had a reason. They had hearings. Dr. Underwager came. And Dr. Erickson. They had gone through preliminary hearings and therapists' reports. Dr. Underwager sat through their experts' testimony as to how the children had been interviewed and spent a day and a half showing them exactly what they did wrong and how they got the incorrect results they did. Nobody wanted to listen to that.

"Finally we got to trial. No evidence. It's funny because public opinion was very much against us until we got to trial. And then, people started saying, 'My God! Where's the evidence?' When the prosecutor presented his case, all he had was the child to say his little catch phrases, and then he called all the other teachers from the school. And they all said, 'No it never happened,' and, 'It couldn't possibly have happened.' That was his case! His case was basically, our case! So we did our part, and he did his rebuttal. And my husband was convicted.

"And he was convinced because the parents that once supported us had now become a militant group against us. They wore 'KIDS DON'T LIE' buttons to court. They intimidated witnesses. Our witnesses would get calls before they'd come. And the police would come, and talk to our witnesses, and do the 'What if we told you' stuff. The day before they were to testify, they would say, 'What if we told you . . . what could we tell you that would convince you that he really did this?' They did all those things. We've got all those things to use on appeal, but the bottom line is that, once the prosecution and everybody is locked in by the news me-

dia, they're going to do anything and everything to win that case.
Their careers are on the line. We should have been granted a
change of venue. All the jurors had heard all about this case on the
media for eight months. No one can be unbiased. Anything you
read, you're going to form an opinion one way or the other.

"So basically what they said, when our attorney questioned them
after they came out with a guilty verdict, 'What were you thinking?' 'What did you convict him on?' They said, 'Well we didn't
believe those kids' stories, but something must have happened.
Because of all the publicity.'

"So my trial was scheduled for May. So I just hit the news media. And I started doing a lot of V.O.C.A.L. stuff and I started
pointing out the inconsistencies in the things they said. And then
they started offering me things, through my attorney, like, 'If you
won't sue us, we'll drop your charges.' 'If you'll wait and be quiet
and not talk any more on the news media 'till after we sentence
your husband we'll drop your charges.' I told them what they could
do! They wanted me to doublecross my husband. They thought
that I'd be afraid, and I'd be willing to do that. Because *they* would
do that. I said, 'No way. Either try me, or drop my charges.
There's no two ways about it. I'm ready to go to trial. I'd welcome
the chance to go to trial!' So they dropped my charges anyway. The
prosecutor had to sit there and eat crow that day and I loved every
minute of it. Young prosecutor about thirty-five. He has dreams of
becoming a district attorney.

"No one understands the political ramifications of these things.
It's careers! Mental Health just got a three-hundred-thousand-
dollar grant, the people who were involved in this, just got three
hundred thousand dollars from the state because of all these kids
who were supposedly abused. We're being sued right and left by
parents who want to collect damages. And unless you're involved
in this it's hard to believe. They say, 'As soon as we get our money,
we're gonna . . .' I heard them when my husband was being sentenced and my charges had just been dropped a few days previous
to this. And I heard them saying to their lawyer, 'Is this going to
hurt our chances to get our money because they dropped her
charges?' The parents who were suing. I was sitting behind this little enclosure, and my charges were going to be dropped, and the

officer who was involved in the investigation, and the therapist who was involved, didn't know I was sitting there, and they got into an argument. She was saying, 'I just spent two months getting these kids ready for this trial. Why did she have to do that? And now you're telling me you're going to drop charges! Why didn't you tell me a long time ago you didn't really want to go after her? I wouldn't have wasted all my time gettin' these kids ready to get her.' They spent two months getting those kids to lie! And I'm sitting there and I'm thinking to myself, 'I don't believe I'm hearing this!' And then my lawyer came out through the door and he says, 'Come on, Becky, we're gonna go in.' Well I stepped out from behind this thing and they almost died! Because here I am listening to them talking about how they got kids ready to lie, against me. They had to work hard on them. And these kids were saying their mothers were there, watching the molestation, and everybody in the world was there, and a lot of nonexistent people, who also had sexually abused these children. If the prosecution had given them your name, they would have said yes. They would have said yes to anything. These weren't even real people! These were just names the kids pulled out of the air. And they'd say, 'Oh yeah, that person was there.' The police spent months trying to find someone named Chris. These kids had named someone named Chris as doing these molestations. There was no Chris there. No one named Chris had ever worked there. No volunteer named Chris had ever been there. They just couldn't get it through their heads. The kids said Chris was there. So there had to be a person named Chris. Who is Chris?

"But they're so illogical. They just don't think.

"The guilty verdict was in April. Sentencing wasn't until June tenth. They gave him fifty to seventy-five years. He had a completely, totally clean record. According to the penal code guidelines of the State of Michigan he should have got zero to five. The judge gave him fifty to seventy-five. So he was transferred to Jackson State Penitentiary, and he's been there ever since. But he's been in jail since October. He was denied bond. He was in the County Jail first. So he's been in jail for over a year now. No bail.

"So then we started the appeal process. We've had all these civil suits that have been filed against us. One of the civil suits was filed

before we had the criminal trial. And once the guilty verdict came
in we had a multitude of other civil suits. So now we're just kind of
working on the appeal process.

"The judge told my lawyer, 'You should have taken a bench trial.
I would have found him not guilty.' I don't think that's true. I think
he knew my husband was not guilty, but I don't think he would
have had the guts to do that.

"It's very hard for me to talk about this tonight," she said, "because tonight is my wedding anniversary. I'm not spending it with
my husband. I'm not going out for a romantic dinner. He wasn't
there for my last anniversary. He wasn't there for my daughter's
Christmas or her birthday. A little over a year ago, government
officials entered our home. They tore it apart. They took the pictures off the walls. They stripped the bedrooms, and they took
everything from the cupboards and the closets. They didn't find
anything, but they still took my husband away. They put him in a
jail cell. For eight months we were only allowed to see him once a
week for twenty minutes. He was behind a glass wall and we had to
talk to him on a telephone. He was not allowed to hold his newborn
daughter. He was not allowed to play with his son. He was not allowed to kiss his wife. After eight months we went to a courtroom.
I can't say that we had a trial. It was more like a hysterical witch
hunt. People testified that my husband—horror of horrors—took a
child to the bathroom during a Christmas program. My husband is
now in state prison and he's serving fifty to seventy-five years for
something that never happened. Every week, the kids get in the
car. We drive two hours. We go through a gate that is watched
over by armed policemen. We're frisked, and we go through a
metal detector. We have dye placed on our hands. We go through
two sets of gates. And for two hours, Richard gets to hold his kids.
He gets to hold them. He gets to kiss them. He gets to catch up on
what's going on with his family. And he must be asking, 'What
country is it that this is happening in?' And what crime could he
possibly have committed? Well, he was accused of anally assaulting
a five-year-old boy. He was convicted without any physical evidence, without any corroborating evidence. He was convicted on a
child's testimony that was very well rehearsed, which was unclear,
impossible, ridiculous. The child insisted the assault happened in a

public place with six teachers witnessing it. He said Richard and I and all the teachers took photographs. My husband was convicted of perpetrating this crime on a day when he was not at this preschool. We were on vacation. We had time-cards to verify that. Sworn testimony, time cards and polygraph exams were not enough to prove his innocence. You may think this couldn't happen in the United States. It did. We were a nice, normal family. We felt really lucky. We had great kids, a job we loved, we had just purchased a home we had worked really hard for. We could even take our kids to work with us! What more could you possibly ask? What happened to us could happen to anybody who works with kids, anybody who spends their time with children, anybody who has neighborhood kids in to play. It could happen any time."

Rebecca's lawyer, Joe Spiezer, joined us. "The things the kids said happened were physically impossible," he reflected. "They said all these sexual acts happened right in front of the police station. This case really bothers me. I've won cases that I should have lost, and I had two guys that should have got the death penalty, and they walked. I wouldn't have felt too bad if they got the death penalty. But this case really bothers me. This guy didn't do it—could not possibly have done what they said he did. I can't imagine what these jurors are thinking! Why can't they just think for a minute? These people don't understand how people engage in sex! I mean . . . I mean . . . these people must be celibate!"

A short, slender woman told me as I sipped my coffee: "My nephew was living in Oklahoma and he heard that the police in California had charged him with child molestation. He thought the whole thing was so ridiculous that he sold a cow so he could get enough money to fly to California and get rid of it. He brought his new wife and his four kids who, it turned out, were the alleged victims. He and his wife both got arrested and they both got three hundred and seventy years." The lady who spoke was Ruellene Pitts, the chairman of the Bakersfield chapter of V.O.C.A.L.

Walter Urban, the attorney representing Betty Raidor in the McMartin trial, said, "Mr. T. made an appearance in the McMartin trial. He told the kids to tell the truth. The kid who was testifying must have taken him seriously, because, after Mr. T. left, he recanted his testimony."

Allen McMahon, a prestigious attorney based in Santa Ana, was sitting next to us. He is active in V.O.C.A.L. and has represented a number of defendants in similar cases.

"Where did all this insanity come from?" I asked him. "Was it Ed Meese? Jerry Falwell?"

"It was Walter Mondale," he told me. "In 1974 the Mondale Act was passed by Congress. And this law provided that huge federal grants to states would be paid if they passed mandatory reporting laws. Millions! So almost all of the fifty states passed these mandatory reporting laws in order to get this money. But in order to get the money, they had to generate new cases! They are fabricating these cases! One of these child abuse agencies got a two-million-dollar grant because they *created* a child molestation case, with lots of victims and lots of suspects, all of them innocent. But they're all facing prison terms. None of the kids said they were molested until they talked with the interviewers. In L.A., the Sheriff's Department spent a million dollars on a Child Sexual Abuse Task Force. They dug up half the South Bay, and all they found were some chicken bones, so maybe Colonel Sanders was the culprit. But they did not find one place of evidence or make one arrest. And that's how we got the child abuse industry.

"Look at it this way. If you're a social worker and you've got a marginal case in front of you. The kid may have been abused but there's not really a lot of evidence, and in fact it's rather doubtful. In the old days you probably would have said to the parents, 'Look, this is what we can do. Under welfare and institutions code, Section 330, we can put you under informal supervision. In other words, I'll come around now and then, and check on the kid, check on the house and everything, and we won't file a petition or anything like that.' In fact, if it were really marginal, you might say, Well, there really isn't enough to go on, so I'm not going to file this case. But under the Mondale Act, the federal government is pumping these obscenely huge amounts of money into the state and local children's protective service agencies. And the amount of money they get is dependent on the number of cases they have filed! So even if this is never actually spoken, if you're that social worker, imagine the pressure on you to open as many new cases as you can. And this is the answer to why these social workers are trying to open so many new cases, when most of them are clearly bullshit, and they have as many as a hundred sixty cases in their caseload already.

"It's money! And money fuels the system. Almost all of the states now have these reporting laws. In 1981 the new reporting law in California became effective. So, suddenly, all these people who have to report under those laws are facing jail if they don't. That's pretty effective. And in addition to that, in 1976 was the case of Daros versus Flood, which was a case where a doctor was sued for not reporting child abuse that was pretty clearly child abuse. And he was found liable for malpractice, and that cost his insurance carrier a lot of money. Since that time, according to a Los Angeles deputy county counsel who wrote a little book on representing parents in juvenile dependency cases, he said in his book that insurance company lawyers, or attorneys who represent hospitals, doctors, schools, et cetera, have been telling their clients to report anything that might *possibly* be abuse. So there again, it's a money thing, you see. These people are afraid of losing money. The real explosion is related to money. It took a few years for it to crank up, but with all this money going into the system, that's what makes the social workers so anxious to start new cases. It's their job that's on the line. Supposedly their job is to protect children, and in many cases the children can be better protected without filing cases and taking children into custody.

"And then you have the ripple effect. The social workers say, 'It's possible this child was abused or molested so how are we going to find out? Let's send the child to a doctor for a physical examination, and to a psychological agency for a psychological evaluation. So then they send the child to one of their favorite agencies or doctors, some of whom—without mentioning any names—have a reputation among attorneys doing juvenile law, as being *professional child abuse finders*. They *will* find abuse or molestation even if they have to grill the kid and put words in his mouth to get him to say it. And these agencies then make a lot of money from the county. They not only get paid per case or per child, but they get grants! One agency of which you and I have knowledge is run by a lady whose only license is a New York State welder's license. That agency, I am informed, also received a two-million-dollar grant. Every city has one of these child abuse agencies, or more than one. They are *creating* these cases.

"The D.A.'s office started trying the McMartin case in the media before they even made any arrests, before the indictments were issued. And now the defense team is bringing out the facts in the media—especially the sloppy way the original evaluations were conducted—and the original tapes show that. They put the words into the kids' mouths. And the kids were young enough that it's very easy to get the kind of answer you want, just by looking a certain way and acting a certain way and giving the kids rewards, ranging from smiles to encouragement, to hugs and pieces of candy, gifts. And they get the questions answered the way they want them answered. And now that the defense team is bringing all this to the attention of the media, the prosecution is screaming that they're trying the case in the media. But that's the only place the case has been tried to date. Kids said they were not molested—until they were interviewed by the evaluators. Two of the parents were on television recently and they said their kids adamantly denied they were molested until they were interviewed by the evaluator, and the evaluator came out and said the child had in fact been molested. And the prosecution talks about their 'solid medical evidence.' I'll tell you what the 'solid medical evidence' is. The medical evidence is written down that the condition is 'consistent with the history of molestation.' The 'history' is that they were told that the child was molested. So they find no real evidence. If they find a scratch anywhere they say it's 'consistent with the history.' In some cases they say it's 'not inconsistent with the history.' Of course all kinds of rumors have gone around that some of the children have gonorrhea. Not true. There was not a single case of sexually transmitted disease in any of these children at McMartin. And I suppose you know that one of the accusations was that all of the pre-schools in the South Bay were part of an international pornography ring. And there was a twenty-five-thousand-dollar reward offered to anybody who could come up with a single pornographic picture of any kids from McMartin. They haven't found a single piece of pornography. And you know how long the case has been going on. And that sheriff's task force. They got the twenty best investigators they could find and they dug up half the South Bay. They went at it for more than a year and they spent a million dollars on the investigation and they haven't produced enough evidence to charge anyone. All they've been able to do so far is to impugn and blacken the name of every pre-school and day care operator in the South Bay, and shut most of them down. They've all had their businesses destroyed.

"I said earlier to look for the profit motive if you really want to know what this thing is all about. Most of these schools carry liability insurance of one million dollars per child. And all these militant parents are pushing and pressuring the D.A.'s office to convict these people so they can sue for millions. Also there's the money they can get from the crime victims compensation law in California. Twenty thousand dollars.

"Even the child abuse industry people are saying that seventy percent of all the child abuse reports are unfounded. And they say that this proves that the system works because they discover that these cases are unfounded. But what they don't tell you is that many of them are not judged to be unfounded until they have ground through the system, the juvenile court system, and in some cases in the criminal courts. And the children are taken out of the home and sent away to live with strangers, and they're told that their parents did something terrible and that they're terrible people. The families are destroyed, people are bankrupted by the expenses of fighting this. And seventy percent of the cases are unfounded. Now, any system that produces seventy percent error is faulty or deficient. A lot of time is being wasted. How about all the time wasted on these unfounded cases when they should be working on cases where there's real danger?

"My client, Elaine Humlen, the case we had killed back in July, the tennis ball case. There was a new filing on her. Someone made an anonymous report that she was beating her kids in her new home. The report was made September twenty-second. They finally got around to investigating in late November. So this woman goes out there, two months after this anonymous report is made, and she looks at the kids, and there's not a mark on them, and they're fat and happy, the house is clean, and it's a nice, security apartment, it's safe, and the report is obviously unfounded. But it took them two months. It was clearly a report made by someone who had malicious intent, or was mentally deranged, but the point is that the social worker's caseload was so heavy that they don't get around to investigating these cases for two months. I read in the paper yesterday that the increase in child abuse reports since 1979 is 879 percent. And seventy percent are unfounded.

"You see, what happened in McMartin . . . they busted Ray Buckey the first time, and they had to release him because there was no evidence. And Buckey sued them. Buckey sued them, and then they really went after him. Then the Manhattan Beach Police Department wrote letters to all those parents and got the kids into evaluation. And they send them to professional abuse finders, and they find something. Were you there when Becky Barkman told about how her husband got fifty to seventy-five years for a molestation that supposedly happened when he was out of town? Her husband was not even there. Little kids are very vague about dates and times. And that's why the complaints filed are so vague. The courts have held that children don't have to come up with an exact date because little children can't come up with exact dates. In this case they narrowed it down to only one date that it possibly could have been. On that date, Becky and her husband were not in town. In addition to which, in order to believe that this kid was molested, you have to believe that the guy who molested him did it on the lawn, outside the school, with all the teachers and students and people walking past, in full view of all the windows of the police station next door. You have to understand the quality of the statements that are believed. In the McMartin case the kids said they were taken up in hot air balloons and thrown out in parachutes and molested on the way down. They were molested in underground caves and cemeteries, where they hacked up dead bodies and they bled. Mrs. McMartin said, 'How could we have done all those things? Some of the kids were only there for three hours a day.'

"The psychologists now want to get a new law passed that would allow testimony from someone who would interpret what the kids mean. Never mind what they say. This is what they mean. So what happens to the Sixth Amendment, and the Fourth Amendment. They don't mean anything any more, in this kind of case. You can't confront your accuser. Hearsay evidence is the rule, rather than the exception. You don't get due process and you don't get a fair trial. Unreasonable search is the norm, and no matter how much it's atttacked, nothing ever happens. It's allowed in. No matter how ethical and fair-minded prosecutors and judges might be in any other kind of case, in this kind of case they go berserk. And by the way, I've seen defense lawyers just sit there and not do a damned thing in these cases. I have seen a number of cases where the defense lawyer has been so overwhelmed and intimidated by these kinds of charges that they have done absolutely nothing for their client.

"I sat and talked with a group of other lawyers the other night and we talked about the common threads in these cases. One of them seems to be very prestigious schools. Like McMartin had a year to two-year waiting list. That was the Harvard of the pre-schools. Another common thread that runs through all these cases is a deranged person making the original accusations. Someone whose sanity is at least dubious. The other common thread, of course, is monetary gain.

"The figures that we hear from the child-saving industry, the most common figure we hear is that one and a half million kids disappear every year. Most of them are runaways. The next largest group are children who have been taken by one of their parents in a custody fight or whatever. But the number of children who were actually kidnapped by a stranger—and this is the FBI statistics for the year 1984—the number of stranger abductions in all fifty states, was sixty-seven. That's what the FBI says."

"Have you spoken with Peggy Ann Buckey since she arrived here last night?" I asked.

"Have I spoken with her! You know . . . Peggy Ann is undoubtedly the sweetest person I've ever met. I can't think of a better word to describe her. Just looking at her . . . it radiates from her. You talk with her for a few minutes and you realize she's still got a sense of humor. She still laughs about this. I guess it's black humor, or gallows humor. That's what her attorney, Forrest Latiner, calls it. She is just a great person! Everyone who met her and talked to her for a few minutes there in Minnesota fell in love with her. She's very shy, but she's the best spokesperson for the defendants, so she's being interviewed on radio and television and by newspapers. She does have a very sweet personality and she's good looking, she's articulate, she's bright. She has an M.A. in special education. And the nicest kid I've ever met.

"We were talking about the common threads that run through all these cases. Another one is that they're using female judges and female prosecutors. Another one is what Walter calls 'dirty discovery.' The prosecutors lie to the judge, they lie to the opposing counsel, they use underhanded, illegal, unethical tactics, they conceal evidence, they manufacture evidence, they lie about whether there is evidence very commonly. Because the evidence is fraudulent. Like all these statements in McMartin by the prosecutor, who said they have 'hard evidence.' And 'medical evidence.' And it just doesn't exist. And thanks to the length of this pre-trial or preliminary hearing, the defense has seen everything that the prosecution has. They think they have. Of course, they haven't seen it all because the prosecution is concealing as much as they can. Ordinarily in a criminal trial what you have to know is—at least in most jurisdictions in California, certainly in L.A. and Orange County— you've got a criminal charge, the defense lawyer walks in to the arraignment and says, 'Not guilty,' and grabs hold of the D.A. and says, 'Let's go to the office. Let me look at the file. I wanna make copies of what you've got, the police report and everything else,' and he says, 'Sure, come along. Here's my file. There's the copy machine.' And you copy everything they've got. And you say, 'Where is your witness list?' Hell, in California, in a criminal case, one of the things they have to give you is a witness list. And you say, 'What else have you got?' And the guy tells you. It's called informal discovery. You don't have to file a discovery motion, in almost any kind of criminal case in California, up to and including first-degree murder. But not in molest cases. They won't tell you anything. You have to get everything by a motion. They hate the defendant so much, because of the kind of case it is, that they'll do anything they can to nail him, regardless of whether it's legal or ethical. Or whether there's any evidence at all. Ray Buckey and Peggy have been sitting in jail for nineteen months. That's longer than they would do on many felony cases, even if they were convicted.

"McMartin is going to be the subject of books, theses, movies, songs, plays, for years. Maybe for centuries. It's the landmark case. The most glaringly common thread that runs through all these current cases is the way the prosecution and the authorities tell us that the more bizarre the stories, the more impossible the stories the kids tell, after they've been led to say them, by the evaluator, the more they are to be believed. That comes from Roland Summit.

He's the king of the child abuse industry. Kee McFarlane is the queen. Roland Summit's Accommodation Syndrome Theory makes a lot of sense in the context of incest cases, but only in that context. In any other kind of case, it doesn't make any sense at all. What's happening in all these cases with the interviewers and evaluators is, if a kid doesn't know the answer to a question, he makes one up. So I think what happened to all these kids in McMartin is they heard the phrase, 'Naked Movie Star Game,' and they tried to think, well, what does that mean? And they figured, well, you take off your clothes and you pose, and maybe some of them danced around to music. Some of them said the teachers were there, and some of them said the teachers weren't there. Of the seven kids, there were seven different stories of the Naked Movie Star Game. Seven different versions. And the tapes suggest that the interviewers may have introduced the name of the Naked Movie Star Game. I looked at the tapes, and in the ones I saw, none of the kids ever said anything about it.

"The interviewers say they didn't ask anything about the Naked Movie Star Game until the kids mentioned it, or the chant. Not true! The tapes show otherwise. They were the first to raise that. I'm not convinced that everybody involved in the prosecution really knows that the charges are a fraud. I think they are so blinded by the *type* of accusations that they can't see what any reasonable person should see. I find it hard to believe that Lael Rubin really believes the charges, but it's possible. I think her career may be trashed by this. I think she's going to be the new Kathleen Morris.* But I don't think there's any way those people are not going to get bound over for trial. I don't think Aviva Bobb has the political courage to let them go. This McMartin case is unlike any case I've seen. Defense lawyers get to be very cynical, and these are all very experienced lawyers. But at McMartin, the defense lawyers are all totally committed to this thing. You talk to these guys, and they are all passionately committed to their clients' innocence. You know when I realized there was something wrong with this case? When I met the defendants! And I knew there was no way in hell they could have done what they are accused of doing! All you have to do is spend a few minutes with them. I experienced

*See Chapter VI.

that. I talked to all of them when I was at the hearing. If you spend half an hour in Peggy Ann Buckey's presence, you'll be madly in love with her. You'll know there's no way she could intentionally harm anyone. And everyone in her family is as nice as she is."

Douglas Besharov was one of the speakers. He was the first director of the National Center for Child Abuse,* and is now a law professor at Georgetown University. He talked about the tidal wave of false allegations of child abuse that has descended on us since the early eighties. He said that reports of child abuse are now seventy percent unfounded, as compared to thirty percent in the sixties.

"Seven out of ten are false!" she said. "The keystone of that was the Federal Child Abuse Act. Walter Mondale was the sponsor of the Federal Child Abuse Act. It's history, unfortunately, was of mixed parentage. Mondale and his colleagues in the Senate wrote a law with a very broad definition of child abuse because they thought they were writing a law for research. What they didn't take into account was that on the House side of Congress there was a parallel effort to develop a law to provide funding to the states. There was a conference, and they decided that the best way to compromise on the two bills was to join them together. In 1975, only three states had laws broad enough to meet federal definitions. By 1979, forty-one states had passed those broader laws. The effect of this has been this phenomenal increase in reports. Child protective agencies grew, their mandates increased, their staffs were enlarged, and their ambitions also. Almost every large population center now has a specialized child protective agency that sees reports, and investigates."

He told us that child protective service workers say that "We need all these unfounded reports. That's how we identify. If we reduce the number of unfounded reports more children will die."

"The truth is just the opposite," he said. "The situation is getting so bad—junk cases flooding the system so seriously that the system's basic ability to function is seriously weakened. A lot of junk is being accepted. And you know what the newspapers are saying: CHILD ABUSE GETTING MORE SEVERE! While the number of re-

*Established by the Mondale Act.

ports has increased phenomenally, the number of kids actually getting help has gone down!

"Now," he said, "all the pressure is toward reporting. If you don't report you are liable, for both criminal and civil prosecution. If you report, you have total immunity." He strongly advocated that states revise their reporting laws to limit liability. "Six states have already done it," he said. "And they have not sunk into the ocean, and they do not have more child abuse than the other states."

An attorney from Sacramento told us, "This is a lot like the Joe McCarthy witch hunt of the nineteen-fifties, when they were trying to tell us there was a Communist hiding behind every bush. Now, the child abuse industry is telling us there's a child molester behind every tree, waiting to pounce on your kid. If you read Roland Summit and the other current literature, it tells you they're everywhere! Even your brother and your uncle are suspect. The problem is . . . they need child molesters to advance their careers, and there aren't many. Maybe two or three guys out of a million are molesters. How many people have you met in your life that were molesters. I'm fifty years old and I've been a lawyer for twenty-five and I've only met one, and I'm not sure even about him.

"But they need child molesters and they are accusing innocent people, and sending them to prison. And this is being done not by greasy, Mafia-type criminals but by well-dressed, well-scrubbed middle-class suburban folks with degrees in psychology and social work, pretty young people who've been to law school and got hired into the D.A.'s office. Judges, and police. They look like anybody else, but there's something missing, some built-in engineering defect. They don't see anything wrong with destroying somebody with false allegations in order to advance their careers. They're psychopaths. They project the appearance of being perfectly normal. But it's unspeakably disgusting behavior. A law that compels people to inform on their friends and neighbors and their own family, is not the best way to deal with it. When you call in the Czar, you stir up a whole new set of problems."

In the morning we dressed and went to the hotel's coffee shop for breakfast. When the elevator doors opened, a group of young girls, about ten or eleven years old, got it. They were dressed in lasciviously brief costumes with panty hose, high heels, lipstick like Las Vegas chorus dancers. Ironically, the national semi-final competition of some dance contest was being held in the same hotel, in the ballroom adjacent to the V.O.C.A.L. Conference. One of the organizers of the conference, a mother of an accused child abuser, looked at the little girls with horror and said, "My God! That looks like child porn to me."

As we walked into the ballroom, a young man was saying, "I always thought that cops and judges were the good guys . . ." I heard that plaintive statement over and over again during the conference. An Ohio attorney sitting next to me said, "These are not hippie radicals. These are very conventional, middle-class people who want to believe in their government, cops and medical practitioners. They want to believe their cops and doctors are people they can trust, like in those comforting TV fantasies. And what this thing has forced them to see is the incompetence and fraud that exists within those professions. Not just incompetence, but the betrayal of trust, the cruelty, the indifference to the ruin of other people's lives. The needless, senseless ruin of people's lives. This molestation mania is a big bonanza for a lot of people who are not overly burdened with ability, and they are willing to make big bucks and score points on the ruin of another person by false allegations because they don't have the brains or integrity to do it in a more legitimate way."

In the afternoon, Dr. Lee Coleman showed two videotaped interviews of children who were witnesses in a child molestation case in Florida. "Most of the people in this room have seen that there is a training process," he said. "That the children are being manipulated. We have quite a job on our hands to convince people of such a thing, which sounds so horrifying, so outrageous on its face—that police, protective service workers, mental health professionals, district attorneys, are actually training a child to believe that he has been molested. Now, I do not make any statement that people are intentionally doing harm. In fact, I always have a working assumption that nobody is intentionally doing harm. Everybody believes that what they're doing is right. So the issue is not accusing anybody of deliberately trying to harm children.

"But the fact remains that if someone's behavior amounts to doing these things, then, that's what we have to pay attention to.

We can't excuse somebody from responsibility for their behavior, in talking about these interviews, just because they may not intentionally be trying to do what they are doing. It's the results of the behavior that we have to look at. There's a lot of material here. But there's also a lot to say and a lot to talk about. Your reactions, your questions, your comments.

"Most of you know that this kind of process is going on, and I don't know how much you've actually had a chance to see it. In some cases you don't get to see videotapes. You see evidence of the process only around the edges. But obviously for you to be able to persuade other people that this kind of process is going on, you've got to understand it yourself. And that's what my hope is to accomplish here this afternoon. If you're going to try to show an outside person that a child is being trained, and it's such a horrifying and unthinkable thought, you've got a tough job on your hands. And if you don't have video tapes in the case that you're talking about, then you may have to take the next step and say, Well, they didn't do any taping. But let me show you what is going on, what has happened somewhere else. Or let's look at the transcript of what was done in this case. And I think we have to build up a library of materials which is available.

"Now, in this case, I can show you these tapes because Florida, which is where this case comes from, allows televising of its criminal cases. So you not only have the fact that a criminal case is open, and a public record, but they actually had the local media television cameras in the courtroom.

"Now . . . I could have edited these tapes down very severely, so that you'd have a minute or two of something, and look at that. But I chose not to do that, because someone could say, 'Well, you're just picking and choosing here and there,' and if you do any editing at all someone could accuse you of that. But I tried to keep it so that you could actually see the flow of significant lengths of time, because, to really understand the process of how the children are being indoctrinated, and are being trained in these cases, it doesn't happen in a sentence or two. It's not as though somebody says something and the child believes that statement. It's a gradual process of learning.

"It's going to take some patience on your part. The first tape that I'm going to show you is twenty-five minutes long. The next segment is an hour and a half, on one child. That hour and a half is actually taken out of an interview that is two and a half hours long, in which the child was with one, or two, or three adults. They were trading off, coming in and out of the room. The child was in there the whole time. Sitting there for a hour and a half can get to be a drag, sitting there with all these people talking at you day after day. I hope that you will really recognize the fact that if you get a sense of what it's like to sit through this interview process for an hour and a half, imagine what it's like for a five or six-year-old child. And you'll see the visual evidence of how fatigued the child is.

"I'm not going to take a lot of time with the fine details of what happened in this case, because, regardless of the outcome of the case, none of that changes the fact of how these children are being interviewed. Now in this case the man was convicted, and has been given over two hundred years. He will be in prison, probably the rest of his life. Whether or not he did anything to any child I really don't know. But that really is not relevant, because the point here is, whether or not somebody did anything doesn't change the question of why in the world would you want to interview a child in such a way? Even if the child *has* been molested in a particular case, we'd never be able to tell whether what they are telling you is because they could actually remember something that had happened—versus all the things that are getting implanted in their minds. So these outrageous techniques are just as harmful in cases of legitimate sexual abuse as they are in cases of false accusation. In both cases we're going to confound the real statements of a child based on what they can remember, versus statements which have come from the learning and indoctrination process that adults put them through. In this case, the allegation was against the husband and wife who had a babysitting service, and the wife eventually testified against the husband. There was a very active plea-bargaining process going on. She ended up with a very minor sentence, and said many things about her husband which raise very serious doubts in my mind, as to whether the things she was claiming happened, could actually have been true. If anybody wants to get into that we can, but I don't think it's worth spending a lot of time on. I think these tapes are what we have to talk about.

"The interviewers are one psychologist and one social worker.

They are a husband and wife team. As you'll see, they work together, sometimes two of them in there, sometimes one. They are
people who are working with the district attorney.

"I think we're going to have to get laws that require that these
interviews be videotaped. You see, the idea of videotaping these
interviews initially was something that was promoted by the sorts
of people who are doing these interviews, because, in their mind,
that's the evidence—in other words, they can actually go to court
and show the child saying it, and this is the way they'll be able to
make the case. When people have had a chance to look at the
tapes, in various cases, and it's been so outrageous, *now* the interviewers are pulling back, and now they're realizing that they better
not tape these interviews, because people are going to see what
they're doing. And that's why I think you're going to see—unless
there's legislative reform to make it mandatory—you're going to
see even less taped interviews than we have now."

He starts the video. A woman is making a long speech to the
child. She is telling the child, "The other kids said it happened
. . ." Coleman stops the tape and says, "That's an out-and-out lie.
Not one of the other children said that." Later on, when the child
tells a wild story, Coleman says, "Prosecutors say that children
don't make up stories like that . . . they're all telling similar stories. Actually, it's the interviewers. They all are being trained by
the same trainers." The interrogation goes on. Coleman comments: "There is a constant going back and forth between what is
clearly labeled as make-believe and what is supposed to be a fact-
finding process. What the hell is a child supposed to do with dolls if
not make-believe? That's what dolls are for." He says that dolls are
not an appropriate tool for a fact-finding process. The woman goes
on babbling, asking the child, "I wonder if they took their clothes
off . . ." The interviewer keeps saying, let's just play a game. Let's
pretend. But it is not a game! They are getting ready to go to court,
and this is the evidence they are going to use to send a man to
prison. This is the evidence!

The interrogation team have gone on and on for a long time now
and they haven't gotten anything from the kid except the statement
that nothing was done to him. She tells him that the other kids
were scared of Frank, the babysitter. Another lie. Not one of the
other children had said that he or she was scared, or that Frank and

Ileana had done anything bad. The child says, "They didn't do any-thing bad to me." She is four years old. The interviewer tells her: "Your mom and dad, they will be very proud of you for telling." The psychologist goes on and on. Coleman comments that almost everything she's telling the child is false.

"It's so terribly important," Coleman says, "to get the judge, the jury, the people who count, to realize the training that's gone on before they have gotten into the case. You can have a D.A. who honestly, sincerely doesn't see, doesn't know about the training. All they know is what they get from the child, once they get into the case. And they have no idea how that child has been trained before that. And even if you don't have the documentation of how the child was trained in your case, if you can convince that person and say, 'Hey, let me show you what is being done!' so that the possibility that it could be done in this case doesn't seem so im-probable to him. The thing to do is to try to prevent it from coming to trial by trying to show this kind of material. Other than that, we're just going to have to try to present it in the case. Some attor-neys are afraid of this stuff because what they see is that the child says something happened, and they think, 'Oh my God! That's prosecution evidence.' I don't agree with that. This is where the truth is. And truth is your strongest weapon."

The videotaped interview goes on and on. The child says nothing happened. The interviewer tells her the other kids say something did happen. She tells the child her parents will be very proud if she tells the secrets. The interviewer asks the child to conjecture: "What do you think might have happened?" And the child begins to conjecture. And all the child's previous statements are ignored, and this is taken as the evidence! The interviewer says, over and over again, "If we just pretend . . ." and "I wonder if they played 'duck duck goose' without any clothes on."

"When I testified in this case," Coleman says, "I said it's not just anatomically correct dolls. I have serious problems with the use of *any* dolls, as a fact-finding process. Because dolls are something children play with. Can you imagine giving a child a doll for a pres-ent, and saying, 'You cannot pretend with this doll. You can only do things that would really happen. No pretending.' That violates the child's entire life experience. That's what a doll is for—to make up stories.

"As for the anatomically correct dolls, I think it is not only child abuse, I think it is sexual abuse. The overstimulation of children, sexually." Several people in the audience told of similar interrogations in which children became obviously sexually aroused.

"You train the children in these interviews," Coleman comments, "and then you send them to a therapist, who gets the child already trained. Then you have that therapist come in and testify, about what the child says. The parents believe that their child has been molested. They've been convinced of this by these interviewers. They think that these interviewers are the friend of the parents. One of the common methods is, that they get a child, and the child, even with these methods, does not say that anything happened to him, for, maybe, two hours. And then they say 'Well, if you think of anything, maybe you could come back, and tell us about it.' And sure enough, two or three weeks later, a parent calls and says, 'She was telling me about something.' And so the next interview starts with: 'Well, your mommy was telling me about some things that you told her. Maybe you could tell me about those things.' And I haven't seen an interview yet where the child actually initiated this. And what I think is . . . the parents are absorbing this material from the interviewer. And the parents are going home and becoming substitutes for the interviewer. So it's coming at the child from several directions at once."

On the television screen the woman tells the child, "You can be a big help to the other kids if you tell . . . You're older than the other kids, and smarter . . . If you don't tell us, you can't help the other kids . . . Do you know what the other children said? Do you believe it? Now let's just pretend . . ." and she starts undressing the dolls: ". . . just make believe."

"Some of the children," she says, "feel that Frank and Ileana were bad."

"Another lie," Coleman comments. "None of the others said that."

"Just pretend," the woman says, undressing the doll. "I wonder if they played the game with their clothes off."

The child is falling asleep. His eyelids are drooping. He's been interrogated for hours.

"Show us what Frank did to you."

"I'll show you what Frank did," the child says. His head is sagging to one side. He's falling asleep! "Here's what Frank did!" He grasps the Frank doll by the penis and swings it around in a circle above his head.

"Where did Frank put his penis?" she asks.

"He put his penis in my nose," the child answers. Everybody laughs. Then he stands the Frank doll on its head on top of the other doll's head. "That's what Frank did!"

After dinner, we went back to the main room to listen to Dr. Lee Coleman's address on False Allegations of Child Abuse.

"The subtitle of my article," he said, "is 'Have the Experts Been Caught With Their Pants Down?' Well, what do I mean by that? The phrase 'to be caught with your pants down' means to be unprepared. And that's really what I think has happened in this field. A certain set of ideas which made some sense until recently are now being applied indiscriminately, even though the situation is totally different. The experts in the field really have been caught with their pants down. They have continued to preach certain things which might have fit in one arena but which really don't now. Times have passed this by and they refuse to acknowledge it.

"Now, before I get into the substance of that, what I want to start with is a concept that has been called 'the banality of evil.' I think that virtually everybody in this room has seen the evil of what is going on. Whether it's your own case, whether in your own life, or whether, as a professional, you have seen the evil of the way the children are being manipulated, of the way investigations are being done. So then you have to say, 'Why? Why is this happening?' And I want to say a little bit by way of trying to explain why it's happening—about this concept of the banality of evil. We think we see the evil. Well, this is a phrase that was coined by the writer, Hannah Arendt, when she wrote a book called, *Eichmann in Jerusalem*. This was when Adolf Eichmann was captured, and brought back to Israel to be put on trial. And the major point that she makes in the book is that the problem of evil in the world is not a problem of evil people. It would be much easier to try to do something about evil things in the world if it were evil people who were doing them. The problem is that ordinary people are the people who are doing evil things. And the point that she makes with regard to the Nazi era was that the holocaust, and all the rest, was not performed, by and large, by evil people. Of course, we have a few people who would certainly qualify for that label. But the masses or bureaucracies which had to carry out the mass murders, were being carried out by ordinary people.

"Well, I think that if you apply that, the evil that is going on in this country around these false allegations . . . I don't think that the way to search for why this is happening is to say that these are evil people who are doing this. I believe the way to start is to say that the people who are doing these things, the interviewers and all the rest, are ordinary people, and, by and large, they are people who are concerned, caring people, people who believe that they are doing the right thing. To me it doesn't make sense any other way. So then we have to say, all right, how could it be that ordinary people, concerned people, caring people, could come to the point where they would end up doing things that seem to be evil? And I don't mean to use the word 'evil' in a religious sense. If some of you want to take it that way, that's fine, but just . . . wrong! Unjustified! Dangerous. Harmful. So how is that happening? Well, I believe I understand why it's happening, and I want to say a little bit about what my feelings are.

"I think that it's amazing that so much influence has come from one particular paper from one particular psychiatrist, and that is the Child Abuse Accommodation Syndrome that was published a few years ago by Doctor Roland Summit. And I want to run through the elements of that paper and try to show you how someone who is trained in the ideas that this paper talks about can come in good faith and good conscience, and with good intentions, to do all the things that we are seeing in these cases. And if I'm right—that this is the source of it—then I think it tells us what we have to do to try to change it. We have to go to the root of the training, teach people why this is wrong, and begin to undo this process.

"I think if I just begin with some comments from the introduction to Dr. Summit's paper, it'll begin to give you some flavor. Just keep in mind that this is what people are getting trained in who are joining the sexual abuse teams in protective services and police, and the mental health professionals who do the evaluations.

"Here are a couple of things that Dr. Summit says about it. He says, 'The explosion of interest creates new hazards for the victim of child sexual abuse since it increases the likelihood of discovery but fails to protect the victim against the secondary assaults of an

inconsistent intervention system. If a respectable, reasonable adult
is accused of perverse, assaultive behavior by an uncertain, emotionally distraught child, most adults who hear the accusation will
fault the child. Disbelief and rejection by adult caretakers increase
the helplessness, hopelessness, isolation and self-blame that make
up the most damaging aspects of child sexual victimization.' He
says later, 'Acceptance and validation are crucial to the psychological survival of the victim.'

"So, you see, right there the mental health person or the protective service worker is being trained that if you do not believe the
child, you are contributing, not to the psychological survival of the
victim, but to the opposite. So you see, the accepting of what a
child says is linked up with caring about the child, and protecting
the child. And he says, 'In present practice it is not unusual for
clinical evaluation to stygmatize legitimate victims as either confused or malicious. Without a clear understanding of the accommodation syndrome, clinical specialists tend to reinforce the comforting belief that children are only rarely legitimate victims and that
among the few complaints that surface, most can be dismissed as
fantasy, confusion, or a displacement of the child's own wish for
power and seductive conquest.'

"Well, maybe at one time that was true in a certain situation that
I'll be describing in a minute. But I think all of you know that it is
one hundred and eighty degrees the opposite of what we are now
seeing, and what we have seen in recent years. But nonetheless, if
this is the way you're getting trained, it says that if you don't trust a
child, then you are just one more of a long chain of people who are
victimizing the child. You join the child abusers, as another
abuser, yourself.

"He also says, 'The purpose of the paper, then, is to provide a
vehicle for a more sensitive, more therapeutic response to legitimate victims of child sexual abuse, and to invite more active, more
effective clinical advocacy for the child within the family and within
the systems of child protection and criminal justice.'

"Well, that all is fine, if we knew we had a legitimate victim.
There is the assumption that we have a legitimate victim. Unfortunately, people who are getting trained in these ideas start off with
the assumption that they have a legitimate victim, and then everything they do goes in this direction. 'Now it is my job to advocate

for this child! I'm not going to be one of those people that fails to protect the child!' So you begin to see how concern about helping a child begins to get molded in a certain direction, consistent with the kind of behavior that many of you are seeing.

"What Summit does, then, is, he has five categories, five components of the syndrome, which I put up on the board. I want to run through each one briefly. As I go through these, keep in mind a couple of questions. Number one: in what kind of situation do I think what Summit is saying makes sense, and in what kind of situation might it not make sense. What Summit is saying is not totally off-the-wall, or inappropriate. What he is saying does make sense if it were confined to situations that were consistent with some of the quotes that I will now give you.

"The first component is 'Secrecy.' Here's what he says about it: 'Any attempts by the child to illuminate the secret will be countered by an adult conspiracy of silence and disbelief. "How could you ever think of such a terrible thing?" the parent says. "Don't let me ever hear you say anything like that again!" '

"Now, in a classic situation where the male figure is the alleged perpetrator, that is the kind of statement you might hear from a mother who is still married to the father, or who is still living with, and wants to continue living with, the live-in boyfriend—yes, indeed, that is the kind of thing that you might hear. That is the classic, intact-family, incest situation. And that is exactly where Dr. Summit's experience comes from. And so many of the people who have been working in this field, that's what they grew up on. Incest! That is where most of the literature was from until the last few years. That's what people were thinking about. That's what was being reported. That makes sense when a mother who hears that her husband has molested a daughter may in fact have more loyalty to her husband than to her daughter, for emotional reasons, for financial reasons, and there may be a lot of other reasons, and as Summit correctly points out, may come to the defense of the father at the expense of the child. And that most certainly is an abuse that anybody who becomes aware of should try to protect the child [from], as Summit says. This is a second victimization. First the child is victimized sexually, and then is victimized by not being believed and is shut down. So far so good.

"Now, we have a situation where the mother and the father have divorced each other. They hate each other. And they are fighting over the custody of the child. Do you think that you are going to hear that mother say to the child, 'How could you ever think of such a terrible thing.'? 'Don't let me ever hear you say that again.'? Well I don't need to tell *this* audience how totally ludicrous that is.

"What if the accusation is against a pre-school teacher? Do you think the mothers are saying, 'Don't ever let me hear you say that again.'? Quite obviously that is not what is going on. Does Dr. Summit or any of the colleagues he has leading this field, ever talk about that? What he's claiming about how 'nobody ever supports the child' makes absolutely no sense, *except* in a situation where the people who might otherwise discredit the child have some reason to discredit the child, like to save their marriage or to save their relationship. So there we have the first component, secrecy. I think you'll see a similar pattern as we go through this.

"The next component is 'Helplessness.' The child not only has to keep his secret, but is helpless to do anything about it. In this part, Summit quotes Ann Landers, who says, 'Father is now fifty-three. To look at him you would think he's the all-American dad. Mom is fifty-one. She would die if she had any idea of what he has been doing to his daughters all those years.' Again, you see, it's the intact family situation. The kinds of cases we've got now, the mother would die rather than believe that the father *didn't* do it. And you all know how true that is. Here again is some of the training that the professional gets. Here's what Summit says: 'If the child's testimony is rejected, in court, there is more likely to be a rejection by the mother and other relatives who may be eager to restore trust in the accused adults, and to brand the child as malicious.' It makes sense in an intact family. It makes absolutely no sense in the kinds of cases that we are seeing so rampantly in the country at this time.

"The next phase is what he calls 'Entrapment and Accommodation.' The child is helpless because nobody will believe him. First, he keeps it a secret, that's the first phase. Then, they're helpless because nobody will believe it. So then, they're trapped and they accommodate to it over some period of years. Well, in incest situations this does happen. A girl is the usual victim who has been molested. You don't have to talk to too many people before you will find somebody who has been victimized, as a child, a girl who has kept it a secret over the years. And I don't think there's anybody who would minimize the trauma and the damage of a child keeping this within himself all these years. And Summit says, 'The only healthy option left for the child is to learn to accept the situation and to survive. There is no way out, no place to run. The healthy-normal, emotionally resilient child will learn to accommodate to the reality of continuing sexual abuse.'

"Then he says here, 'The child is given the power to destroy the family and the responsibility to keep it together.' If the child says anything the family will be destroyed; if the child holds it in, the family will stay together. And again, that's true, if the family is already together. But what if the family isn't together? What if that's long gone? Then that just simply doesn't apply! But there's no mention, no recognition, by Summit or anybody else that I see, who are being accepted as leaders, that it doesn't apply when the family isn't together.

"Or take that to one of these pre-school cases. It's totally irrelevant to say the child is given the power to destroy the family, and the responsibility to keep it together. Michael Ruby, down in Los Angeles, he's not in the family. Neither is Claudia Krikorian or any of these people who are being accused, so it just totally does not fit.

"All right, the next category is 'Delayed, conflicted and unconvincing disclosure.' The child finally does come out and say something. And of course in many cases of incest the girl never will say anything. She just grows up and keeps it to herself. And who can ever measure how much damage that does? We have to assume that it can't be good, to have kept that inside all those years. But Summit says now, 'The mother typically reacts to allegations of sexual abuse with disbelief and protective denial. As someone substantially dependent on approval and generosity of the father, the mother in the incestuous triangle is confronted with a mindsplitting dilemma. Either the child is bad and deserving of punishment or the father is bad, and unfairly punitive. One of them is lying and unworthy of trust. The mother's whole security and life adjustment and much of her sense of adult self-worth demand a trust in the reliability of her partner. To accept the alternative means annihilation of the family, and a large piece of her identity.' That makes sense. The mother's married. She wants to hold on to her husband. Does it make any sense when there's a divorce already taken place, there's a bitter custody fight, or the teacher is in a pre-school, and none of these allegations are going to apply. It's based on incest cases. The connections between the Parents United group and Roland Summit are very strong. A lot of this experience comes from cases where there's no question that there's acknowledged sexual abuse. The perpetrators admitted it—and not under the kind of heavy-duty plea bargaining that we know can happen. But the experience comes out of cases where they really can, with some reasonable sense of it, start off with the finding that there has been a molestation—again, totally different from what we're talking about, where that is the question: whether the child's been molested.

"No real experience in actually interviewing children. I would think that in itself would not have to mean that what he would say would be invalid. People can come up with whatever ideas from whatever source they get them. It's the ideas that we have to check out.

"So, again, we see every one of these categories so far fits with the intact family, and does not fit with either custody disputes, or pre-schools or other professionals who are accused—which is the two main categories of cases that we are seeing as the focus of these false allegations.

"Finally, 'Retraction.' And this is the big one. Summit says about retraction: 'Whatever a child says about sexual abuse, she is likely to reverse it. Beneath the anger of impulsive disclosure remains the ambivalence of guilt and martyred obligation to protect the family.' Again, that assumes that there *is* a family, meaning mother, father or father substitute, and child. Okay. Summit goes on to say: 'The message from the mother is very clear, often explicit. "Why do you go on telling those awful stories about your father? If you send him to prison, we won't be a family any more. We'll end up on welfare with no place to stay. Is that what you want to do to us?" ' And what Summit says is, 'Unless there is special support for the child and immediate intervention to force responsibility on the father, the girl will follow the normal course and retract her complaint. This restores the precarious equilibrium of the family.'

"Now, obviously you can see that it's the intact family he's talking about, but notice some things here. 'Unless there is immediate intervention . . .' Do you begin to see where some of these people are coming from? This is not capricious. This is not coming out of nowhere. This is not because these people get their jollies out of coming into your house and violating your civil rights. That is not why they're doing it. They're doing it because they have been trained to believe that they have to do it if they care about children, if they want to protect children, if they're going to be better than the last generation who didn't believe the children. They're doing all the wrong things for the right reasons. And this, in my opinion is where those reasons are coming from.

"Now, Dr. Summit tells us some things about that famous idea that children don't lie. He doesn't actually say they don't lie. Even that category of experts doesn't go quite so far as to say that children don't lie. They just say they don't lie about sexual abuse. Well, I've already commented at some meetings to some of you that I think it's a grave mistake to cast the problem in terms of whether the child is lying. And I urge you, don't let yourself get caught in that trap. Because you then get seen as a stigmatizer of the child. You're calling the child a liar, and, given all the emotion that's being generated, that is not going to help intrude a little rationality. And it is not accurate to think of the child as lying. If a child believes in Santa Claus, there are other choices besides believing in Santa Claus or believing that the child is a liar. The obvious truth is that the child believes in Santa Claus and therefore they're not lying. They believe what they're talking about. So this is the absurdity that is being foisted on the nation by these experts when they talk about 'children don't lie,' as though the question is whether or not they're lying. *The question is whether or not what they believe is in fact true. And if they believe it and it isn't true, how did they come to believe it?* Now here's what Summit says. He says, 'Very few children—no more than two or three per thousand—have ever been found to exaggerate or invent claims of sexual molestation.' Now is that out of touch with reality or isn't it?

"Now this paper was written about five years ago. We might be able to excuse Dr. Summit, based on the date of the paper—and when I say Dr. Summit, I . . . it really isn't just limited to him. He stands at the center of the people who are leading this field, so I really mean all of them. If they were to come and say, 'Well, yes, we did believe that, but obviously there's something more that's going on,' then we could say, 'Beautiful! Now let's talk about that.'

But that's not what's happening. They are digging their heels in. They are simply saying, 'No! Children can be relied on!' You just heard this morning Dr. Ray tell us, after going to Chicago, that the latest evidence is that children are basically telling the truth. So he and people who are leading the system are saying, 'We have to go to Chicago to find out from the "latest evidence" what we think about what the children are saying. We can't believe our eyes and our ears, and what we're seeing right in front of us.'

"So they are not taking into account what is happening. They're simply sticking to their position that if the child says that anything happened it has to have happened. And he goes on to say, 'It has become a maxim among child sexual abuse intervention counselors and investigators that children never fabricate the kinds of explicit sexual manipulations they divulge in complaints or interrogations.'

"It's getting so bad that a lot of the training and indoctrination of the children is not even happening in the office. It's happening in homes now. It's happening in ways that we can't document at all.

"In some of the Southern California pre-school cases, as you heard last night, the police sent around a letter to the parents and said, 'We have reason to believe that your child has been molested or has witnessed children being molested,' and they gave them a long shopping list of behaviors which could show that the child was molested. Nightmares, temper tantrums, all this long list of things that could come from any number of causes. And then they also said, 'You parents will be the last to know, the last ones that the children will tell, so you need to bring the children in for experts who are trained how to get the children to tell,' so you know that the parents are going to start trying to ask the children all these questions, and to begin the process in ways that I'm sure are not all the same, but also I think the evidence is overwhelming that a lot of the training is coming from parents. And that's why I insist upon calling parents victims as well, even though, at one level, they are victimizing their own children, but they really are victims first. They have been led down the path and they are doing things to their own children which—I just keep waiting for some of the parents to recognize what they have been trained to do, and at least begin to start undoing it.

"To say children never fabricate these things reminds me of

when Jimmy Carter said, after he was inaugurated, and he had his first press conference, he said to the press, 'You know, I'll never lie to you.' And that was his first lie. And that's nothing against Jimmy Carter. It's in the nature of the business. And to say that children never fabricate, is a fabrication in itself, obviously, a fabrication which is being maintained by the leaders in the field.

"I want to finish with just a few more quotes of how Summit finishes up his paper, because now it's time, after developing the five components of his 'syndrome' to really lay the pep talk on the reader of the paper. That is, Summit is now telling people who have come to his paper to learn how to do a job of protecting the child, to really drive the message home and get that person to a point of view where they're not going to fail to protect the child, in Summit's terms. He says, and these are just a few quotes, he says, 'Acceptance and validation are crucial to the psychological survival of the victim.' Next: 'In a crime where there is usually no third-party eyewitnesses and no physical evidence, the verdict, and the validation of the child's perception of reality and acceptance by adult caretakers, and even the emotional survival of the child may all depend on the knowledge and skill of the clinical advocate. Every clinician must be capable of understanding and articulating the position of the child in the prevailing adult imbalance of credibility.'

"Next: 'Clinical experience and expert testimony can provide advocacy for the child. They need an adult clinical advocate to translate the child's world into adult acceptable language.' Next: 'As an advocate for the child, both in therapy and in court the more illogical and incredible the initiation scene might seem to adults the more likely it is that the child's plaintive description is valid.'

"Next: 'Unless there is expert advocacy for the child in criminal court, the child is likely to be abandoned as the helpless custodian of a self-incriminating secret which no responsible adult can believe. The psychiatrist or other counseling specialist has a crucial role in early detection, treatment intervention and expert courtroom advocacy. The specialist must help mobilize skeptical caretakers into a position of belief, acceptance, support and protection of the child.'

"Next: 'It is counter-therapeutic and unjust to expose legitimate

victims to evaluations or treatment by therapists who cannot suspect or believe in the possibility of unilateral sexual victimization of
children by apparently normal adults.'

"So, in other words, if you are somebody who doesn't see that
the child has been molested often enough, you simply won't be
sent these evaluations. And I know people who have been edged
out of their positions because they, too often, said, 'I don't think
the child's been molested.' I don't get into that because I would
never accept an evaluation to see whether a child has been molested, because I don't believe that there are any such evaluations
that mental health professionals can do, so I don't do it. But I know
people who will honestly try, and once the county sees that they're
not giving them a high enough percentage of 'It happened' evaluations, they simply won't send any more to that therapist, and this is
the kind of training that they would have got, to believe that's what
they have to do. They just don't send people to therapists who
don't believe in the possibility.

"Finally, Summit says, 'The justice system can rarely prove guilt
or impose sanctions without preparation and continued support of
all parties within an effective treatment system.' What does all this
add up to? What it all adds up to is that a person who goes to their
training and gets exposed to all this comes to believe that 'if I talk
to a child, I hear the allegation, I look into it, and I do not believe
that the child was molested, then I am an uncaring professional,
and not only am I uncaring, but I am incompetent . . . that I simply have not been well enough trained . . . that I am one of the
stupid ones, one of the people who has no mental acumen and no
moral sensitivity.' I hope you can see just how strong this message
can be. You've got to believe the child, if you care about children
and if you're doing your job well.

"The whole idea of saying, Well wait a minute, it's not a question
of 'do I believe the child?' It's a question of what has happened
with this child. How has this child been influenced? Who has
something to gain, something to lose, by what is being said? It all
goes by the wayside because this whole thing sets in motion a
knee-jerk reaction, and I think that's what it's coming from.

"Okay, what do we have to do? Obviously we've got to begin to
educate people about why the system is being trained the wrong
way. And we cannot fall for this shibboleth: more training. Because

the ideal training workshop, as things stand right now, would be to have Kee McFarlane, of the Children's Institute International in Los Angeles, to do the training of how to interview the kids with the dolls, and to have Roland Summit lecture on the theory and some of the issues of his syndrome. And you see where we would end up. More training means more of the problem. So what we've got to do now is go out and start educating people about what's wrong with all these theories.

"The whole problem of this hysteria is pretty new, and therefore the problem of how to get people to look at it sensibly is even newer. People are just beginning to fight back, whether it's in the cases in court or whether it's in the media. My view of how to attack these claims is not to do other psychological evaluations and say that our psychological evaluations are right, and theirs are wrong. In my view, you are validating the process of the evaluations by doing that. That is, you are further convincing a court that, Gee, these evaluations must be awfully important because both sides are doing them. And I think that encourages the court to abandon their common sense, and the facts. So the only approach that I would be willing to use, and the one I urge on people caught in these situations: Do not use psychologists or psychology for ANYTHING. If you're absolutely forced to, by a court, do it under protest, because you must do it, tactically, but go on record before anything is done, that you will not accept the results because you do not acknowledge the validity of the methods, and that you intend to call people who will question those methods. That approach is a very new idea, so that, I think, is something that we have to bring out, more and more.

"But I think one thing we certainly have to know is how to cross-examine the other side's doctors. We've just got to make sure the attorneys know who's out there to help them. And we are busy trying to get more of us available to help them. We've got to expand our club."

During the social hour after the evening's program had ended, a woman from California told me of a recent case in one of the West Coast cities.

"Ken is thirty-two. He was recovering from open-heart surgery. The sheriff's detectives came in and arrested him and pulled him

out of his hospital bed. They actually pulled the tubes and i.v.s out
of him, arrested him and took him down to county jail. They later
came to his house and removed three of his children and put them
in protective custody. His wife was eight months pregnant with the
fourth. They arrested her and put her in jail too. It was his ex-wife
who made the complaint. She wanted full custody of their kid by
his first marriage, so she accused him of molestation. While he's
being booked they go to his home and arrest his pregnant wife in
her nightgown. They take her down to county jail, they hold her
there for four days without allowing her a telephone call. She
started having pain and they released her, in the parking lot. She
was having premature contractions. She sat in the parking lot for an
hour before anyone knew she was there, barefoot, pregnant, and in
a nightgown. When the baby was born, the baby was twelve hours
old, the detective found out the baby was born, and they took that
baby too! They said that the wife knew that the father had molested
his kid and therefore she was guilty of child endangerment. They
still have her baby. It's been eighteen months. Now *that's* child
abuse!

"They released his wife, and dropped all the charges against her
in criminal court. Recently, she went back to court. Her husband
has since been convicted. There is no evidence, but her lawyer
didn't bring in any experts. He thought it wouldn't be necessary
because the charges were obviously unfounded. Which was naive.
They didn't contact V.O.C.A.L. until after the conviction, which is
unfortunate, because there were a lot of things they overlooked.
The fact that there was a vindictive ex-wife trying to get custody
was not allowed in. So therefore the jury's only getting part of the
picture. They see the child, but they don't see what's causing the
child to say it. So they got a conviction. There was also testimony
from this woman detective who arrested them and took their kids,
who said she was an expert on child abuse, and that she knows a
child molester when she sees one, and that this Ken is definitely
one. It was nonsense, but the jury bought it.

"His wife recently went back into court to try and get her children because her husband is going to prison for forty-three years.
And he never molested anyone! She went into juvenile court to try
to get her children back, and the social workers told the judge that
she should not have the children back because she was passive and

allowed the children to be molested, and therefore she is capable of endangering the children further. And when the maternal grandmother stood up and said, could you please let them stay with me, the judge looked at her and said, 'No. Look what kind of monster you've raised . . .' They still couldn't understand that it was the vindictive ex-wife who started all this with baseless allegations.

"What had happened was, the ex-wife had remarried, and she wanted her new husband to adopt the nine-year-old boy. Ken refused to sign over and terminate his parental rights. He said, 'No, I want to keep contact with my son and have joint custody.' And two days later he was arrested. By this time, the nine-year-old boy is saying, well, yeah, he saw something happen. This woman detective had had him all this time. We're getting a lot of taped interviews from other kids she's had in her custody. She screams at the kid and says, 'You're a liar! I know this man is a molester. You better tell me or I'm gonna hafta give you some problems!' She scares the kid to death. And he's only a little kid and he's away from his parents and he finally makes some kind of statement that he was molested. And she said, 'Now you're telling the truth and you better stick with the truth, or you're in big trouble!'

"We're getting that on tape. I've got interviews with children who've even been bribed by this detective. She's the head of the child sexual abuse unit. She just got a commendation from a women's organization. She and her partner were described as being the Cagney and Lacey of molestation. Her partner is not as bad as she is, but she works under this woman and has to go along with this bribing and threatening of witnesses. But I've got some of these kids on tape, and we're gradually building our case against her."

It was beginning to snow in the morning when we got into the cab and headed for the airport. Minneapolis is a beautiful city. We drove past lakes, lovely old houses, lots of elm trees everywhere. We drove alongside the Mississippi River. You never see litter or garbage on the streets and sidewalks of Minneapolis.

We got out at the airport, went inside, and waited.

VI

Jordan, Minnesota

"Children Never Lie . . ."

"Back in September, 1983, Christine Brown and Judith Kath made the first complaints," Lois Bentz told us. Mrs. Bentz was one of the principals in this story, the first to be put on trial in Jordan, mother of three small children. "Kath talked to her daughter and her daughter told her that James Rud had been fondling her. Christine Brown and Judith Kath were friends and had daughters the same age, and they hung around a lot together. So Christine Brown asked her daughter if that was happening, and she said it had, so they went down to the Jordan Police Department and made a complaint against James Rud. He was a young man, about twenty-six, I think. He had had two prior convictions for molestation. Rud was arrested. He was the first arrest. That was in October.

"After that it just started to snowball. His neighbors, a cop, a sheriff, and both of the two mothers who made the original complaint were arrested. They arrested Rud's parents, the Germundsons. . . . They were, basically, women who all knew each other, and neighbors of Rud, they arrested all those people.

"And so when they arrested Chris Brown, and our neighbors, Tom and Helen Brown, went to fight for custody of Chris Brown's five kids. And they were supposed to have a home study completed on the Browns by January fifteenth, and they arrested them on the eleventh.

"We felt they were innocent. My husband, on January sixteenth, went to a town meeting, and basically stated that, you know, why did they have to put these people through the news media every night? If you're gonna arrest them, just arrest them. We felt they were innocent, and they were on a witch hunt. And, basically, we just stuck up for the Browns, and it was kind of a supportive group that went down to the town council that night. The next night we got a call. They wanted to talk to our children. The Scott County Attorney's detectives. And that Friday we were arrested and after we were arrested, Greg Myers, the Jordan cop, was arrested. Then Don and Cindy Buchan were arrested and Terry Morgenson. It was just one after another. Don Buchan was a deputy sheriff.

"First we had two attorneys, Freeberg and Mozig, but we couldn't afford them. So they got us two attorneys, Earl Gray and Barry Voss. And we just decided that we had had enough. We couldn't get in to see the children. We were totally isolated from them. No phone calls, no nothing. Our parents couldn't get in to see them. We even tried to get a priest in to see them, Father Tom. We have three sons. At that time they were six, eleven and thirteen. We realized then . . . we decided back in April, that we were going to be first to go, because the children were totally isolated from us. We could have no contact with them whatsoever, so we decided that   you can't hang in limbo like that forever. You can't see your children, you've got this hanging over your head, you know you're innocent . . . We decided to go, set a trial date, and go for it.

"We knew they had a weak case. No case. We were totally innocent. So that's what we did. We set it for August twentieth.

"The trial started on August twentieth, last year, 1984. There was no evidence at all. They had our two sons, and the two neighbor kids, and one neighbor girl. And then Chris Brown's daughter. And what happened . . . they ended up dropping two of our sons, right away. They dropped half of the counts, right after the children's testimony.

"My middle boy, whom they ended up dropping charges on, stated that I had done it once to him while his dad was at work, and his dad had done it once to him while I was at work, and when we asked him why he told them that, he said, 'Mom, they question you and question you and question you and question you. Finally, when I said that, they finally left me alone.'

"They were being questioned by the Scott County Attorney, by detectives, by social workers, even the drivers who drove them back and forth, over and over again. Seven months, that's a long time for an eleven-year-old. He was sticking to his guns, but, how much can a little kid take? By the time it ended up, they had him from January to February of the next year. Thirteen months. We were found not guilty September nineteenth, and we did not see our two youngest until the middle of December. We asked them to give us back our kids after we were found not guilty and they would not cooperate with us at all. Kathleen Morris, the prosecutor, had stated to the news media after we were acquitted that just because we were acquitted doesn't mean that we're innocent. She said she was fed up with the presumption of innocence. She vowed to keep our children away from us. We finally got the kids back in January and February.

"It's something to go through a thing like that. You don't know if you're going to go to prison for something you didn't do. You don't know if you're going to see your children again. I realized a lot of those people I didn't know were innocent, because we'd sit and read these complaints, and you were supposedly at all these parties, with people you didn't even know! People you'd never even met. And yet you were supposedly all together at these bizarre parties, molesting babies. And something else—these children, all their findings, the girls were virgins, and by the time they got done with them, they said there was just nothing out of the normal, no evidence at all. Someone had a six-year-old daughter, she had gotten out of the bathtub, and she was doing cartwheels and stuff like that, and he thought it was kinda cute, and he took pictures of her. Somehow, they got hold of that, and they successfully prosecuted him, for child pornography. He was very much respected in the community, and he ended up losing everything. And he had a nervous breakdown. He was convicted, but I don't remember how long he got.

"The ones that accused us were Christine Brown's daughter and the neighbor boy. They were scared. And by that time, Chris Brown's daughter, they had worked on her so long that whomever they mentioned, she said they did it. They offered Rud a deal. He went for a long time and said, 'No, I've never seen any other molestation, I don't know these people,' until it got down where they started putting a lot of pressure on him just before our trial. Kathleen Morris, the prosecutor, figured if she had an adult witness to corroborate the children's testimony, because there was no evidence, she would get her conviction. He accused about twenty people and worked them all in there and made up all these stories.

"We had never met Rud, so when he got into our trial, they said if he cooperated, he would get leniency. He had nothing to lose. He had two prior convictions. So he was trying to save his skin. He ended up apologizing. He told our investigator to tell everybody he was sorry. He did go on TV too and said that he did lie. He got forty years.

"But he got on the stand. He was supposed to identify us. Well, I was very easy to identify. I was the only woman up there, aside from Kathleen Morris, the prosecutor. But when it came to identifying Bob, he couldn't do it. So that hurt her case. And then she didn't want the murder allegations brought out, so she ended up dropping charges against everyone.

"When it first happened, they called us on the phone. It was a cop. He said, 'We have your children. We've been to your house. Get a hold of your husband, drive yourselves down to the police station. You're under arrest for child sexual abuse. Park two blocks away on Holmes, because the news media is here.' The news media were informed that I was being arrested before I was informed. The media were always there when anyone was arrested. They knew before the people, themselves. I tried to call the attorney. He wasn't in. My husband had called a neighbor, and they said, 'I hate to tell you this, but there's four squad cars up there, and they've taken your children.'

"We got nailed because we were disagreeing with them. We didn't think Tom and Helen were guilty, and it had gotten so it was like Nazi Germany down there. Nobody knew who was next. Kids were terrified to go to school. Parents were terrified to send their children to school. They didn't know if they'd be coming home at night.

"But now that it's over, and it's been thoroughly investigated, and it's so obvious that there was such an abuse of power . . . We had death threats on the phone, nasty letters. . . . We had twelve people sitting in there. They heard all the facts. And we were found innocent. What more can we do? The attorney general has investigated it. But it was a nightmare. It still is. We were arrested January twentieth. January fourteenth they took my thirteen-year-old away and put him in a foster home. They put them in separate homes. They would go back to Tony and Billy and say, 'Well, Marlin said that your parents did this and that' . . . and they'd go to Marlin and say, Tony and Billy said this and that' . . . . And the children couldn't communicate between each other. They didn't believe it, but after a while they didn't know what to believe. They hadn't seen us in months. They hadn't seen relatives in months. The only people they're seeing are these Scott County People.

"You know, what bothers me so much . . . as a child, I remember you think your parents can protect you from anything. 'There's nothing can get me, my mom and dad will chase 'em away.'

"What happened here, as far as I'm concerned, they lost all that security because they were taken away, and Mom and Dad couldn't do anything to help them. I don't believe they'll ever get that security back again. They've lost this image of mom and dad as being able to protect them. And they don't understand. They will eventually believe how hard we fought, to get them back . . . But how do you explain that to a kid? They would not even let Father Tom Carroll in to see the kids. Even P.O.W.'s get to see a priest in there. We told him, 'We want you in there and just tell the kids we love them, and we're fighting to get them back, and keep their chins up.' They wouldn't even let a priest in to see them.

"All this, just because my husband got up in front of the City Council meeting and spoke, because Tom and Helen Brown were our neighbors, and we felt they were innocent. And he said, 'What are you doing with these people, smearing them across the media every night, and dragging the town through the mud? If you're gonna arrest them, just arrest them, don't do all this smear and everything.' . . . Next night we got a call. They said, 'We want to talk to your children.' That's all it took.

"And it worked! Because people would come up to us and say, 'Hey, we know your innocent!' And I would say, 'Okay, let's get something going here.' And they said, 'No way! I've got kids. I don't want to be arrested.'

"And I worry about my kids. I worry about what happens ten years from now. Is it going to be like the Vietnam vets? All of a sudden all of that stuff builds up and they snap? What is the psychological damage that's been done to them? And there has to be damage because I know the way *I* feel. And it's always on my mind because I'm a mother, and I worry about my children."

Scott County Attorney Kathleen Morris, who prosecuted this case, was widely known for her excessive zeal in prosecuting alleged child abuse cases. When the Bentzes were acquitted, she made the enraged statement that ". . . we live in a society that doesn't believe children."

More than forty children were questioned, and there is documentary evidence that they were interviewed a total of 128 times, but it is known that they were interviewed many more times than that.* Twenty-six children were taken away from their parents. Some were isolated from their parents for as long as a year, some in communities outside the county. Parents' letters were intercepted and withheld, gifts were not delivered, and phone calls were not reported to the children. According to the Minneapolis *Star & Tribune*, in the case of at least one family social workers were told by Morris's office to route all requests from parents, in regard to the children, through her office and to refuse the parents any information about their children. Tom and Helen Brown were told they would be allowed visits with their children only if they admitted their guilt. According to one deputy who worked on the case, Morris rewarded the children with Cokes, cookies and birthday cakes. Child witnesses told that they were led to believe if they accused their parents, they would be allowed to go home. One child was questioned forty-five times by a therapist, and at least twenty-nine times by social workers and detectives.

The questioning spun out of control. Children who had made allegations of child sex rings and mass molestations of children, satanic and sadistic ritual sex, now began telling their interrogators of mass murders of infants. Kathleen Morris began calling the defense attorneys and offered their clients immunity if they would

*Minneapolis *Star & Tribune*, May 26, 1985.

tell the prosecutor about the alleged murders. None offered to do so and Morris dropped the charges against all twenty-four defendents. She said she was dropping the charges to protect "an active criminal investigation of great magnitude," but detectives involved in the investigation said Morris told them that the witnesses had lost their credibility, and that was why the charges were being dismissed.

According to the *Star & Tribune,* Morris tried to suppress evidence "and tried to hide the full extent of what [the witnesses] had said." The newspaper stated that "One reason for Morris' willingness to proceed is her belief that children almost never lie about sexual abuse." The newspaper also stated that "Accusations were drawn from the children in an atmosphere of isolation, pressure and rewards. Interviews were more numerous than officials have said, and as the sessions continued, the children's claims grew more bizarre. Some children said they believed that accusing their parents would hasten their return home."

There was also evidence that at least three of the child witnesses had been involved in sexual activity with other children. Two stated that they were relieved when the investigation focused on adults rather than what the children were doing.

One child told that he had attended parties where large numbers of adults would torture and kill children. He said he saw three children murdered at a sex party and was forced to copulate with animals. Police investigating the allegations began to doubt the credibility of the children's stories. Records show that this child once tried to retract the murder claims, but was persuaded by a therapist to revert to them. Another therapist said, "The witnesses have been interviewed so many times . . . so many of them have recanted or altered their stories."

When Tom and Helen Brown finally got their children returned to them, they asked their daughter why the children had told the stories they had told. The girl's face fell and tears began to run down her cheeks. The girl sobbed that she had been afraid that Kathleen Morris and the others would hurt her.

One of the children said his interrogators ". . . wouldn't let me out of the room until I said yes. It would have gone on forever." Another said he was told that he would never see his parents again unless he accused them of sexual abuse.

Once they were taken out of their homes, the children were questioned endlessly, day after day, month after month, and whatever they said was treated with great importance because there simply was no evidence against anyone except Rud.

On October 11, 1984, the Minnesota Bureau of Criminal Apprehension and the FBI took over the investigation, and the Attorney General's office assumed responsibility for the cases. On February 12, Attorney General Hubert Humphrey III released a 29-page report explaining why none of the defendants could be prosecuted. He cited the lack of evidence and said the children were questioned too often and in a way that risked false accusations. Kathleen Morris accused Humphrey of having political motives for his statements.

The report states that "During the week of October 15, 1984, the Minnesota Bureau of Criminal Apprehension and the Federal Bureau of Investigation (FBI) began investigating the alleged homicides, pornography and child abuse in Scott County." The report stated that the investigation involved over a dozen state and federal investigative agencies. The juristictional focus of the FBI effort was on allegations of homicide and pornography.

"At the conclusion of their investigation the FBI/BCA agents submitted their investigative findings to Attorney General Humphrey. Their findings are as follows:

1. There is no credible evidence to support allegations of murder which arose during the sexual abuse investigation.
2. There is insufficient evidence to justify the filing of any new sex abuse charges."

The investigation involved an enormous number of criminal investigative agencies and personnel, both local and federal.

". . . Interviews with the children," the report stated, "resulted in three individuals recanting their earlier allegations of killings. Four other children who had been identified by Scott County authorities as having given statements regarding homicides stated they had never actually witnessed any killings. The only child to continue talking about murders gave investigators three entirely different versions of what she claimed happened, all within the course of one interview session. In sum, by November 14, 1984, there was no credible evidence to believe homicides had occurred.

"The first interview with a twelve-year-old boy who had provided the most graphic details of homicides took place on November 2, 1984. During the interview the child described in detail seven children being stabbed, mutilated and/or shot during the spring and summer of 1983. This contrasted with his statements in July, 1984, to Scott County investigators. At that time he had described three homicides. He also indicated at that time that at least fourteen adults and eleven children observed one child being mutilated and killed.

"When interviewed in November, 1984, he indicated that five bodies had been disposed of in the Minnesota River. He described how a caravan of cars had gone to the Lawrence Campgrounds and that the group involved in the homicide walked across a walkway bridge. This description of a caravan of cars traveling though the streets of a small Minnesota town on a summer's eve caused the investigators to question . . . the allegations in that no witness had ever reported seeing such a caravan of cars. The youth went on to describe the disposal of one of the bodies. He stated that the group involved in the homicides carried a body to the park, while armed with flashlights. He stated that . . . the bodies of the alleged homicide victims were disposed of in the river.

"On November 3, 1984, BCA agents accompanied this boy, his guardian, *ad litem* and therapist to the area where the child said bodies had been dumped. He stated that some of the bodies had been placed in an inflatable boat, paddled out and dumped in the middle of the river.

"Shortly before a November 6 interview with this boy, state/federal agents spoke with a park ranger who had kept a diary noting the depth of the river and certain occurrences there in 1983. The park ranger indicated that in March of 1983 the river had flooded over its banks and had swept away the walkway bridge, which was not replaced until late summer of that year. He stated that during much of the spring and early summer of 1983 the trails or paths which are located next to the river had been impassable because the river had flooded those areas. This was the same time period during which, according to the boy, bodies were carried along the paths and over the bridge. The physical impossibility of such events during that period raised severe doubts as to the boy's credibility.

"On November 6, 1984, the agents met with this boy in the presence of his therapist. Again, he spoke of bodies being disposed of at the campground site. Agents asked the boy if he still remembered bodies being placed in inflatable boats which were then rowed to the middle of the river where the bodies were dumped. This was asked because agents had been informed by law enforcement personnel familiar with the river that currents would have pulled any inflatable boat downstream, making it unlikely that a boat could have been rowed to the middle and back. The child began to change his story about where the boat took the bodies. The agents told him that the walkway bridge was not in place when he said a body was carried across it. At that point he broke down and cried. He admitted that he had lied and stated that there were no murders. He stated that he was still telling the truth about the sex abuse but that he had invented the murder stories because he didn't want to go home.

"The agents also interviewed another child who had made allegations of homicide. When interviewed in July by Scott County investigators, this individual told of three or four killings. He told of victims being shot or stabbed, and of one being drowned in a neighbor's pool. He described one of the victims as a drummer in a rock and roll band, who was playing at a party when he (the drummer) was killed. When told that the purpose of the agents' interview was to discuss the alleged homicides, the child immediately stated that he had lied about the cutting and the torture and death of any victims. He stated that the idea of homicides came into his head when Scott County investigators questioned him about a black or mulatto boy who may have been cut or tortured. He said he got the idea of ritualistic torturing from a television program he had seen. He stated that he lied about the murders because he wanted to please the investigators.

"On November 6, 1984, state/federal agents met with a nine-year-old girl who had made allegations of murder in July, 1984. In July she had stated that her father shot and killed an eight-year-old black boy in the kitchen of their home. She did not describe any other children being present, nor any mutilations or sexual abuse accompanying the killings. The residence where she stated killings took place was not the site of any alleged sex parties or ritual killings described by other witnesses.

"When she met with state and federal agents in November, 1984, she immediately recanted all allegations of homicide. She stated that the reason she made up the story about someone being killed was because her 'very good friend' told her to say those things. This friend was the child who first made mention of killings in July, 1984.

"The child who first mentioned killings is a twelve-year-old female who met with Scott County investigators after she had talked to her therapist about homicides. This child had been sexually abused by James Rud over an extended period of time. By July, 1984, this child had been interviewed no less than twenty-three times about the sex abuse allegations. She had accused eleven adults of sexually abusing herself or other children.

"When questioned in July about homicides, she told Scott County investigators that she had seen a person stick the broken stem of a wine glass into the vagina of a baby girl, then stab the baby in the chest and bury it. She stated the child's mother was told that day that the baby was dead.

"She also told of a woman in her thirties who had been sexual with her and then was killed by the same person. A third victim she described was a young mulatto boy killed after having sex with her.

"When this witness met with state/federal investigators in November, 1984, she vividly described very different homicides. She again told of a baby being killed—this time with its head partly cut off. She stated that the child's mother had dropped the baby off at her friend's house, where her friend's father was going to babysit. She stated that her friend's father killed the child because he could not tolerate the baby.

"She spoke of a three-year-old black boy being stabbed. The child was killed, she stated, because it had gotten into her father's shed and started a fire. She stated that this aggravated her friend's father so he killed the child with a pocket knife and buried the child in his back yard.

"The next victim she described was a four-year-old boy who, she stated, started a fire in the street and then was stabbed in the heart by her friend's father because he stated that the child deserved punishment.

"The fourth alleged victim was an eleven-year-old boy for whom the girl said she was babysitting, even though she was only ten at the time. She stated that this child had taken some pills from a cabinet and got intoxicated from them. She stated that her friend's father revived him and then killed him with a knife.

"She told investigators that all those killings took place on the very same day. She also made no mention of the woman in her thirties she had said was killed during her July, 1984, statement.

"During the interview the girl was at ease and extremely talkative. In each case she talked about the victims being cut and stabbed. She was asked by the agents if there was any shooting involved, and she said 'no.' One of the agents then pointed out to her that earlier police reports showed individuals being shot. She then described the four homicides again and this time changed her story, stating that all the individuals had been shot rather than stabbed. Her therapist then asked a question, and the child said that the individuals had been stabbed rather than shot. Because of the demeanor of this child and as a result of the shifts in her story within a relatively short period of time, it became clear to investigators that this child was simply not believable as to those stories.

Three other children who had been described in police reports as having discussed alleged homicides were questioned. They told state/federal investigators that they had not observed homicides but rather talked of people being hurt. Therapists informed these investigators of a fourth child who said that he had never used the word 'murdered,' but rather 'hurt.' State and federal investigators attempted to interview this particular child. The child indicated that he would only be willing to talk to the agents through puppets. He indicated that he would nod the head of one of the puppets yes or no. At some point in the interview the agents asked him if he had seen any kids that were killed. This child shook the puppet's head 'no.' When questioned by his therapist as to whether he had spoken last summer with a Scott County detective about homicides, the child indicated through puppets that he did not remember that conversation.

"When state/federal agents first began investigating the alleged homicides, they planned a search of the Minnesota River. Investigators consulted with pathologists to determine what, if any, evidence of a body would still exist after being in a river for an extended period of time. They spoke with the Army Corps of Engineers to determine if any evidence, assuming it existed, could be discovered through such a search. They spoke with law enforcement representatives from other Minnesota counties who have had experience with river search operations. They were informed that the possibility of finding such evidence was extremely slim. However, it was felt that every reasonable investigative effort should be made. Plans were made to begin the river search in early November, 1984. Bad weather forced a postponement of that search. It was at this time that investigators discovered that the walkway bridge had been washed away months earlier and children began recanting allegations of murder. As it became clear that there was no credible evidence of murders, the river search was canceled. In the absence of any credible evidence, both the FBI and BCA felt it would be inappropriate to risk injury or potential loss of life in a river search.

"In addition to planning a search of the river, investigators had prepared search warrants based on the original statements of the children. However, as the stories collapsed and as the physical impossibilities of the original allegations piled up, it was concluded that there was no probable cause to justify the filing of any search warrants."

After concluding that there were no murders, the authorities then turned their attention to the allegations of sexual abuse and pornography. They continued to interview the children, and their investigation included contacts with law enforcement officials in New York, Alaska, Utah, Kansas, Iowa, Washington, D.C., Georgia, Missouri, California and Texas.

The original investigation did not produce a single photograph containing child pornography, despite the fact that many children had mentioned photographs being taken at the alleged sex parties. The only evidence of pornography and sexual abuse of children rested on statements of children who were unable to provide credible testimony.

"The credibility problems," the Attorney General's report

stated, "result from repeated questioning, a lack of reports, and cross-germination of allegations."

"A therapist's report," the report said, "notes that one child had been interviewed by nine individuals about the alleged abuse. The mother of another child indicated that her daughter had been interviewed as many as fifty times by law enforcement or Scott County authorities.

"In many cases children were removed from their homes and isolated from all family contact for prolonged periods, even though the children denied having been sexually abused. In some instances the children did not 'admit' their parents had abused them until several months of such separation, marked by continuous questioning about abuse. In the most extreme cases, these children were also told that reunification with their families would be facilitated by 'admissions' of sex abuse by their parents and other adults.

"The problem of over-interrogation was compounded by a lack of reports. For example, Scott County investigators' notes show that one nine-year-old girl was interviewed by law enforcement authorities approximately twenty times and yet there were only four written reports concerning those interviews. In addition, her meetings with the County Attorney are undocumented. The pattern was not at all unusual. Investigators' notes show that another child was interviewed by law enforcement officers over twenty times and yet there are reports from less than half of those interviews. In addition, on at least half a dozen occasions she met with the County Attorney, again with no reports on these meetings."

"The children who told the homicide stories had been questioned repeatedly, over an extended period of time, about sex abuse. Some had initially denied being sexually abused by their parents until questioned over a period of months. In some instances, over a period of time, the allegations of sexual abuse turned to stories of mutilations and eventually homicide.

"The Scott County experience has demonstrated that in some instances prolonged interrogation of children may result in confusion between fact and fantasy."

In addition to the problem of over-interrogation and lack of reports, another problem that undermined the credibility of the child witnesses, according to the report, was "cross germination." "In some instances, witnesses were informed what other witnesses had stated. Sometimes the witnesses would be interviewed together . . . during one case, child witnesses were provided with the same motel accommodations, ate meals together and were otherwise permitted to have contact with each other."

"Representatives of the Scott County Attorney said their office felt obliged to arrest suspects and remove children from homes with great dispatch whenever a new adult was identified as an abuser. In many instances, this resulted in persons being charged with abusing children at a time when these children had either denied the abuse or had not even been interviewed.

"For example, the neighbors of two former defendants described a meeting with the defendants following their arrest to discuss and review the complaint. During the meeting the neighbors learned for the first time that their own child was an alleged abuse victim of those very defendants. At that time, neither the children of the accused nor the neighbors' child had been questioned by authorities.

"In several other instances, parents were arrested and charged with abusing their own children, even though those children denied the abuse through several weeks of interrogation and separation from their parents."

The report also said that Morris sought to compensate for an absence of evidence by trying to get defendants to testify against each other in exchange for the standard plea offer of no jail time, psychological evaluation, and a misdemeanor rather than a felony record. The defendants were also told that if they did not provide the information, the prosecution of sex abuse charges against them would go forward. They refused the offer, saying they had no information about any homicides.

"In sum, with the single exception [of James Rud] none of the efforts to obtain incriminating evidence of sex abuse from the defendants or from other potential adult witnesses produced any fruit whatsoever."

Rud made a 113-page statement in which he implicated eighteen defendants. He was given polygraph examinations, one of which was inconclusive, and a second one which he failed. He then recanted his statements about adults being involved in child sex abuse. He denied attending any sex parties or that there was a "sex ring." He said he knew several of the defendants but denied that he had any knowledge of any of them abusing children. Rud said he was pressured to fabricate the story.

The law enforcement authorities interviewed other juveniles who admitted having sexual involvement with other children. They were offered immunity from prosecution in exchange for testimony regarding other alleged molesters. They too changed their stories and then recanted. In spite of the intensive effort of state and federal investigators, no evidence was uncovered that would corroborate the allegations of the children.

The Humphrey report recommended that prosecutors should seek to protect children by means other than removal from the home, and that "perpetrators, rather than victims, should be removed from the home." It also questioned the propriety of the therapists' role as part of the prosecution and suggested that their role ought to be a more neutral one.

Finally, it stated, ". . . the City of Jordan should be listed among the victims of the so-called sex-ring cases. Over sixty of its citizens were either charged with or suspected of abusing over one hundred children. State/federal investigators simply do not believe that accusations of such widespread abuse were accurate. The citizens of Jordan . . . have suffered as a result of these public accusations. The impact those accusations had on the community may well be extensive and far-reaching. . . . We have an obligation to the citizens of Jordan to help address, treat and learn from these unfortunate events."

But the most memorable statement was made by one of the therapists who said, "I think what was done to the families, the long separation and isolation of the children, the instigation of accusations by the children against their own parents, has done a great deal more harm than molestation."

VII

Bakersfield Baby Snatchers

"Where Are the Bodies?

GONZALES

"Gerardo "Johnny" Gonzales had it made. He had an exquisitely pretty wife, Cheryl, two small children and a comfortable home in a good neighborhood. Since his honorable discharge from the army in 1973 he worked his way up to a $40,000-a-year job in the oilfields of Kern County. He believed in the American dream.

The American dream ended for Gerardo Gonzales on June 26, 1984. "About 8 p.m. we were all at home eating peach cobbler and ice cream when there was a knock on the door and my wife answered, and told me there were three sheriff's deputies. I answered the door where I was met by Deputy Bill Rutledge. He then informed me I was under arrest for child molest. I could not believe what I was hearing.

"He then asked me if he could come in and talk about it. I said yes. They came in. I asked Mr. Rutledge who was I supposed to have molested. He refused to tell me and said, 'Let's go outside and talk.' I stepped outside with Mr. Rutledge. I asked again, 'Who was I supposed to have molested?' He again refused to say and told me to let him search our house. I asked if he had a search warrant. He then grabbed me around the neck and asked me if I was a lawyer. I told him if he was going to act like that he would have to get a search warrant. He then led me to his squad car and put me in back, rolled all the windows up and went back inside the house.

"About five minutes went by and I saw Rutledge and my wife and another officer coming out of my house. He led her behind my service truck, but he stopped directly behind it. I could look in the front windshield and see out the back window of my truck, since our driveway has an incline down toward the street. I could see he was yelling at her and she was pointing to our house.

"He grabbed her by the arm and twisted it behind her back. I heard her yell, 'Okay! Stop!' He then handed her what looked like a piece of paper and a pen. I later found out it was a consent form to search our house. I later found out they were looking for pictures and syringes and pills. They found nothing of what they were looking for after two hours of searching because we have never had any syringes or pills in our house. Deputy Rutledge then told my wife that he was taking our children, and he did. While I was at the sheriff station Rutledge kept telling me to confess and he would talk to the judge and he would take it easy on me. I told him I could not confess to something I had never done. He then left the room and I could hear him questioning my little girl in the next room. My little girl was crying, telling him I never done anything to her."

After two days in the jail Gonzales was released. Then the officers came back to his home and arrested him again. This time he was in jail for eight days, and the bail was $50,000. He bailed out. They also arrested a Rev. Will Thomas who, Gonzales said, had never been at the Gonzales home. While he was out on bail he complained to the Attorney General and his State Assemblyman "about what this deputy and a welfare case worker, Cory Taylor, were doing with our kids." Gonzales and his wife went to a juvenile court hearing at which his daughter said that no molestation had occurred, but that Rutledge and Cory Taylor had told her to say that it had.

About four days later, they came back, and Gonzales was charged with about one hundred counts and his wife with seventy-five counts of molestation. The original charges were only nine counts. Later, they twice added more counts.

"I went to the bedroom and told Gerardo there were some officers out front," Cheryl Gonzales told me. "He went to see what they wanted and I went to the bathroom. When I came out I went to the livingroom. There was an officer standing in the middle of the livingroom and a woman I hadn't seen before, sitting on the couch with my kids. I asked the officer what was going on. He told me that my husband was being arrested for child molesting. I shouted, 'WHAT!' and asked if they were kidding. He said no. I turned to the woman and asked, 'Who are you?' She said she was from C.P.S. and her name was Cory Taylor. Then she asked an officer named Bill Rutledge to take me outside because I was overly upset. So we went outside. I asked him who had said this had happened, and that I wanted to go back in and be with my kids.

"He grabbed my arm and twisted it behind my back. He told me I was getting too loud. Then he told me he had a piece of paper he wanted me to sign, and that if I didn't, he would 'haul my ass to jail' along with my husband. The paper was a search warrant for my house. During this time, he held my arm behind my back.

"He also kept asking me who was a black man named Thomas. So I signed the paper because I was afraid of what would happen to my kids if they took me to jail. I told them I did know a Will Thomas. He is a minister and my karate teacher. We finally went back in the house. Tyson, my son, came and sat on my lap while my daughter, Melissa, sat beside me. Then I looked over and asked Cory Taylor who had said this. She told me it was a little girl named Brooke. I turned to Melissa and asked if she knew a Brooke. She said yes. Then Cory Taylor started asking Melissa questions about this Brooke. She asked if Brooke was Melissa's friend and she said yes. I asked Melissa if she went to school with Brooke. She said no, that Brooke was just a little girl that lived down the street. Then Cory Taylor looked at me and said, 'You really don't know what's going on here, do you?' I said no, and that I thought it must all be some kind of big mistake. The officers were still searching my house. Tyson fell asleep on my lap. Bill Rutledge, the officer, came out of the bedroom and told Cory Taylor that they didn't find what they were looking for, but that there was other stuff they were taking. He didn't tell me what it was.

"Then he looked over at me and said that I had two beautiful kids and that he was taking them. I told him, 'No!' I wouldn't let him. He shouted back, 'I am taking them whether you like it or not! Do you hear me?' He looked over at Cory Taylor and they started talking. He told her he would take the kids in his car. I asked where they were taking them. Cory Taylor said she would be taking them to shelter care. Melissa was crying. Tyson was asleep. I told Melissa that I'd see her tomorrow and to take care of Tyson. As I turned to go back into the house I saw Gerardo sitting in one of the sheriff's cars. Then Rutledge came over to me and asked me if I liked the idea of my husband putting his dick in my daughter's face, ass and cunt. I told him that it hadn't happened. Then he walked off and got in his car and they all left. I went back in the house and called my mother."

"We have just finished the prelim," Gerardo said. "They have now involved all of our friends and about eight to ten children. Another little girl, Crystal Prescott, got up on the stand and, under cross-examination, started saying that nothing ever happened and that Cory Taylor and Susan Skabeland [a deputy D.A.] made her say those things [the accusations]. She told that to my lawyer, then to the D.A., then to judge McNutt [sic]. The judge then called a recess. When we came back in, the D.A. told the judge that Crystal couldn't testify any longer, that she broke down in her office and couldn't return. But the little girl was smiling and cheerful.

"My little girl and Crystal have had no contact with each other since this began. Why did two little six-year-olds say exactly the same thing? But that's not all. Now we have an eight-year-old boy who is saying the same thing—that Cory Taylor made him say those things. He also said that Cory Taylor would lock him up in a room until he said what they wanted him to say. We also had another deputy sheriff admit on the stand that she lied to a little girl to get her to say those things. But I have been bound over on over one hundred ten counts. My lawyer says the D.A. is scared that we will sue them because we lost everything we owned. I just want you to know that, as God is my witness, we are innocent, and I have been willing to take polygraph, truth serum, hypnosis or voice stress tests to prove we are innocent. I pray every day that all these lies will be exposed. This county has more molest cases than any other place in the country. Nearly every day you see a new case in the paper. What makes these people think that two happily married people who believe in God and still have sex every day would do something like this to little children? These people are brainwashing our children!"

When the officers searched Gonzales' house, they seized his camera, miscellaneous bills from his dresser drawer, a cedar chest, and various personal effects. They also took away his dog "because of his possible involvement in the case."

"That's ridiculous!" a neighbor told us. "That was the meanest dog that ever was. The kids were all scared to death of him."

Dominic Eyhrabide, Gerardo Gonzales' attorney, told me:

"In June, they go to Gerardo's house and put him in jail, and take his kids away from him. That's June the twenty-sixth, of 1984. Gerardo bailed out. Charges weren't filed right away. Then he was rearrested and charges were filed and he bailed out. So for the balance of June and July, he's out of custody, and his kids are originally placed with the grandmother. Then they're taken away from the grandmother and are now under the welfare department's control. Now, on August the twenty-fourth, Gerardo—and you have to understand, he's a high-strung guy—Gerardo went down to the welfare department. He walks in and said, 'I want to talk to the head guy.' He doesn't mess around. He says, 'I want to talk to the head of the welfare department.' He was angry about the lurid sex education they were giving his kids.

"That same day, August twenty-fourth, a social worker who is an employee of the welfare department, and a member of the sheriff's department, go back down to the neighborhood. They start knocking on doors. Why, we don't know. They go to Crystal Prescott's house, and Suzanne Garrison. And they say, 'We'd like to talk to your kids.' I think that's highly unusual. I don't think any kid named Crystal or Suzanne had ever been mentioned. Why the hell did they go to their houses? It looks like Gerardo pissed them off and they were looking for complaining witnesses. Once you get into this case, you may find more connections than that. But in any event, they go to the neighborhood, and the following Monday, they interview Crystal and they interview Suzanne. And Leroy's name comes up. Leroy's kid was called Tootie. They go and talk to Tootie and they claim that, somehow, Tootie says that his dad was involved. The next thing you know, boom, he's in jail. That's the first or second week in September. That man is innocent. He's been convicted already, but he's innocent. My client, Gerardo, didn't even know Leroy Stowe. When they went out and filed charges on Stowe, they went out and added more charges on Gerardo. They filed a whole second case, on Crystal, Tootie and Suzanne.

"Now, Gerardo's back in custody, and he can't make bail any more. That is the first time Gerardo ever met Leroy Stowe. They lived about two blocks away, but they just never got to know each other. They had nothing in common and my client didn't know him. He can't say that he never saw him, but they didn't know each other.

"I think there's been a concession by the prosecution that the investigation went haywire. They don't believe the satanic rituals and the cannibalism. Those kids accused a D.A. also. At that point they had to pretty much disavow the investigation. The deputy D.A. they accused was Sara Ryals. And they accused Cory Taylor, the therapist.

"I wondered, back in the prelim when there was no suspicion that this was anything but a garden variety molest case, I wondered, why in the hell is Cory Taylor always running around, leading the investigation? Number one, she's a social worker. Number two, she's an intake worker. Intake workers don't run around knocking on doors looking for kids to say they were molested, trying to instigate new cases. I don't think that's part of her job. But she is always there, in these interviews.

"Something went haywire, so all the people that were named, after about five months into the case, there's really a doubt as to whether they're involved or not. That gets rid of all these parents. However, Gerardo's been named from day one. And that's the theory they're going to try Gonzales on, next year."

These events were triggered by a telephone call made by a teacher at a day care center who had in her care a five-year-old girl who had complained of an itchy vagina. The woman felt it was necessary to report this circumstance as evidence of possible child molestation. This was Brooke. According to the authorities, she accused virtually everyone she knew, including her parents, her grandmother, and her aunt. In all of the reports and statements of the Sheriff's Department and C.P.S. workers, the accusations were treated as fact rather than unproved allegations—this in spite of the fact that every one of the children alleged to have been molested was taken to a pediatrician, and no evidence of sexual abuse was found. The accused adults took polygraph tests, all of which indicated they were truthful when they said they had never engaged in any kind of child sexual abuse. Also, the children failed to identify the accused adults in police lineups. Law enforcement and C.P.S. workers ignored all of this and zealously went forward with their prosecution of the accused.

Brad and Mary Nokes were implicated by a five-year-old girl. They were attending a court hearing for Gerardo and Cheryl Gonzales who were awaiting trial on multiple counts of molestation.

"They are good friends of ours," Mary said. "We were there because we believe they are innocent." One of the children testifying pointed her out as being the wife of an unknown man allegedly involved in the molestations, and a sheriff's deputy immediately demanded her name and address. She left to pick up her children, Michael and Angela, from school. The detectives were already there when she arrived, and told Mary they were taking her children to a county juvenile detention facility.

"Michael started crying," she said. "I told him, 'whatever you do, tell the truth, and don't let them talk you into anything.' " Mary was allowed to visit Michael and Angela once, then the county social workers stopped all visits. She has not seen her children for a year.

When detectives began interrogating Michael he flatly denied that he had ever been molested by anyone. According to the officers, six days later, Michael stated that he and his sister had been molested by Gerardo Gonzales, Cheryl Gonzales, and by his father. Three weeks later he denied that he had ever been molested, saying that Cory Taylor made him say those things.

After being held for two months at the county facility, Michael was released and placed in the custody of an aunt. His grandfather, Roy Nokes, hired a private investigator who interviewed Michael on tape on November 16. During the interview Michael told the investigator that while he was at the county facility, Child Protective Services workers refused to believe his repeated statements that he had never been molested or seen anyone else molested:

"She'd say, 'Come on. You'd better start telling . . . or I'll keep you in this room all day,'" Michael told the interviewer.

"How did that make you feel?" she asked him.

"Rotten," Michael replied.

When the county C.P.S. workers learned of the interview, Michael was quickly taken from his aunt's home and returned to the Jamison Center. Later, he was placed in a foster home, but separated from his sister.

Carolyn Heim, according to a court transcript, and according to her own notes, stated that she gave Michael "hypnotic messages" during her therapy, when he had been in custody for almost two months and was still denying to her that he had ever been molested.

Brad and Mary Nokes and other family members believe the sheriff's officers and C.P.S. workers kidnapped their children in order to brainwash them, along with dozens of other children, to program them to testify against their parents.

"What in the name of God have they done to these kids?" Mary said. "This is not the kids' fault. I feel anger toward the people who are doing this to them. I cannot understand why or how the authorities can be doing this to children. Before they were taken away from us they were normal, happy, healthy, well-adjusted kids." Her husband, Brad, 27, said "They have to know they are doing wrong. They can't be doing this awfulness by mistake."

Brad and Mary Nokes were arrested shortly after their children were taken away. They were charged with 130 felony counts of child molestation. Along with five other Nokes family members, they passed polygraph tests which showed they were truthful when they said they had never molested any children. In May, a Superior Court judge dismissed the charges against Brad and Mary, but the District Attorney is appealing the dismissal in an effort to reinstate the charges.

As the counseling went on, Michael accused his parents, his aunt and uncle, Jack Cummings and Jackie Nokes, and all four grandparents. He also accused a deputy district attorney. The accusations became increasingly bizarre, some of them strikingly similar to those in McMartin and other cases, tales of infanticide, drinking of blood in cannibalistic rituals, threats, knives, swords, robes, children being forced to ingest feces and urine. Michael said he and other children were forced to murder infants and drain their blood. Then, he said, the infants were roasted and eaten. The children alleged that at least twenty-seven babies were killed. At least two of the infants said to be murder victims were found to still be alive, and a third had died in 1972. After dredging two lakes and digging up Gonzales's yard, no dead babies were found. Members of the Nokes family stated that the bizarre stories came after the children had been cut off from their families for months and interrogated endlessly. Kern County Sheriff Larry Kleier said he believed the children's stories.

In a written report, Carolyn Heim states that she interviewed Michael Nokes when he was first taken into custody:

> Michael is a very withdrawn, pale, little boy who is having a great deal of difficulty dealing with his parents being in jail. When I explained that I work with children who have been molested, he immediately told me what molested meant and said his parents had never molested him. . . . He said his parents told him that the 'cops' would try to 'brainwash' him into saying that things had happened. When I asked him what brainwash meant, he said confuse him and make him believe things that weren't true. He repeatedly said in a very loud voice, 'My parents never did anything.' When I finally said that I thought that he had been molested, he again withdrew and said nothing. . . . He expressed concern and worry about his parents being in jail.

In her report, Heim stated that Michael's problems were "lying," "worry," "low self-esteem," and "has been sexually abused." She further stated that "As the therapist for Michael Nokes, I strongly recommend that Michael have a complete psychological evaluation. Michael is exhibiting severe symptoms as a result of his molest which greatly concerns me. I feel that this complete evaluation should be done as soon as possible. These symptoms become even more pronounced after visitation with his relatives, and I feel, as a result, these visitations should be suspended. . . ."

The transcript of a sworn deposition of Pam Ninefeldt sheds some interesting information about what happened to Michael and his sister, Angie, after they were taken from their parents. Ninefeldt is the foster mother in whose care Michael and Angela were placed.

(FROM THE DEPOSITION)

Q. Can you describe for me what you recall as far as your impressions of Angela when you first met her?

A. She was very pale and she was very frightened. She cried and cried and cried and cried, and I finally got her to stop crying. She wanted to know when I was going to molest her. And I said, nobody is going to molest you here. And she looked like oh, sure, sure. Then she wouldn't talk about it for a long time. She wouldn't say anything. She demonstrated a lot of angry behavior.

Q. When you said at some point she wanted to know when you were going to molest her, she said some words to that effect to you?

A. She said, if I can remember, she said, when are they going to do it, and I said who is they, and she said, you know, the people, when are they going to do it? And I said, when are they going to do what? And she said, you know, the sex stuff, when are they going to do it? And I said, it's not going to happen here. You're safe. And every time I would tell her she's safe, she would start to cry again.

Q. When was it that she said this to you?

A. I had her about two weeks.

Q. So mid-December?

A. Yeah.

Q. Did you notice any change in Angela's appearance and behavior between the time you first saw her in the beginning of December 1984 and June of 1985.

A. Oh, absolutely.

Q. Tell me about the changes.

A. Well, she smiled a lot more. She was beginning to develop a real cute little sense of humor. She would tease. She was beginning to stop soiling herself, which was a daily thing. She stopped soiling and smearing it on my bathroom walls, which I appreciated a great deal.

Q. With regard to her brother, Michael, can you describe what he was like when he first arrived in your home?

A. Michael was—Mike was crying. He was very withdrawn. He was very tense.

Q. It is my understanding from reviewing somebody's words someplace that in December, Michael, at least at the Child Guidance, was denying that he had been molested. Did he deny to you that he had been molested?

A. Yes.

Q. Was there ever a time when you made a statement to him to the effect, Come on Michael, I know you were molested, there is no point in saying that you weren't or no point denying it.

A. I said . . . he said all these kids are talking about my parents and saying they did terrible things. And nothing ever happened to me . . .

(Several pages later she states)

". . . I told her about the exam about a week ahead of time. The day we were leaving, I said, Now, you're not going to school because this is the day we're going to go down and see Dr. Woodling, remember? And she said, Okay. We drove to Ventura and we got to Dr. Woodling's office, and I said, You know why you're here? Huh-uh. We're here because this is the doctor who's going to examine you. Oh, he's going to molest me? No, he's not going to molest you. He's going to be sure you're okay, all right? Uh-huh.

(Twenty-three pages later she is asked)

Q. Has there been some time in the recent past when he's been so withdrawn that he has drawn up into the fetal position and didn't want to—

A. Yes.

Q. When was that?

A. I really wouldn't want to get into. . . . I don't want to get into that.

Q. I want to know the time frame of when he's exhibiting symptoms like that.

A. I know. But I just feel that's kind of . . . I would need some advice before I could answer that.

(And, twenty pages later)

Q. You mentioned—your expression, I think, was Michael's card collection. I dimly recall—believe it or not, back when I was ten years old myself, and the card collection that I had was always somehow associated with bubble gum. Now Michael's seem to be associated with . . . he's got the beginnings of an attorney file?

A. No, every office . . .

Q. What's in Michael's card file?

A. Every office he goes into, or attorney's office or doctor's office, they have the little calling cards. Well, Michael collects them. That's his card collection.

(Still later)

Q. Your best estimate, if you can make it, including his testimony and judicial proceedings, his talks with you, his talks with law enforcement, Deputy Sheriffs, talks with district attorney people, talks with Carolyn Heim, both individually and in group therapy, are you able to estimate how many hours Michael has been talking about child molestation since he became your foster child?

A. I couldn't even begin.

Q. Would it be in excess of a hundred hours?

A. I don't know. I really don't.

Q. That's fair enough. Basically the same question, including . . .

A. We don't talk about it a lot at home. We just don't.

Q. Including testimony, including talks with Michael, including law enforcement, including district attorney's people, including Miss Heim or formerly Miss Calgar, how many hours . . . are you able to estimate how many hours you have spent talking about child molestation since Michael came into your home?

A. I can't. I have no idea. I didn't clock it. I mean . . .

Q. Would it be . . . again, I ask you, would it be unreasonable to suggest it would have been in excess of a hundred hours?

A. I don't know.

Q. All right, if you don't know, you don't know. Thank you. I have no further questions.

Members of the Nokes family told me Angie had said, "They're on me all the time. They never stop."

Then, Michael accused Cory Taylor. In the Sheriff's Department's written report of this incident, the investigating officer states: "Michael said that he wanted to give me the name of a woman who was involved in molesting children as much as any of the other adults whose names he had given me in the past. Michael said he had not given me the name of this woman before now because he was very threatened of her [sic] and he had thought she was our friend.

"I asked Michael what was the name of the female he was talking about and Michael said, 'Cory Taylor.' I asked Michael if he was sure that Cory Taylor was involved with the other adults in molesting him and the other children involved. Michael stated that he was. I asked Michael if he was telling the truth about Cory Taylor, because if he was not, this was very bad to say that a person was involved when they really were not. Michael looked me in the eyes and said, 'I'm telling you the truth about Cory.'

"Michael said he has known Cory for a long time, that he knew Cory Taylor from before Gerardo and Cheryl were arrested. Michael said that Cory Taylor would always bring another woman a lot when she would come to the places and molest him and other children. Michael said that he had seen Cory with Will Thomas and the white pastor, later identified as Farrell Neeley, many times before the Gonzales's were arrested.

"I asked Michael if he could give me a list of the places that he had seen Cory Taylor at prior to the Gonzales's being arrested for child molesting. Michael said that Cory Taylor was at, and had molested him and other children, at his mom and dad's apartment, the Gonzales's house, Leroy Stowe's house, a foster mother's house by the name of Wanda, unknown last name, at Will Thomas's and Farrell Neeley's 'bad church,' and at Kathy Scott's house. Michael said that these were all of the places that he was molested at by Cory Taylor.

"I asked Michael if he could give me a list of the children that he had seen Cory Taylor molest. Michael said that he and his sister Angela were molested by Cory Taylor, Melissa Gonzales, Suzanne Garrison, Tyson Gonzales, Brooke Hastings, Crystal Prescott, Leroy Stowe III, Armando Warrazas, Donnie, Joe and Jonathan McGee, Leslie Cari and Mary Green. Michael said that these were all of the children that he could remember right now.

"Michael said that Cory's involvement in molesting children was the same type of involvement that he had described several of the other adults doing. Michael said that Cory had given him drugs, as did most of the other adults, and saw Cory taking pictures, as did most of the other adults.

"Michael said the molesting of him was done in much the same manner as he had described the other adults doing, including putting her fingers in his behind and putting her mouth on his front and behind, and him having to do the same to her.

"I asked Michael about when the first time was, if he could remember, that he had been molested by Cory Taylor at a particular house. Michael said he thought the first time that he had been molested by Cory Taylor was at the Gonzales house around January of 1984. Michael said that Cory Taylor had always threatened him like all the other adults and said, 'When I saw Cory Taylor at Jamison I was surprised because all of the good people were telling me I was safe there.' Michael said when Cory Taylor would come and talk with him either at the sheriff's station or at Jamison, that she would tell him what he could or could not say. Michael said that Cory would tell him that he could tell that he had been molested, but he had better not tell that she had molested him."

Like the other children, Michael denied that he had been molested until he had been in custody for some time. After several months in custody, he began telling spectacular stories of satanic rituals and the slaughter of animals and babies. None of the children told of devil worship and murder until they had been in custody for a considerable length of time. Then came the tales of sex orgies with all of the parents present, taking pictures, killing babies and animals. Nevertheless, dozens of children were taken from their parents, many of whom were never charged with any crime. Twelve children identified eighty adults as participants in the satanic rites, according to the Sheriff's Department and C.P.S. workers.

Leroy Stowe was thirty-five years old. He was born in Kern County and had lived there all of his life. He had been a basketball star in high school and had subsequently attended Porterville College. His wife was thirty-six. They had met when they were five years old. They married in 1968 and their first son was born in 1969. The following year twin daughters were born. In 1978 another son was born, Leroy Stowe III, whom they call "Tootie." Stowe worked at a hospital and his wife worked for the telephone company. They were buying their home and had lived in it for nine years.

At about nine in the evening two sheriff's deputies came to his door. Stowe was asleep. The officers asked to speak to Stowe and his wife awoke him. They asked her and the daughters to leave the room.

"After my wife and daughters left the room, Deputy Rutledge said, 'You are under arrest for molesting a Mexican girl around the corner and for taking your son around there for money. You have been named as a suspect in this case and we are arresting you.'

"I couldn't believe what I was hearing and I asked him to repeat what he had said. Then I said, 'Let me get dressed and we'll get this all cleared up. I thought then it would be easy to get this cleared up because I knew I hadn't done anything and I didn't even know the people who lived around the corner."

Stowe went into the bedroom and told his wife. He asked her to call his mother who lives nearby, while he got dressed. Stowe was taken outside and put into a police car. His wife returned to the living room where the deputies had been joined by Cory Taylor, the Child Protective Services worker. They asked to speak with "Tootie." Mrs. Stowe told them he was asleep. They told her to wake him up. He had been given medication for coughing, and it was difficult to awake him. According to Stowe, Rutledge became impatient and said he would take him in his underwear, as he was.

"My wife became extremely frightened because, until then, they had said nothing about taking him away. They had only said they wanted to talk to him. She asked if they could talk to him here. Deputy Rutledge said no, 'We have the right to take him.' They said they were putting him into protective custody. Protective custody from whom? If I was arrested and the other people who were supposedly involved were in jail, who were they protecting him from? Deputy Rutledge said, 'Just put him in a blanket and we will take him like that.' My wife said he was sick and insisted that she be allowed to dress him. Deputy Rutledge kept asking her to hurry up.

"My wife told Tootie not to be afraid, and to tell the truth, and she would come and get him in the morning, because Cory Taylor kept saying she could pick him up in the morning. Then he was taken outside. Cory Taylor then said she would explain what had happened. She said, 'You know, some children in the neighborhood have been molested.' My wife told her she knew nothing about it.

"Cory Taylor said that some children had been molested and

they had said that a little boy named Tootie had been there and also had been molested. She said that the children didn't know Tootie's real name but they knew he lived in the neighborhood and was starting first grade. She said they had done some investigating and found out that our Tootie was the one they were looking for. They also said that Tootie's father had been taking him over to the Gonzales house on Johndra Avenue over a long period of time and molesting him there, then passing him to the Gonzaleses for them to molest him, and that he had molested the Gonzales child. My wife told her that we knew no one in the neighborhood named Gonzales and she didn't even know which street was Johndra. The twins were starting to cry again and Cory Taylor ordered them to go to their room. They said to her, 'You can't tell us what to do.' She later wrote in her report that they were hostile.

"By this time my mother, father, brother and sister were arriving. The deputy kept trying to hurry Cory Taylor up. She told my wife that they just wanted to talk to Tootie and she could pick him up in the morning. She gave her a number to call in the morning and they left.

"I was taken to the Sheriff's Department downtown and put in an interview room. Deputy Rutledge said to me, 'Sit down and be quiet and let me do all the talking and don't interrupt me. Why don't you just go ahead and confess. It will be easier on you. Since you have a problem we will get some help for you.' He said he understood people like me because he had taken a course in psychology. I told him I hadn't done anything to confess to. Then he got up and left the room. He left the door ajar. I could hear Tootie's voice coming from the next room. I heard him say, 'My daddy didn't do anything.' I also heard Cory Taylor tell Deputy Rutledge that Tootie said his father didn't do anything.

"The deputy closed the door and I couldn't hear any more. After a while he came back in and said, 'Your son's in the next room spilling his guts.' I told him again that I hadn't done anything."

Leroy Stowe was booked and his bail was set at $75,000. After talking with his lawyer, he decided to wait until the arraignment in the hope of getting his bail reduced, before trying to get out of jail.

His wife called the number Taylor had given her, but got nothing but a runaround. The people she spoke to said they knew nothing about the case. Finally, she was told that Tootie was not being released. She asked if she could be allowed to see him and she was told that she could. She went to talk to the worker in person, a Mrs. Kanital. She told her that she loved her son and only wanted to protect and care for him, and that she was worried because he had been ill, and had always been afraid to sleep alone. She felt he would be frightened, having to spend the night in a strange place with strangers. Mrs. Kanital was annoyed and tersely told Mrs. Stowe she would not be allowed to see Tootie.

On September 14, 1984, Stowe was transported across the street for a bail hearing. His attorney asked that his bail be reduced but the District Attorney objected. The judge said that the seriousness of the charges was sufficient reason not to grant a reduction. Like the other defendants, Stowe had little hope of coming up with enough cash to pay the bail and the attorney's fees he was facing.

In September, Tootie was released to the custody of his grandmother, but Mrs. Kanital visited her and told her that Tootie was not to talk to, or visit, any of Stowe's relatives. She was warned not to discuss with him, anything about what had happened. Tootie asked her why he had to go to the Jamison Center, which he referred to as a "jail for kids."

Tootie's grandmother said that he was very upset and cried for his parents and wanted to go home. Just prior to the preliminary hearing, he was picked up and taken to the district attorney's office early in the morning and kept there all day. Stowe believes that his son was kept there to be coached for his answers in court.

On October tenth, Tootie was taken to the Sheriff's Department to look at lineups in which Gerardo and Cheryl Gonzales were to appear. The people he picked out were not Mr. and Mrs. Gonzales. Stowe was put in a lineup for Melissa Gonzales to look at.

"While I was standing in the lineup I could hear arguing but I couldn't hear what was being said. Later, my lawyer told me that when Melissa said she didn't know anyone in the lineup, Deputy Bill Rutledge asked her if anyone in the lineup looked like anyone who had done anything bad to her. Then, when she said no to that, he said to her angrily, 'You know it's number four! Why don't you just go ahead and say number four!' That's when my lawyer and Deputy Rutledge began to argue."

Melissa was the first to testify. Gonzales's lawyer asked her if she had ever lied in court and she said yes. He asked that she be disqualified but the judge denied his motion. She stated she had had intercourse with her father, a Reverend Thomas and Stowe, but a medical report brought into evidence later stated that there had been no penetration of any kind.

Tootie testified that he was molested by the Gonzaleses and that Stowe had been there but had not done anything to him. He said he could describe what happened to him but was unable to tell in what order or manner these things had happened or what was said. During all the time he was questioned, not once did ne say that his father was ever inside the Gonzales home. Two other children said that the police came to their school and questioned them about the Gonzaleses. They said the police described "nasty things" and asked if the Gonzaleses did those nasty things to them. Both said no.

"The investigators and law enforcement officers are describing sexual acts to all of these children, over and over, until they agree to say they were molested," said Stowe.

In November, fearing that Stowe's wife, Pat, would be picked up too, the Stowes sent their other three children to live with their great-grandparents to keep them from being put in juvenile hall and separated. Later, they brought them home, thinking the danger of Pat's being arrested had passed.

In December the District Attorney offered Stowe a plea bargain; if he would plead guilty and testify against the other adults accused, they would not file charges against Pat. He rejected the offer. "How could I testify against people I didn't know and had never met. Why would I confess to something I didn't do?"

Stowe's lawyer asked to have the case continued because he had other cases pending. The judge said he would only agree to continue it on a daily basis. "We had to come to court each day and have the case continued to the next day. Since I had to leave work each day to do this, Mr. Mitts asked Judge Stewart if I could have a waiver so I wouldn't have to be there each day. He refused. This continued through December.

"While Tootie was visiting in Fullerton, Pat asked her brother to have him examined by a specialist whose findings couldn't be questioned. We had thought that in these kinds of cases a physical examination would be part of the investigation process, but with the way the laws are now there is no need for physical evidence. It's like somebody accused of murder but no one has to produce a body. Just as long as someone says you did it you can be arrested and tried. Pat wanted to have Tootie examined by someone outside of Kern County, someone who had nothing to fear from the officials here, a doctor who wouldn't take sides but would honestly report his findings.

"He was examined at Children's Hospital of Orange County. The doctor checked him and talked to him privately. Afterwards she told my brother-in-law that she could find no signs of molest. When she questioned him he had told her that no one ever touched him or bothered him in any way. There were social workers at the hospital who interviewed him, and he told them the same thing, that no one had molested him. The doctor and the social worker both gave Mr. Wright [Mrs. Stowe's brother] a very optimistic report of their findings. They said they couldn't give us a copy of the reports because they had to turn them over to the Children's Protective Services in Kern County. They said that our lawyer would have no problem in getting a copy. Both said they could find no reason to believe he had been molested.

"When Mrs. Kanital received the medical reports from Fullerton she called Mrs. Porter [Tootie's grandmother]. She was very upset. She told Mrs. Porter not to take him out of the county or let him see Mr. Wright again."

In January Stowe's wife took a second mortgage on their home to pay for bail and legal fees. His lawyer tried to get a copy of the medical examination from C.P.S. He did not succeed.

In February, jury selection began in Superior Court for Stowe's trial. Three days before Tootie was to testify, he was taken from his grandmother by the District Attorney's office. That evening police called Mrs. Porter to tell her that Tootie would not be returned and was being placed, once again, in Jamison, the county juvenile facility. They offered no explanation and gave Mrs. Porter a number to call. They called the number but were given no answers to their questions.

The trial started. Melissa was the first to testify. She contradicted all of her previous testimony. She said that all of the alleged molestations occurred in the early afternoon. Stowe had time cards to prove he was at work during the time these events were going on.

"I had a lot of family present during the trial," Stowe said. "We all got to go out on a break, but my mother-in-law decided to stay and sit in the courtroom. The D.A., Sara Riles, didn't realize she was there, still in the courtroom.

"When the bailiff asked Sara Riles how Tootie was doing, she told him that she had him picked up because he kept changing his story. Sometimes he would say yes, and sometimes he would say no, he hadn't been molested. When she realized she had been overheard, she quickly changed her story and said that he was being threatened, and that that was why she had picked him up. Later, when we asked Mrs. Kanital why Tootie had been picked up, she said it was because Mrs. Porter was letting him visit with some relatives he wasn't supposed to see. We asked her who. She said his uncle, Mr. Wright. We told her they hadn't seen each other since December. Why, two months later, would they come and get him for that? Then she said it was because he was visiting his other great-grandparents who live just down the street. We reminded her that she had said it was okay for him to visit them.

"A new hearing was set for February 27 in the morning. We reminded her that we were in trial in Superior Court and couldn't be in two places at once. She said we could be there or not be there, but she was going to have a hearing regardless.

"We asked to have Tootie assigned a lawyer to look out for his welfare because it was clear the D.A. and the welfare department didn't care about him and wanted only to use him for their purposes. Tootie was brought to court by the D.A. and attorney McKnight, his new lawyer. He was brought in wearing clothes that were too small, shoes which were too big and second hand. His hair hadn't been combed in days. He testified that the Gonzaleses molested him and that I was there, but didn't molest him. When he was told for the first time that the people he picked out from the lineup were not the Gonzaleses he was truly surprised. He said that all the bad things happened on May 20, 1984, before school was out, in the early afternoon. Again, my time cards showed that I was at work.

"We had an investigator go to Orange County to interview the doctor and social worker about their findings to see if they could help us by testifying. Surprisingly, they both did a 180-degree turn. The doctor said she couldn't help us. The social worker said she didn't even bother to make a report since the case was being handled in Bakersfield, and anything she had written down had been thrown away. She too said there was nothing she could do to help us. We have no way of knowing why they both changed their story—whether it was just that they didn't want to get involved or because they didn't want to come all the way to Bakersfield to testify, or because someone talked to them and intimidated them or pressured them not to get involved. We have no way of knowing."

Susan Garrison testified that she had been molested and that Stowe was there. She said that one day at least five adults were present and each of them gave her a shot. Stowe's lawyer had transcripts of other hearings and pointed out the contradictions in her testimony.

"Michael Nokes was the next to testify. We feel that the D.A. brought him in because I was at work at the times Tootie and Melissa said these bad things happened. Michael said that all these things happened on a Saturday morning when only my family could verify that I was at home. He said he was molested by the Gonzaleses and his parents. He also testified that I, along with other adults, threatened him with a knife. The D.A. asked him to point out Mr. Stowe. I was the only black man at the lawyers' table and the only black man in the courtroom. Before court started that day Michael Nokes arrived at the courtroom before I did. When I entered, I was pointed out to him by the person who brought him. My relatives witnessed this.

"During the defense portion of the trial my older children testified that they watched Tootie too closely for him to have been gone for the length of time he claimed. My wife testified to the fact that we didn't even know the Gonzaleses and that Tootie wasn't allowed to leave the block for any reason.

"My attorney called Carol Muse as a witness. She works for the Sheriff's Department on some of their cases. He questioned her about the tapes that were made of some of the conversations with the children. He read excerpts from some of the tapes proving that the children had said in the beginning that I wasn't involved and they didn't know me. Also, they had said that Tootie hadn't been at the Gonzaleses house or been molested. But later, after continuing interrogation, they changed their story.

"The jury convicted me of sixteen of the eighteen counts of mo-

lest and aiding and abetting. My family and I were completely devastated by the conviction. We felt there was enough evidence for a
reasonable doubt. Now, everything seemed hopeless. We had a
meeting with a lawyer and he explained the appeal process and
gave us some hope that I might be granted an appeal bond. This
would allow me to stay out of jail during the appeal to support my
family. We also discussed what had gone wrong in the trial. He had
talked to some of the jurors about their decision. They said they
based their decision solely on the testimony of the children. They
didn't take any of the evidence we presented into consideration.
They had made up their minds as soon as the children finished testifying. The way things are now in Kern County, the D.A. has only
to put on children. . . .

"Pat talked to Mrs. Kanital about seeing Tootie. She said that I
would no longer be allowed to see Tootie. Period. She said that Pat
and the other children would be able to see him for a supervised
visit only at Jamison. Pat asked her again about getting someone to
help Tootie and explain to him what was happening and why.
Merely the fact that a child is taken out of his home and kept from
his family is enough reason for someone to sit down and talk with
him honestly about what is happening and answer his questions.

"Pat, and my older children, and two neighbor boys were allowed to visit Tootie at Jamison for about an hour. He was glad to
see them. Toward the end of the visit he asked his mother if he was
going to go home soon. Mrs. Kanital was quick to jump in and say,
'Some day, not yet.' He needs more than these vague answers.

"My nephew came home from school today and told his mother
Tootie was back at his old school in Bakersfield. Tootie said he was
living in a foster home. Mrs. Kanital had told us that nothing would
be done with him until the hearing on March 22, 1985.

"We went to Juvenile Court. When my lawyer, Mr. Tello,
arrived he went into the back to check in and see when we would
get started. When he returned he asked us to come outside to talk.
He showed us a report in which charges were being filed in Juvenile Court against my wife, Pat. She was going to be charged with
child molestation of some of these children. The report also stated
that she, along with some of the other adults charged, went to Melissa Gonzales's school while she was waiting in line for the bus to
go home, and threatened her if she continued to testify.

"All I can say is, here again, we don't know any of these people. We haven't molested our son or any other children. They are just going to do the same thing with Pat that they did with me. They will say the kids are too young to know exactly what day or time, and our evidence will mean nothing. This is just another measure used by the D.A. to keep Tootie away from his family. Otherwise, why would this so-called 'new evidence' surface just three days before Tootie's placement hearing? Before today I felt that these people had done just about all they could do to us. They have taken my son and practically sentenced me to life in jail. They're going to make me leave my wife alone with a mountain of debts and little hope.

"Now it seems that this whole nightmare is starting all over again. Is this what happens to relatives and friends who believe in you, and try to stand by you and help? They get arrested and prosecuted too. It's the D.A.'s contention that anyone who shows concern for the accused must be involved in some way. And they will stop at nothing to scare off anyone who tries to help me or any of the defendants in cases like this. They use this weapon to make the accused look alone and guilty to a jury, and frighten off anyone who might help the accused prove their innocence.

"Today I got a copy of the report of the charges that are being filed in Juvenile Court against my wife. They charge her with molest and threats against Melissa Gonzales. The D.A. has accused more adults, some related to other defendants. They have involved new children and even alleged that the acts took place at different houses, not just the Gonzales house. They allege that the children were molested in my home. I'm afraid that the next step they take will be to involve my other children in some sick way, and I am powerless to stop them. Dear God, isn't there anyone out there who cares enough to help save my family?"

Jackie Nokes [Brad Nokes's sister and friend of Bill Thomas] and her husband, Jack Cummings (they live together but are not legally married), decided to leave Bakersfield. "We heard that Brad and Mary Nokes had been named as suspects. We knew then," Cummings said, "because all our children had been friends, and cousins to the Nokes children. On October 2, Jackie, Mary Nokes, Juanita Green and Roy and Rita Nokes prepared statements to be submitted to the County Grand Jury for investigation. That night I packed as many things as possible, and Jackie and myself and our three children left town within an hour. We headed to Mount Shasta where my mother lives. There we borrowed a twelve-foot travel trailer and took off again for the Eureka area where I might find work on a drilling rig. At the time we left I was making about $35,000 a year running an oil production rig.

"At the time we left our seven-year-old was making A's and B's in school and our five-year-old loved his new kindergarten. Our baby was not yet two years old, and we feared that they would be taken from us. We live for our children and could not bear the idea of losing them. We knew that any day our children might not come home from school, and our precious baby might be taken.

"Within two weeks we heard that Michael and Angela Nokes, our children's cousins and best friends, had been taken from school by the county workers. We knew then that our worst fears were true, and they were rounding up everyone they could, whether friend, relative, or neighbor. We moved on to Cloverdale and I got a job at the Geysers on a rig and worked for a month before the rig shut down. We returned to Mt. Shasta and spent December there. We spent January in a trailer in the Mojave Desert and lived off my unemployment. In February we returned to Mt. Shasta. We still had not been named or sought to the best of our knowledge. A few days later I received a job offer in Portola, California. We were still fearful but, reassured that we were not suspects, put our two older boys in Portola Elementary. My job folded up after six weeks and we were forced to return to Mt. Shasta one week before Easter vacation.

"On April ninth we received a phone call telling us that we had been named on some reports. That night we left Oregon and camped out in our trailer in different areas until April 28, when I foolishly returned to Mt. Shasta to pick up my tax return check. The local police had been notified to look for my car. At two a.m. the police knocked on the motel door where we were staying and said that Kern County had a hold on our children. And took our kids from us.

"The nightmare we feared for so long had come true. We had no words. Only tears. Our lives were shattered. We were told they would be placed in a foster home and then transported back to the hell we had left. On April 29 at 1:30 p.m. we contacted an attorney and he informed us that the children had been taken without benefit of a 300 petition. Mr. Stein [the attorney] filed a writ of *habeas corpus* ordering the children to appear at a hearing to determine jurisdiction on May 7. This was duly signed by Judge Cleaver.

"On May 1, based on the deception that the children would be returned on May 7, the judge gave a verbal order that if the childen were returned, he saw no reason not to allow it.

"That morning, Coral Cooper handed my children to *them!* At the hearing on May 3, all proper procedures were ignored and the illegalities of kidnapping. In re Singer it has been held that it is illegal to keep and detain minors for the purpose of using them as witnesses. This was ignored. On May 6, our lawyer, Mr. Stein, assured me they had to return our children. On May 7 the writ of *habeas corpus* was ignored and the judge said he had no choice but to turn the matter over to Kern County. As of this date we remain uncharged of any crime and intend to fight for our beloved children."

Their lawyer, Charles Stein, wrote to the Los Angeles ACLU, asking for help. In his letter, he stated that "The Bakersfield Child Protective Services is apparently taking custody of children without benefit of warrant or 300 Petition, and sequestering them in a place where they can be questioned at great length and under onerous circumstances until they implicate, in some manner, their parents with child molestation allegations. Petitions are apparently drawn up after the fact, and then upon date of hearing the parents who attend are arrested and charged on 288-type charges. It is my understanding that this has been going on for some period of time and that approximately twenty-five to thirty families have now been involved in arrests and prosecution."

He stated that "I obtained a writ of *habeas corpus* with the intent to keep the children in Siskiyou County and ask that Siskiyou County assume jurisdiction over the matter . . . in a forum not tainted with the allegations of impropriety which exists in Kern County. Through a series of colossal foul-ups, the children were released to Kern County by Siskiyou County C.P.S., anyway. Kern County then refused to release the children pursuant to the writ and held them and continue to hold them in custody in Kern County.

"The Cummings' children," he stated, "are still being held in Kern County in violation of a plethora of statutes and Constitutional parameters, and the Cummings have expended their meager resources on attorneys fees to no avail. It was for that reason that we sought out the help of the ACLU.

"Certain persons in the Kern County District Attorney's Office, in C.P.S., and at the Sheriff's Office, all female, have taken it upon themselves to initiate a crusade against child molestation. They have apparently chosen to ignore legal niceties to accomplish their ends. Unfortunately, the Cummings family, and others, are caught up in the middle of this malfeasance of office."

The Los Angeles ACLU did not reply.

PITTS

Ricky Pitts and his new wife, Marcella, were living in Oklahoma. They had moved there recently from Bakersfield, California. They were trying to get custody of her three sons who were living with their father in Bakersfield, who knew that Marcella and Ricky were coming to file for custody. Notices of the hearing had been sent out to all parties involved. Ricky and Marcella believed this custody hearing would help them get custody of the boys. They never got a chance to be heard. They were arrested as they got off the elevator, at the courthouse.

Ricky's aunt, Ruellene Pitts, told me: "Ricky had his two girls from a previous marriage with him, and they snatched them and took them away too. Ricky thought, 'If I just go to California and tell the truth, that'll straighten it out and we'll get the boys.' Instead, he got 373 years. His wife got the same, and his wife's mother, Grace Dill, got 405 years.

"Ricky, his wife, his wife's mother, brother, sister, brother-in-law and a friend all got convicted. The friend got 405 years. Her brother got 405 years. The one who got the least was the brother-in-law. He got 285 years.

"The cops' story was that they were a pornography ring and that they were using these kids for sexual exploitation, having sex with the kids and filming it, and selling the films. They never found one piece of pornography. One of the deputy district attorneys was going around offering money to some of the other people who had been accused, although they weren't charged, offering money if they would come up with photographs. And they still came up with nothing. But they got a jury to vote guilty, because some of the kids said there was cameras there. Everybody has a camera.

"Ricky was a farmer, and he had to sell a cow to get enough money to come back. He brought four of his kids with him, and it turned out that those were the alleged victims. They were his two daughters and his two nieces. They said, all along, that no molestation ever happened. They still say it. They were examined by a doctor," Ruellene said. "And he testifies only for the prosecution. When the natural mother took those kids to be examined, he told her that the kids were not molested. But, by the time he got to court, they *were* molested. He and the prosecutor were buddies. They went to school together.

"And then the other two girls that he brought back with him, his nieces, they also said nothing happened. In fact, Chris held out for seven months. Finally, she said something happened, and then the other one did too. They worked on them for a long time.

"They arrested Rick and Marcella first. Then they went out and arrested her sister and brother. Then they came back a few months later and arrested the grandmother, and then, a few months later they arrested the brother-in-law. They arrested seven people. But they also have a warrant out for my other nephew and his wife, who is Marcella's older sister. Two of my nephews married two sisters. And so anybody who was in the family or married into the family was arrested.

"My other nephew and his wife, they were getting ready to come to Oklahoma when somebody called them and told them that Rick had been arrested, and so they decided they better not come out. They would just get railroaded, like the rest.

"They went into the preliminary, and only one child testified. The oldest boy. And, incidentally, it took them three months to get him to say anything happened. What he said in the preliminary was totally different from what he said in the trial. Several times the judge told the D.A. not to talk to that boy. Whenever the boy would get stumped for an answer, or would answer the wrong way, that D.A. would take the child out of the courtroom, and when the child came back into the courtroom, his testimony was totally changed. So the judge ordered that nobody could talk to the child outside the courtroom, but the D.A. just went ahead and did it anyway. And the judge didn't do anything about it.

"Gina Miller was a friend. She was picked up on a warrant for somebody else, someone who was accused of molesting. They picked up Gina by mistake! And she was pregnant at the time. They had to get a court order to get the shackles off her because she was falling all over the courtroom, and falling all over the jail cell. She was eight months pregnant! They let her out on bail so she could have her baby.

"They kept trying to make deals with her, that if she would testify against the others they would give her total immunity, and she said, 'I *can't* testify because I know they didn't do anything!' So her attorney tried to have her declared mentally incompetent because she refused to testify against the others. He tried to knife her in the back.

"And then they made the women strip down, because the kids said they had tattoos, which they did, and they admitted they had tattoos. It was a family joke. Grandma had a cherry tattooed on her behind. But they made these women strip down and they took nude pictures of them. The cops did that. So the only nude pictures that were in there were the nude pictures of the grandmother and the sister and the brother-in-law, because he had a lot of tattoos too. They got a surprise in the preliminary, because they kept asking about tattoos and the kids said, 'Oh, he doesn't have any tattoos except on his arm.' He is tattooed from one end to the other! Even his penis is tattooed. But the cops wanted to use the tattoos to make them look bad. It was irrelevant, but they did it anyway.

"Then, one of the witnesses in our group, they were threatening her! Her name was Carla Joyce. I have a very interesting tape of what they did to her. She had been named, and in fact it was Gina Miller who was mistakenly picked up on Carla Joyce's warrant. But they threatened Carla Joyce with 'If you don't testify, we're gonna put about sixty counts of child molest on you.' This was the Sheriff's Department and the prosecution. The D.A.'s office. She finally said, 'All right, I'll do it, I'll do it,' because they threatened to take away her kids. So what they finally did to her, when she agreed to do it, they took her to a motel room, handcuffed her to a bed overnight. She had not even been booked. They handcuffed her to a bed overnight, got her up in the morning and took her over for questioning. They transported her to an entirely different county, booked her in a jail there under a false name, and she got so hysterical there that they had to take her to a psychiatric ward and started giving her medication. They took her back to jail. She reacted to the medication, so they gave her more.

"Carla Joyce is out now. They got scared because she raised so much hell, they were afraid she would wreck the whole case. They let her go, out of the county, and she had no money to get home. But Gina Miller, the one who was picked up by mistake, on Carla Joyce's warrant, got 405 years.

"Then they brought in some more witnesses from the jail cell, saying the girls had confessed in the jail cell, and that they had done these things. In the first place, it was a lie. In the second place, one of these women had testified in four other molestation cases saying exactly the same thing. She was in for child molest herself.

"And there was another one in the men's section. They had a man in there. His name was Willy Pitman. And he testified in court that the Sheriff's Department and the D.A. came in there and handed him a script, and told him to memorize it. And he was going to testify. He was in there for robbery or something like that. And he just absolutely refused to do it. And he came in and testified about what happened, and the judge would not allow the jury to hear that! Judge Friedman.

"All of the defendants had taken lie detector tests—and passed them. But the judge told us that if even one of us mentioned in court that we had passed a lie detector test, we would get an automatic six months in jail. There were well over a hundred motions made by the defense, and only three were granted. Anything the D.A. wanted was granted. The jury spent as much time out of the courtroom as they did in. Anything that came up that the D.A. didn't want, the jury was immediately sent out of the room.

"One of the defendants, his name is Wayne Forsythe, the brother-in-law, he has been charged in another molest case which is kind of an offshoot of this one. He was living with a woman at the time the charges were brought. She too was questioned and asked to testify against my nephew and his wife. She said, 'I have never met those people in my life, so I couldn't say anything.' Another one who was threatened with thirty counts, unless she testified against them, she said 'I can't do it. I don't know anything about them.' And as soon as she got out she immediately wrote an article in a newspaper. Within eight days after the newspaper article came out, she was arrested and charged. And almost everybody in her apartment complex has been charged. The cops call it 'another ring,' 'another child pornography ring.' Her name is Stephanie Jenkins.

"We wanted to bring in Marcella's ex-mother-in-law, who wanted to come in and testify in Marcella's behalf, because she knew that the accusations were false, but one of the D.A.'s investigators went out and talked to her, and scared her half to death. Then he went back to court, and lied to the court, and said that *we* were trying to pressure her to come in and testify. And that was not true. She called us and begged us to let her testify on Marcella's behalf, because she knew the accusations of molestation were not true. But they wouldn't allow her to testify. They wouldn't let us present any testimony on our behalf at all.

"And the prosecutor kept changing the dates when everything was supposed to have happened, so it's very difficult to build a defense when you don't know when these alleged acts occurred. They kept switching it back and forth in a span of about two years.

"One of the jurors was a friend of the step-grandmother, who was a witness on the prosecution's side.

"Ricky's mother and father have lost their property, their ranch, their savings, everything. It cost them $150,000 to pay for defending him in the case.

"Even Rick's ex-wife, she wanted to testify in Rick's defense. But they threatened her. The deputy D.A. They were threatening to drag her into the case, and they took her husband aside and made the threats to him. And he was so frightened he wouldn't even tell his wife what the threats were. So he got up and testified for the prosecution, on the D.A.'s promise that they would not bring charges against his wife, who was Rick's ex-wife.

"They had Rick's daughters locked up for a while, and they had them in a foster home, so Rick told his ex-wife he would let her get custody, just to get them out of the foster home. And the D.A. was using the girls as a lever to get Rick's ex-wife to testify. And she wouldn't testify, but she was scared to death. And when she got the girls, the attorney—they had appointed attorneys for the girls—the attorney told her not to let the girls be examined, and she was scared that if she did, the social workers would come back and take the girls away from her.

"And the D.A. came in and talked to her new husband and said, 'These girls have got to be examined, and if they aren't we're gonna drag her in.' And this was after the D.A. got a court order saying that none of the kids could be examined. And he's the one who told the mother, 'Get 'em down there and get 'em examined.' And he gave her the name of the doctor who was their hired man, who always finds abuse. A professional abuse finder. And the D.A. violated his own order, and then he said that she voluntarily did it, which was a lie.

"And when the girls found out that that doctor got up there and testified that they had been molested, they were furious! Now they don't trust doctors any more. They wanted to know how a medical doctor could get up there and lie like that. The prosecutors have their favorite doctors they can always count on to find sexual abuse, no matter what.

"It's totally destroyed the whole family. And the funny thing is, Rick's father, my brother-in-law, had always taught them to respect the law. And it's totally destroyed any illusions they had about the American justice system.

"You know what this judge did in the case? He bought two dolls for one of the witnesses, and gave them to her in the courtroom. All the girls that testified for the prosecution got cabbage patch dolls. And there were three girls who got up and testified and said, 'No way!'—that nothing like that ever happened. And they didn't get anything. They were called liars.

"There are so many things wrong with this case they ought to be able to win it on appeal. But it'll take a long time. There's over 20,000 pages of transcript for the lawyers to go through.

"It costs a lot of money. My brother and sister-in-law are going to try to auction off some more of their farm equipment, but I don't know if it'll be enough. We'll need at least fifty thousand dollars.

"The kids who talked about all the satanic rituals . . . The D.A. said they had no contact with each other. But they all went to the same therapist. Carolyn Heim was the one, at the Henrietta Weill Child Guidance Center."

DOMINIC EYHRABIDE, Colleen Bennett's attorney:

"Something strange is going on. I don't know what. Something extremely sinister. And weird. I wish I could reach down into my attorney's bag of tricks and pull something out that would explain it. In Kern County, everybody's getting convicted. Kids are coming up with the most bizarre stories in the world, but the defendants are all landing in jail.

"I'll say one thing about the Pitts case, and here again, I don't say this too often. I think they have a very good chance of getting their case reversed on appeal. When the Fifth District Court of Appeal sees what happened in that trial . . . that trial was a joke. Now, that case wasn't as bizarre as Gonzales. It wasn't even close. But, thank God, those people at least have something to hope for. There were any number of legal flaws in the case, but if you just want to talk about facts, here's one pretty good one: The kids said they were molested every other weekend, which coincided with when the three Martin boys visited with their natural mother, Marcella. That was about September, 1982. And then Rick and everybody moved about June, 1983. That was the ten-month period. And they're saying it happened every other weekend. And they claimed that all of this same group of people came together.

"Now, the grandmother, Grace, she had time records that showed that on most of these Saturdays she worked. The kids said it happened in the daytime. And that poor lady, she worked until 3:30. She didn't even have transportation. She either gets a ride, somehow, or takes the bus back, or her son, Wayne, would take her, and they also said he was supposed to be involved in all of this. And that was just bull! And here's another thing. My client, Colleen, didn't even start dating Wayne Forsythe until about February. And then they moved. So it wasn't really until April or May that all of this group could have been together. They're claiming that this group came together every weekend for ten months. That did not happen! This isn't just speculation. These are established facts.

"What you have to understand is . . . when these cases go to

trial, those kids . . . they are scripted! That doesn't mean rehearsed. That doesn't mean they brainwash the kids, but what it
does mean is that they prepare the kids, they interview the kids,
basically with a view towards, 'How do we make this plausible to a
jury?' And they tie in the original denials by the kids, and what was
said at the preliminary hearing, and the medical examinations, if
there were any. . . . And now at the trial, where you might have
originally had ten kids that didn't agree on anything, now you get
to trial, and all the kids agree, On everything. And it's bullshit.

"And the people who wind up on juries don't have many experiences with kids talking about sex. And their belief seems to be that
if a kid can discuss sex, if a child can describe a sex act, that proves
that he was molested, and that proves it must have been you, unless you can prove that he was molested somewhere else—which,
in the Pitts case, the judge wouldn't let us do, even though we
tried over and over again.

"I can't imagine anyone getting a more unfair trial. Almost every
avenue of cross-examination was cut off. The trial was an absolute
farce. And there was one allegation that the D.A. knew we could
prove was baloney. And that's when the three Martin boys said
. . . on the week that Rick was arrested . . . and through all this
psychological reinforcement, or whatever's going on with these
kids, and the kids feel that they have to report more and more
spectacular stories, and the closer Rick Pitts gets to coming back to
California, the stronger the allegations get. So now, on the eve of
Rick Pitts coming back to California, they come up with the biggest
story of all. They say that they're swimming, during the daytime,
in a public pool at the North Bakersfield recreation district
swimming pool. So you've got all kinds of parents there. Now, this
is a very well-run pool. They've got lifeguards. Now, the kids said
that they went in the bathroom. And that Doug and Steve and
Carla met them there, and Doug and Steve were dunking them in
the pool, and then Doug and Steve individually took the boys, one
at a time, into the restroom area, which is just a stall. It's right out
in the open. And the boys said they had to orally copulate Doug
and Steve, and Doug and Steve sodomized the boys, and that,
while this was going on, other children and parents walked by and
saw this, but didn't bother to say anything.

"Now, that tied into our theory that these kids were being fed a bunch of B.S., and that this was just the culmination of all of it. The judge would not let us put this into evidence. I think that was serious error. And there was a lot more.

"The D.A., if you can believe this, got an order which straightjacketed us that said that any time we want to ask a child a question on cross-examination, and it would subject the child to embarrassment, we would have to ask the judge, at sidebar, or ask for a hearing outside the presence of the jury, to find out if we could ask the question. Try to ask kids questions on those terms. You don't even know when you're in violation of the order. Theoretically, the whole subject is embarrassing to them. I was so frustrated I made the same motion, directed toward the D.A. I literally copied the prosecutor's motion, word for word, and said what's good for the goose is good for the gander, but the judge denied it.

"I've seen a lot of cases where there was a little bit of error, a little hearsay or some prosecutorial misconduct, but in this case the error was beyond prejudicial. The jury convicted, and it surprised me when they convicted everybody. Now I wasn't that surprised when my client, and Rick Pitts and Wayne Forsythe and Marcella, got convicted, because their own natural children got up there and pointed the finger at them. But that wasn't true with the other three. I was really surprised that Grace Dill, the grandmother, got convicted. And Gina! That was really interesting. She was picked up by mistake on somebody else's warrant. The whole thing was a big mistake in her case. And she had an excellent attorney who did a good job for her.

"I believe that the jury was poisoned, after sitting in on this hearing for three months. Four months. It was obvious that the judge thought our clients were guilty. His rulings and his comments from the bench reinforced that all the way through. I think the jury was just poisoned. But when they convict someone like Gina Miller! The kids didn't even recognize her! Didn't even know her. Her attorney didn't even ask questions a lot of the time because—why should he? The kids didn't say anything against his client. She got 405 years, the same as Grace. And they had virtually no evidence against her!

"Another thing. The prosecutor in the Pitts case is a very strong attorney. I mean, strong in the sense that he really knows what he's doing. Also, he's very strong-willed in the courtroom. He puts on an Academy Award performance. He has a very commanding, dominating presence and he just got the judge to go along with him. He got the judge to adopt his position one hundred percent of the time. And he did some unethical things in the trial. I mean, he's too smart to really believe in some of the legal tactics he was engaging in. But he was very artful, and dominating, and the judge went along with him, and we'll just have to wait to see about that on the appeal. There's no doubt that the prosecutor controlled that court. I'd be asking questions, and he'd say 'Objection, your honor. Didn't the court rule on that in chambers? Isn't Mr. Eyhrabide in contempt of court for asking those questions?' Now that was totally untrue and he knew it. It was a perfectly proper question. But when he did that, the judge would say, 'Yeah, Mr. Eyhrabide, didn't we go over that?' And it made it look like I did something really wrong, and he made me look really bad to the jury. But the D.A. was well aware that that was the dynamics going on out there, and he used it to the hilt.

"Another thing that's really crazy. . . . the concept of 'discovery' is that the prosecutor has got to disclose whatever evidence he possesses, both favorable and adverse, to the defense. And in this case there were about ten witnesses they called to the witness stand, and we didn't even know who they were. So as soon as we'd hear the name of the witness I'd say, 'Your honor, can I approach the sidebar?' And we'd go to sidebar and I'd say, 'I have an objection, your honor. We had a discovery order. I've got discovery as to this witness. I'm moving for discovery, or a continuance, or something. I don't know what this witness is going to say.' And the D.A. would say, 'Oh, Mr. Eyhrabide's gotten everything,' or, 'We didn't have any written reports on this witness.' And the judge would say, 'Oh, that's fine. You'll get discovery right now, Mr. Eyhrabide.' Things like that happened constantly. Some of it was significant, some of it wasn't. There was a lot of dirty discovery. And I've learned, the hard way, that every time a prosecutor starts to ask a question— like he's going to elicit an act of sodomy—like, he'll say, 'Did he put it in your butt?' or something like that. And let's say that no-where in the discovery is there any reference to that sort of an act. Now, I always jump up, and make ten motions because I never had discovery of any of this. And then, the D.A. will come back and say, 'Well, the child just told me this last night.' Then you've got to ask for a hearing to find out what was said. Why would he wait until the night before a trial, after a nine-month investigation, to tell this?

"But there's something strange going on here. I believe there's something worse going on than just suggestive interviewing, or psychological reinforcing. Carolyn Heim, in her notes in her log, at the clinic, said that by hypnotic suggestion she was able to help Michael Nokes remember certain things. Her deposition was taken in one of the juvenile court cases, and they confronted her with her log, and her explanation was, 'I do not know anything about hypnosis. I have never had any training in hypnosis. I do not know how to hypnotize anyone. All I meant by that entry was that I was trying to help Michael recall certain things because he was having a problem with it. . . .' I don't think she will ever be able to satisfactorily explain that statement.

"Henrietta Weill Child Guidance Clinic needs to be checked out in terms of what was going on in 1984, and 1985. Carolyn Heim came from Santa Clara County. And she was involved in some kind of child protective services up there. And she come down here. And she has been schooled in all this stuff, the grants and everything, and I think that's where Henrietta Weill's coming from. They've now got some grants. And every one of these people knows that their job security entailed generating cases to justify reapplication for new grants. There's no question about that.

"This is kind of an aside, but my child's in a day care place, a pre-school. They had a woman come to the school to ask the parents to give their consent to let them give the children a seminar on child molesting. And these kids are only three years old! So they're going to give this little puppet show, about good touching and bad touching, and all that jazz, to these three-year-olds! So what you've got here, you've got the people that run around to all these schools. Not only are they reporting agents, but they go around and give these lectures to kids—knowing they're going to generate something. And they are out there, just generating business! I can just see this little kid raising his hand and saying, 'Oh yeah. I take baths with Mommy and Daddy. My daddy, I get in bed with him sometimes.' Next thing you know, they've got the kid aside, and he's in therapy. And Dad's in jail. I wouldn't give my consent for my kid to see the lecture.

"What's crazy about it—they claim that about eighty-five or ninety percent of all molestation is done in the home, by a person that's known to the child. And if you don't have a history of that stuff going on in your family, do you really want to educate your kid sexually, starting at age three, only on the remote chance that the old man down the street might molest your kid?

"I asked this lady, at the meeting, if she knew anything about the Gonzales case, and I told her that I was representing Gonzales. And I asked her, I said, 'Are you aware of all the allegations of cannibalism and infanticide?' And she said, 'Yeah.' And I said, 'Just tell me, what do you think?' And you know what? She looked me straight in the eyes and she said, 'It's all true. The public's just not ready for it yet.'

"So what you're dealing with there is a mentality of people that are just going to believe anything, elicit anything! It's terrible to think that people of that mentality are interviewing those kids.

"But it's generally thought, around here at least, that if you're accused of molestation, you're marked for life. You're cooked. And don't rely on the presumption of innocence. Just being accused of molestation changes everyone's perception of you.

"And who has the resources to defend themselves in this kind of case? If you get arrested for molestation, it's going to take the attorney seven or eight weeks to put on a preliminary hearing. You have one hundred counts, ranging over a period of a year or more. How many people could afford an attorney for eight weeks? It would bankrupt almost anybody. And when they charge, they charge in groups, and they charge lots of counts, because then the D.A., in effect, picks the attorney. Because he knows this defendant is not going to be able to go out and hire a world-class attorney. And those guys are going to charge a lot.

"There's another real problem with all this. You try to find a doctor that wants to testify for the defense in a criminal molestation case! They ain't around. But the prosecution has this industry going! Doctors. But there is no defense industry. And the local pediatricians in town don't even want to see their names mentioned in the same breath as molestation. They don't want to see their names in the newspaper.

"We filed motions for disqualification of the D.A.'s office. Those motions were denied in the local Superior Court. We filed petitions for writ in the Fifth District Court of Appeal, and they have ordered the opposing side to respond. They usually don't. They usually dismiss them out of hand. In other words, they're entertaining it. They think there's some merit to this. If those petitions are denied, I think we can go, this time. If either one of those motions is granted, then I think it'll be continued, out of necessity, to set us up in another county, or get the A.G. in here. Or both. If either one of those is granted. It's going to take the A.G. at least three months to get ready for this. I don't think the A.G.'s going to want to fool around with the mess. I feel sure they'll make a definite effort at settling the case. If Gerardo gets convicted, that will be about the sixth molestation ring conviction, and over-400-year sentence coming out of this county, that they're going to have to deal with on appeal. God, I would think that would sure raise some eyebrows. I don't think, as far as crime is concerned, Bakersfield is any worse than anywhere else.

"I have handled cases where the kid really was molested. In a lot of these cases, there are two things you notice. One is that when the kid has to tell about it in court, he appears to be going through a lot of pain and emotion. When the kid has to talk about Daddy doing something to him, it looks like he's actually reliving it! There's real emotion! But consistently in these current cases you do not see that. These kids are emotionless. They just go in there and recite. About penises, and vaginas, and holes . . . I don't know if it's because they've been interviewed eight hundred times, or . . . but . . . it's like they don't even know their mom and dad any more. After a while, it's just very cold, and that really, really bothers me. In the Pitts case, one of the things that really hurt the defense . . . we had my client's daughter on the witness stand. Her name is Amanda. Amanda was about five at the time she testified. But relatively immature. Not a very bright girl. She testified—and she was rather bizarre in what she was saying—they got her to say that she was touched, but it was kind of vague and didn't amount to anything. At the end of her testimony they had her start at one end, and start identifying the defendants. She looked at Gina Miller, and she said, 'I don't know who that is.' Then she looked at her grandmother, and she said, 'That's grandma.' Then she looked at her uncle, Wayne Dill. She didn't recognize him either. Then she got to Rick Pitts, and when she could see Rick, I mean to tell you, that kid just cracked up! She started yelling and screaming. And I tell you, I've never seen anything like it before. The kid just freaked. And I do not believe it was phony. That kid just shrieked. It was as if she'd just seen her father killed and was all alone in the world. She started running. She grabbed the judge.

"Now, that incident—I am absolutely convinced—was based on eight or nine months of them telling that kid how bad Rick Pitts is. I am absolutely convinced that you can take a kid, and if you talk badly enough about a third party, when that kid finally sees that third party, she's going to think that's the devil personified. And I don't think it's hard to believe. If I started talking to my daughter today about Mr. Jones down the street, about how he comes out at midnight and does unspeakably horrible things . . . she's going to be petrified of him.

"And the reason I believe that—all the more—is that my client told me . . . Now I don't know if she always told me the truth, I mean, how do I ever know? But she would have no reason to tell me that Rick and Amanda were really good buddies. She told me that before that incident in court. She told me that afterwards. She always told me that . . . that Rick and Amanda had a really good relationship. And she didn't tell me that about her other daughter. And she didn't tell me that all her kids loved her boyfriends, or husbands, or family. Colleen would have no reason to lie about that. It wouldn't make any difference. To this day I know that Colleen's in prison wondering, Why in the hell did Amanda freak out when she saw Rick? And that was the kid that said that Rick was arrested by the bailiff.* That kid was in another world. She wasn't even dealing in reality any more. I think she was a kid who was neglected, and kind of living in a dream world. My client ran around with a lot of men. She wasn't very stable. In fact the grandmother more or less took care of the kids. My client really never did. But Colleen would really have no reason to lie about Rick having a good relationship with Amanda. And I really believe they worked on her for nine months and told her Rick was someone to be terrified of. And that was a powerful piece of evidence, against

---

*A bailiff is a guard who works only in the courtroom to protect the judge, jury, witnesses, maintain order, etc. He does not go out and arrest people, like a policeman or a sheriff.—Ed.

Rick and against everybody, by inference, I guess. All the older kids said that Wayne Forsythe was really the mean guy, and Rick was much nicer. So why would Amanda like Wayne and freak out when she saw Rick? They told her some horror stories. And she hadn't seen Rick for a year. And that wasn't an act. She had been taught to be afraid of Rick.

"Up to that point, there was no evidence. That incident was the strongest piece of evidence in the whole case. Half the jury was in tears. They cried for that kid.

"Lucky for Rick, I don't think the Court of Appeal will stand for it. In fact, I'm hoping that we'll get a published opinion reprimanding the court. That case must have cost the county several hundred thousand dollars. And it was just wasted.

"But even in cases where there really was molestation, the cure's worse than the disease. What they ought to do, when there is a molest in the home—and I'm not talking about those cases where there's violence or brutality—if that happens, sure, they should be prosecuted. But in these cases at home, I haven't seen one yet that I thought was a lost cause. These children would be better off if they would try to salvage the family relationship. And I'm not saying that out of soft-heartedness. These kids are going to go into foster homes. They're going to get knocked around. In a foster home, the child's just a paycheck. He's not really their kid. And they destroy the kid's family, and get him to accuse his own father and mother, and send them to prison.

"They ought to try to save the family. In the long run there would be less harm done. But in this county they want to terminate the parental rights and lock the people up for as long as possible. And that's not an exaggeration. They have no soul or humanity in the D.A.'s office here.

"I would like to see a study done, a follow-up on what happens to these kids. The D.A.'s, the investigators, the sheriff's investigators, they mother the kids! I mean, like the kid has six parents during the trial. He's never got so much attention in his life. They take him to toy stores. They never had so much attention and gifts showered on them.

"I'd like to know what happens the day after sentencing. 'Good bye, kid. See ya later.' It's nice to play with a kid for a while, but what happens when the kid gets sick, or when the kid's in a bad mood, or the kid's bad? They don't have to deal with that. They don't have to be with the kid twenty-four hours. It's easy to come to court with the kid. This is a special occasion, and you keep the kid happy. But at five o'clock, it's adios, and I'm going home. The kid goes back to her foster home or county facility. They use these kids, for their own ends, during the course of the prosecution, and once it's over, it's 'Good bye, kid.' I don't think there's any follow-up, or any lasting interest in the kid."

ANDREW RUBIN, Attorney for Ricky Pitts:

"Ricky Pitts and Marcella Pitts each had been married previously. They get a notice that Marcella's ex-husband—his name is Johnny Martin—is going into court in an attempt to cut off her visitation. All of her visitation. He was in Bakersfield. He had the kids, the three boys. She had visitation with them, and she was planning to come back to California to fight for custody, probably six months after that or maybe a year after that. She gets a notice in the mail that there is going to be a hearing, the purpose of which is to terminate her visitation rights.

"In the papers it stated that this was based upon allegations that there had been some molestation, although nothing like what ended up being brought out in the trial. That notice was, more likely than not, a ruse to get her and maybe Rick Pitts back to California. Now it is possible the the original filing might have been serious—to the extent that the Martins really did want to have this hearing to cut off the visitation rights. But it ended up being a vehicle to get Rick and Marcella back to California, where they were arrested when they went to the hearing.

"They arrived in California two or three days before the hearing. They bring Rick's kids from his first marriage, whose names are Carol and Lisa, back as witnesses that there wasn't any molestation, but, I think, more as character witnesses. They're very unsophisticated people and I think their feeling was that they'd show the court how well Rick's kids were doing, and that would obviously prove to the court that there couldn't have been any molestation. It's sort of naive but that was what they were trying to do. Rick and Marcella go to the hearing. There is no hearing, and in fact they are arrested. I think by that time the whole thing had mutated into a way of getting the Pittses arrested.

"The police then went to the place where the Pittses were staying for those few days, and arrested Marcella's sister, Colleen Bennett, picked up Lisa and Carol Pitts, and also a couple of other kids who were there, who ended up being witnesses. Charges were then filed alleging multiple counts of lewd and lascivious conduct with kids, and a few other things.

"Now we have to back up in time to February. The arrest took place in July. Going back four months before that, Marcella's youngest boy is caught with several other kids, fooling around, in some kind of sexual game. Bryan, at that time, was like six or seven. They were playing post office or something, in the oleander bushes at school. They get brought in, several of the kids get brought in to talk to a school counselor. The school counselor believes that Bryan is showing more sophistication with regard to sexual terminology than is normal for a boy of his age. Bryan also allegedly said that his mother had done something to him. And the counselor's initial reaction was that that had happened to him very recently. Now his natural mother, Marcella, hadn't had any contact with him for several months because she's been in Oklahoma. But it was the counselor's belief that this had happened very recently. Which would mean that Marcella couldn't have done it.

He said something to the stepmother, Janice Martin. At that point Janice talks to each of the boys. And Johnny, who's the oldest boy, who's like maybe nine years old, maybe eight, denies that anything happened. Bryan, who at that point is about six, talking with the cops, accuses Rick of doing something. The cops come out. The cops interview the three boys individually. These were Sheriff's Deputies. Johnny, the oldest boy, denies anything happened. One of the other boys said his mother did something to him. This is still in early February. In the period between, the cop decides to call somebody from the sexual abuse team in. He calls in a guy named Bob Fields, who's also a Deputy Sheriff, who's apparently not had much training in interviewing kids or doing child molestation cases either. Fields and then another guy, during a period of about a month and a half, interview these kids several times. They were still living with the Martins. Temporarily they were moved to a foster home right before Rick and Marcella moved, the previous May, a year before they were arrested. They were seeing the kids the night before they were leaving. They left the kids with a babysitter and went to have a few beers. Somebody called the cops on the babysitter. The babysitter was about sixteen years old, and was smoking marijuana. They arrest him and they take the kids to shelter care, where the kids remained until the Martins picked them up, four or five days later. Now I think at some point while these molestation allegations were made, the kids were also taken to shelter care, but, again, they don't stay there for very long. And the Martins get them back, because they're not involved in the alleged molestation. Then they file this action for changing the visitation. Now that brings us back up to June.

"In June of 1984, Rick and Marcella are arrested. Several other kids are then interviewed, including Rick's two kids. They deny anything happened. Then his nieces, Colleen Bennett's kids, are interviewed. Initially they say nothing happened, but later on, they say things happened. After many interviews. Maybe twenty. According to the sheriff's people, there were about twenty contacts—they admit that—but they say there were only one or two conversations about the case. There's this woman named Carol Darling, and it's actually her husband is the other guy who does the interviews. Brad Darling. Carol Darling is the juvenile 'nice guy' at the sheriff's office. She admitted seeing the girl twenty times—between twenty and thirty times—but said, 'I just wanted to be her friend, and told her if she wanted to talk to me, she could, and most of the time she didn't talk about the case until she decided to open up.'

"I don't believe that.

"In July of 1984 there's a preliminary hearing. The only witness is Johnny Martin. He's the oldest boy, and the one who originally said nothing happened, but who, through several interviews, not only gilded the lily but did several other things to it too. He went from 'Nothing happened' to unbelievable orgies, pornography. He's the first one who talks about that, and he's the only witness at the preliminary hearing. There ended up being seven defendants. They were charged in three different groups. Johnny Martin was the only witness at each preliminary hearing. They get bound over into Superior Court, and, to a large extent, they've got the three

Martin boys and one other witness at this point—maybe—and I'm not sure even of that.

"Now I came into the case in October of 1984. The case was set for trial in November. Interestingly enough, two days before the case is set for trial, a couple of the girl witnesses who denied anything's happened, suddenly come forward and say 'There's something I want to tell you that I haven't told you.' And they corroborate, to some extent, what the Martin boys have said. Now, this Carol Darling denies that there's any causal link between the trial date and the fact that they come forward within two days of the trial date, saying, 'Well, you know, these things don't really go on the trial date . . . you knew there'd be a jury to pick, so you really can't read anything into the fact that. . . .' I think it's a bunch of crap. I think they were looking for more witnesses whom we would not be able to attack as being under the influence of the Martins. I have trouble believing that this was just a coincidence.

"The case gets continued into the middle of December. We started. The Judge decided that we wouldn't get a jury because of the Christmas holiday, and continued the case until right after New Year's. Picking the jury took six or seven weeks, and they led off with a girl named Christine Hays. Although she contradicted herself several times, she wasn't a bad witness. Then they went through various kids, and they all testified that these things happened, every other weekend. Now, there was a wide variance as to when these things supposedly happened. The original allegations were that they happened during a two-year period, when Marcella had visitation with her boys. That period got truncated considerably, depending on which witness you listened to. And some of the witnesses talked about it happening for about a year, some of them talked about it happening for a couple of months, or just a short time. It's real hard to figure out just what's happening.

"All the kids talked about there being lots of people there. They all mentioned six or seven of the defendants. They did not all mention the grandmother. In fact, some of them specifically said the grandmother wasn't there, and a couple of them said Marcella's brother, Wayne Dill, wasn't there. Who was the leader depended on which kid was talking. Some of them said my client, Rick, was. Some of them said Wayne Forsythe was. Some of them said there were these two guys who either didn't have names or sometimes they were called Doug and Steve. They were the leaders. It varied from child to child. Each kid told a different story.

"After the preliminary hearing of Rick, Marcella and Marcella's sister, Colleen, shortly after that, there was another preliminary hearing. That happened, because, after a while, these kids started mentioning other people being involved. This preliminary was Wayne Dill, who's Marcella's brother; Grace Dill, who's her mother; and a woman named Gina Miller. When the kids started talking and expanding the list of who was there, and it became a spectacular orgy, instead of just one or two people doing it once to one kid. Initially, just the one boy said that somebody . . . not even sodomized him but just touched him. Then it just started growing, like bacteria, and going crazy. And they started mentioning other people. Now, Bryan, the youngest boy, also mentioned that he had been molested several years before when he was an extremely little kid, by Wayne Dill, back in Oklahoma, and that he had been burned by his mother, Marcella, with a spoon. They claimed they had records of this. When you go back and look at the records, what the records seem to indicate is that he was burned, but you don't know by whom. Maybe it was a spoon; maybe it was a knife. Tommy, his brother, admitted burning him with a knife or a spoon by accident. He had been playing with a spoon. It was hot. He dropped it and it hit Bryan on the leg. There's a group back in Arkansas called SCAN, I think, that did some sort of an investigation of this, and came up with nothing.

"This, however, the prosecution alluded to several times during the trial, in a way that made it appear that there had been allegations that were sustained. That's not what the record says at all. And they insinuated that Marcella had moved around so that she couldn't be found. None of that was true, but they brought it in front of a jury anyway. It was objected to but we were overruled by Judge Friedman. The kids talked about a Carla being involved. And when they're driven around they point to a Gina Miller as being Carla. They also claim that in June, after Rick and Marcella and Colleen were arrested, and in jail, the Martin boys claim they went to a high school swimming pool, and were confronted by this Doug and Rick, at the pool, in the changing room, sodomized and orally copulated in the changing rooms, with people wandering by, doing nothing about it . . . that they were thrown off diving boards into the pool, in front of the lifeguard, who did nothing. (By the way, the lifeguards were interviewed and this never happened.) And they said they were then taken by Doug and Steve into a car that was being driven by Carla, and that Carla's son, Jed, was in the car, and while they were driving around, Doug and Steve orally copulated and, I think, sodomized them again, and then threatened them and let them out.

"Two of the kids later claimed to have seen Doug and Steve at a gymnastics meet. The cops are called. The cops arrest these two guys, put them in a lineup, and most of the kids can't identify them. Now, interestingly enough, Bryan and Tommy, the two Martin kids who picked them out at the gymnastics meet, one of them identifies them at the lineup, which is not surprising, since he picked them out at the meet. And the other one can't—despite the fact he just picked them out at the gymnastics meet. None of the other kids recognized them at all.

"Now that evidence—the evidence of the swimming pool incident—was ruled inadmissible as to all defendants, except Gina Miller. Because she was the only one engaged in that particular incident. It was ruled tangentially admissible to her, so that her lawyer could go into it, not totally, but in some detail. We were not allowed to go into it at all. That's the same as saying you couldn't impeach the Gonzales kids, with all the satan worship, devil-murder stuff that they came up with later. Anyway, that was the ruling.

"I interviewed Jed, who was Gina Miller's son, who denied any of this took place. He denied any molestation took place. He denied the incident at the swimming pool took place. He denied knowing anybody named Doug and Steve, and barely knew the Martin kids. But we were not allowed to bring him in as a witness because that was all tangential.

"Now, while all these people are in jail, Wayne Forsythe comes to visit Colleen Bennett who's, I guess, his wife. And eventually he gets arrested, and they put on a preliminary hearing with him, and he ends up being joined in trial with us. That becomes important because Wayne Forsythe is a defendant in another child molesting case. The one with Lecain and Jenkins. The prosecution was allowed to bring in our trial a couple of witnesses from that case who testified against Wayne Forsythe that he was involved in a 'ring' that was similar, with Alan Lecain and all those other people. We were not allowed to put on any of the other kids from his case to say none of this was true. Because none of the evidence had come in against us. So all of this evidence came in, with an admonition that it was not to be used against anyone except Wayne Forsythe. Well, you know, that's a lot of crap. Anyway, that was part of the evidence. The Martin boys all told stories that were much more detailed than what they told in the preliminary, with the exception of Johnny Martin, who had already testified three times. They were allowed to testify in a way that it would be impossible to tell whether the incidents they were talking about were the same incidents the others were talking about. In other words, none of the kids was asked what happened on a specific date. None of the kids was asked about a specific time. Each of the kids was, basically, asked, 'Think of a time you remember best, and tell us what happened.' There wasn't any attempt to pin it down in terms of what month, or what day. We asked the kids, and the kids didn't know.

"One kid testified that he snorted a nine-inch line of cocaine that was half an inch wide. That's impossible, as our expert testified. Even an adult would be dead if he did that.

"The kids who 'admitted' being molested were never given physical examinations. The only physical examinations they ordered were on the two girls who denied anything happened. And when you talk about discovery being hidden, in *February* they ordered these examinations. They did not make that discovery available to us until two or three days before the doctor testified, which, I believe, was in June. We believed that they had these examinations, although we didn't have any hard evidence of it. We had made several motions to have the children examined, all of which were denied. And as far as I know, to this day, the kids who said it happened have never been examined.

"Before trial, we had a polygrapher run my client and his wife, then Colleen Bennett and one other defendant. I think it was Grace Dill. They all came up as being truthful when they denied any involvement in any molestation at all. This was a lie detector test. We ran a motion that this should be allowed in as evidence, and we lost. And I assume that'll be taken up on appeal. I don't know.

"There were many contradictions between what each child said earlier and what they said later, in the trial. What I'm talking about is what they said in the initial interviews, and what they eventually said. It was very different. The way the prosecution explained it was: 'It took them a while to open up.'

"One kid said that this happened every other weekend and each kid was given two shots, injections. He said they were lined up on a bed, on their stomachs, given two shots in the behind. Two kids testified that there were no shots. Another kid said there were shots only once and only two or three kids got the shots. And the only way they knew this happened was because the other kids told them there were shots. None of the kids evidenced any show of needle marks or bruising, either at home, according to the parents, or at school, according to their teachers. And we're talking about allegations of these things happening over a period of five or six hours on a Sunday. Kids being sodomized fifteen times, being given shots, being given cocaine, drinking alcohol, smoking marijuana. At least the Martin boys, we had their school records, and there was nothing unusual about their Monday school attendance. In fact, there was better attendance on Mondays than on the other days of the week. The kids said they were sodomized very violently, but there was never any evidence of soreness or anything like that.

"There was supposedly a board there that the kids were tied to, or strapped to. A couple of the kids said they never saw a board. A couple of kids said there was a board but it wasn't used, or was used with only one kid. Christine said there was a board but it was never used on her. One of the other kids said she was put on the board every other weekend. There were inconsistencies from beginning to end.

"Some of the kids said they saw the videotapes afterward, and others said they never saw the videotapes—despite the fact that the first kid said the second kid was there, and the second kid said he never saw the videotape.

"And there were some things they said that were just inherently ridiculous, that couldn't have happened. The kids started off saying these things happened in a certain bedroom in the house. The dimensions of the bedroom were something like nine by eleven [feet], but it was not quite that big. There were several things sticking out from the wall—like a closet in the next room. In that bedroom there was a king-sized bed which everybody agrees was there, and three or four other pieces of furniture. In other words you would have to walk sideways to get through the room, there was so little space. The kids said there were about fifteen kids and fifteen adults in the room at the same time—with a camera on a rolling tripod, or a dolly, with the big wheels. Some of the kids said two tripods. All at one time. I've been in that room. The jury was in the room. It physically could not happen.

"During the course of the interviewing, when the kids first started talking about sexual orgies, they talked about it happening in this one small bedroom. Then, later, things migrated so that it sometimes happened in other rooms. That came much later in the interviewing process, because the investigators realized that all the things these kids were talking about could not have happened, so the kids got led into saying it happened in other rooms.

"Emotionally, the most damaging bit of testimony was this girl who was five years old whose testimony was really bizarre. This was Amanda, the daughter of Colleen. First of all, she was so little she couldn't even see people who were in the courtroom. So she kept saying, 'Where's my mommy? I want to talk to my mommy.' And her mother was in the courtroom. She just couldn't see her, the way the courtroom was set up. Her testimony was ridiculous. She claimed to live in the house where all these things took place. She referred to it as the green house. She had never spent a night there. We verified that through numerous independent witnesses. She claimed that she lived there with her mother, her father, her mother's first husband, her grandmother and two or three other people. And then moved to: her mother never lived there, her grandmother never lived there. *She* never lived there. Her sister never lived there. They didn't live there at all. Who lived there was my client, Ricky, Marcella and Ricky's two daughters. It seemed real clear to me that she was fantasizing living there because it was a stable home. She had been kicked around. She had been the subject of a custody fight. Her father had kidnapped her for a while. The mother kidnapped her back. She was obviously looking for a stable home environment that didn't change, and was normal. She also testified that she was present when all of these people were arrested in the back yard of this house—which wasn't true. She was present when her mother was arrested, but Rick and

Marcella were already in custody. She testified that the person who arrested Rick was the bailiff in the courtroom. She testified that Rick or someone had tried to poison her with a piece of poison candy which she knew was poisoned because it had little speckles in it, but that she wouldn't eat it and it stayed on a table in her bedroom, and that she left it there for two years and then her mother threw it away, after Rick was arrested.

"It was so clearly obvious that none of this was true. She was up there fantasizing, having a good time. But, a couple of times, she said, 'Rick's not here, is he? I don't want Rick to hear this.' Then they brought her off the stand and tried to have her identify the defendants. The defendants were seated behind the attorneys. The first person she sees, she says, 'Oh, I don't know, that's some woman . . . I think she's a friend of my aunt's. I don't know what her name is.' Then she said, 'That woman's my grandmother. Hi, Grandma. How are you?' Then she looks, and it's her uncle, Wayne Dill, and she says, 'I'm not real sure . . .' And then she saw Rick, and she went into hysterics, and started screaming, 'Oh God! It's Rick! Don't let him kill me. Don't let him touch me.' Running around in circles. This little tiny five-year-old voice. Running in front of the jury, screaming bloody murder! 'Don't let him kill me! Oh, God, It's Rick! Help! Help!' The judge tried to get somebody to quiet her down. She wouldn't go with the witness coordinator, she went running up to the judge, grabbed his robe, gasping and hyperventilating and said, 'Don't let him near me! Don't let him kill me!' And then the judge took her behind the courtroom. He forgot even to recess. He just took her back into chambers. We're all sitting there. The jury's sitting there. And he came out about fifteen minutes later and said, 'She's too upset to testify but she'll be back tomorrow. She's a real trooper.' And he said court was dismissed for the day.

"That piece of testimony had more impact than anything else. It was really disturbing because, up to that point, I didn't really care about her testimony. She wasn't believable at all.

"And then they had a doctor, and the doctor testified that he had examined Carol and Lisa Pitts, and that each of them showed signs consistent with being molested. The defendants claim that the doctor substituted, in his testimony, photographs of molested kids, in place of their kids' photographs, based on two facts: number one, because they didn't molest their kids, so the signs couldn't be there, and number two, based on the fact that the older daughter's photograph had much more pubic hair than she actually has. That was their statement to me. I've talked to several reputable doctors in the field whose position is that most doctors, doctors who will examine kids, are likely to find the same evidence. There's damage or there isn't damage. But, they say, this doctor is much quicker to jump to the conclusion that the damage comes from molestation rather than any other cause. I wanted to have another doctor listen to this doctor's testimony and then help in cross-examination, but we weren't able to do that.

"Another thing this doctor does that's somewhat in dispute . . . he uses a thing called a colposcope, and it's basically a magnifying glass with a light. My understanding is it was developed in Brazil in the sixties or seventies. It was developed as a tool to see whether women were virgins, because in a strongly Catholic country, people don't want to marry non-virgins. There is a debate in the scientific community—not as to whether the colposcope works for what it was designed to do, but as to whether it has any value at all in examining kids. I made an objection to any testimony given with regard to the colposcope without laying a foundation that it's accepted in the scientific community. That was *before* I knew that it wasn't accepted in the scientific community. That was, of course, overruled. Courts let in all sorts of stuff that is supposedly expert testimony that just does not have any scientific validity. There's supposed to be all sorts of foundational evidence that comes in before new procedures and new techniques get utilized. One of the great examples of it is the old powder burns. For years the paraffin test was used and considered really good evidence. And it turns out that it's totally worthless.

"I have a lot of problems with the kids' testimony. Too many things that just don't jibe. All of the kids. The defendants, during the entire course of the trial, all of them, never gave one hint of being guilty. Not once! There were a couple of them who were given really good offers to testify against the others. They said, 'How can I do it? I don't have anything to tell you.' That's certainly inconsistent with guilt. And a couple of them who were offered the deals . . . the lawyers who represented them would have told them enough about the benefits of doing what they had to do, to get around any resistance they might have had. And the lawyers would rather not have been sitting there for seven months. I don't think any of us wanted to sit there for seven months. I sure didn't. In other words, if they had any information to give, they would almost certainly have made a deal and testified against the others.

"Another thing. The kids' stories become more and more embellished, more and more spectacular as time went by. Murders and cannibalism. One would think that they would talk about that earlier—that that would make a bigger impression on them, more than the other things. The way these things expand and migrate is not logical.

"I have a secondary problem. I don't have kids. I don't like kids. I'm never around kids. I particularly avoid kids, and I avoided kids when I was a kid. And it may be that kids think like this and I don't know because I'm never around kids. But I don't think so.

"Let me tell you a brief story and then I'm going to have to go. There was somebody who was a potential juror in our case who was excused, early in the jury-selection process, because she said she couldn't possibly be fair. She liked kids too much. She worked with kids. She was a teacher. So she gets excused for cause. Later on— maybe a month or two later—she called me, saying that she needed to talk to me and could we go out and have a drink together. We did, and she told me a teacher she knew had been accused of molestation. And she asked me what type of thing she might be doing with the kids that, if given the wrong interpretation, would put her at risk. She'd never thought about it before, but she was now very concerned, about touching the kid, being affectionate with the kid, being supportive and positive toward the kids, because this could be misinterpreted. And what should she do, in terms of her actions with the kids, to make sure that this didn't happen.

"I think that that's an unbelievably sad commentary on our society, because, although I don't like kids and don't want to be near them, I think that, when you have somebody that really does like kids and wants to be with them, and teaches kids and wants to help them, to make it difficult and dangerous for them, and to deter them, is really a tragedy, because, I think, predatory child molesters are not deterred. It doesn't matter how draconic the laws are, those people are not deterred. It's to a large extent a sickness, or a misorientation, which is what I prefer to call it. And they're attracted to kids, and you can tell them they're going to be put away for the rest of their lives, and it's really not going to deter any of them.

"But the people you deter are the people you really want to be with kids. And so what ends up happening is that this type of draconic law—and not just the penalties, but the whole scheme—what ends up happening is counterproductive, because you drive away and scare off people who really want to be with kids and really like kids, but who are afraid. And you don't scare off the people who are predatory child molesters. And so you end up with a higher percentage of child molesters than you had before. The overall number of them remains the same. But the overall number of good people diminishes. And I think that's a real tragedy. Children should come into the world loved and supported, and the people who want to do that are being scared off."

"They've gone crazy here," Jackie Nokes told us. "There's a man in the city jail charged with child molestation. He's a paraplegic. There's another one they arrested for molestation. He was wounded in Viet Nam. He has no genitals." We met another Bakersfield woman who told us that she had been charged with molestation. She is an epileptic. When she denied the accusation, C.P.S. workers told her, "You don't remember. You molested your child while you were having an epileptic seizure." The county has taken away two of her children and had them adopted. She is pregnant, and they intend to take away her baby when it is born.

"If you really want to get to the bottom of this thing," Jackie told me, "check out the Henrietta Weill Child Guidance Center. That's where they interview all these kids."

There are numerous other purported child molestation cases pending in Kern County, too numerous and too lengthy for inclusion in this book, with compelling evidence of flagrant misconduct on the part of prosecutors, judges, law enforcement officials and C.P.S. workers.

VIII

Montessori

"We Need More Victims"

Claudia Krikorian is owner of two pre-schools in the South Bay suburb of Los Angeles County. In April, 1984, accusations of molestation were made by the police and the Department of Social Services. She has been involved in lengthy court battles to keep her schools open, after court action by the D.S.S. to close them down. I spoke with Krikorian on two occasions, and this is what she told me:

"On April 30, 1984, I received a telephone call from the Lomita sheriff's officer saying she wanted to meet with me. I didn't know what it was about, but I did go to the station. And she took me in a little room, and there was no one else present, so no one else heard our conversation, unfortunately, and it wasn't taped. And she told me about the allegation and I was really shocked. The allegation was that there was sexual molestation at my Rolling Hills school. She said that one of my teachers had shown children pornographic pictures, and perhaps fondled the child. She didn't tell me who made the accusation, but I guessed. First of all, it was a woman who had two children so that narrowed it down a lot. Her child had been in the school for not even one month. She'd been there for three weeks, and the child had exhibited on the playground some unusual behavior. She would always wear very short little dresses that wouldn't cover even her underpants. And she was obsessed with her body. We'd find her putting sand into her panties and then accusing other kids of doing it. She would climb up to the top of the slide and then say, 'I can't come down. Somebody will look at my panties.'

"So we contacted the parents on October fourth, and told them, 'We don't want to make a big issue of it but perhaps the problem would be lessened if she could wear long pants to school—like maybe cords or something . . .' And the mother said, 'Oh, don't worry. She's acting this way because she was molested, just last August.' And she's just telling us this, and I thought this was pretty strange, because that's important information when you're first admitting a child. Anyway, that hit me when I was sitting in the sheriff's office, and I said, 'By chance is it Mrs. So-and-so?' and the sheriff said, 'Well, yes, it is.' And I said, 'Well, I really feel I should fill you in on a little bit of background. The reason I was able to guess who it was out of all these families is because we were the ones who contacted the mother and told her the child was exhibiting some strange behavior.'

"And the sheriff said, 'Well we're aware of that. She has accused a Sunday school teacher of molestation. She's made other accusations.' So I said, 'I think you should handle this very delicately,' because in light of the McMartin hysteria that was going on at the time, 'I think you should handle this with great care.' She told me she wanted a list of every child who had attended a Christmas arts and crafts program where this particular employee had worked, at our school. And she ordered me not to tell anyone of our conversation, and I said, 'Not even my husband?' and she said, 'Not your husband. Not anyone. And be back in my office tomorrow morning at eight a.m.' And I said, 'Well I don't know . . . I think it's very unusual that you're telling me not to tell anyone about this.' She has no authority to tell me what I can say to my husband. And I'm not getting very good feelings about this.

"So then she said to me that she had proof that the man had been showing pornographic material. And she said she had been investigating it for over a month, before she contacted me. On March 27 she had received the allegation, and it wasn't until April 30 that she notified me. So, then, I got really mad. I said, 'Do you mean to tell me that you're holding evidence of molestation for a month, and that this teacher has been there, and you haven't done anything to insure the safety of the kids? You mean to tell me that you're convinced that he's guilty and you haven't even been at my school! I've never seen your face. I've been there every day. You've never had anyone undercover putting surveillance on him! This is disgraceful! I have to let him go immediately if you're holding proof.'

"She wouldn't show me the proof, by the way, because, she said, there was an investigation pending. But she said, 'Although I can't reveal to you what my evidence is, but I have it!' She was lying to me. Not one piece of pornography was found. She never had one piece of evidence. Nothing.

"So, when she said she was holding evidence, I said, 'Well I'm going to have to let this man go, because I can't jeopardize the safety of my kids.' And then she put her finger in my face and she said, 'You will not!' She said, 'We need more victims.'

" 'We need more victims.' That's what she said! I said, 'Well, I'm sorry but that is out of the question. And I'm appalled that you've known about this for a month, and now you're telling me to keep him!' I said, 'I'm sorry but I'm not going to jeopardize the kids' safety for the sake of your case.' And she said that if I interfered with the police investigation, she would have me arrested. So she started threatening me. So I left and I contacted my husband. And immediately we got an attorney. I went in the next morning at eight o'clock like she said, with my attorney—and she was angry! In fact, she testified in court that she had told me not to tell anyone. And she testified in court that if I had not had anything to hide, then I would not have needed an attorney. My attorney wanted to find out what was going on, and she told him basically the same thing, that she had evidence, and for them to continue their investigation, I had to retain this individual. And my attorney said, No, that's not possible, unless you want to assume all liability and you want to put somebody in to watch, we're not going to assume that kind of responsibility. And she said, 'Well, we can't do that, but he is not to know about this investigation.'

"Well, my attorney said he didn't want to antagonize her. He realized what kind of person he was dealing with, and he said we would see what we can work out. He said, 'Let's schedule a meeting for two o'clock.' And we called in the head of the Montessori

Teacher Training Institute, under whom I had hired this employee. He was a teaching intern. So we scheduled a meeting for two o'clock with the deputy and the heads of the Montessori Teacher Training Institute, in my attorney's office. And at that time I was supposed to turn over the list of all the names and addresses and phone numbers of the children who had attended the Christmas arts and crafts program. And I didn't feel good about doing that, because that's confidential information. I'm not at liberty to give out the names and addresses of my students.

"So we went back at two o'clock and we tried to devise a scheme to assist her, because she was threatening me with arrest, and he, the teacher, couldn't know that he was under investigation. I thought perhaps we could remove him from the school without his becoming aware of it. So I gave him work to do. I said—because I believed in his innocence, and I believed that they would discover his innocence, and it would all be cleared up. I gave him two weeks. I said, 'Moson, I want you to take two weeks. You've got papers to do to complete your written portion of your teacher training program. I want you to take time to complete those papers, and you will be paid in full.' And he was so happy. He said, 'Oh, thank you so much! I really appreciate it.' It was nearing June. I said, 'Complete your papers, and take the two weeks. I'm going to be trying out a new intern for next year.' So, the next day, he arrived back at school, with his three-year-old son, who was a student at my school, a darling little boy. I think if he had been guilty he would have known something was up. He would have known. But he didn't. And he said, 'Gee, thanks for your generosity.' And he said, 'Part of doing a teacher's training program is that you have to observe ten schools, and you have to do a write-up on your observations.' And he said, that morning that he brought his son in, 'I've made appointments for three schools this morning. I'll be going to three schools to do my observation.' And my mind is going, 'Oh my God! She's got evidence that he's molesting children. I can't have him around children!' So I called my attorney, and my attorney said, 'Listen, he's got to know. First of all, the guy has a right to know. Secondly, now that you know, you have liability too.' So my attorney advised him, 'I would advise you to get yourself an attorney, and for your own sake, do not be around children.' He

notified him, and he told him. Even after he told him, I continued
to see him because I believed that he was innocent.

"He was devastated. And when the police found out that my attorney had told him, oh! it was terrible. They went to his [Moson's]
apartment and they arrested him. They handcuffed him and they
took his three-year-old son away and put him in a foster home.

"But I have to tell you how they did that, because it's so cruel.
He and his wife are divorced, but they have a very amicable relationship. And they share all responsibilities for their son. They live
close to one another. She's a C.P.A., and he was an intern teacher,
and the son would come to school with him. And in the evening
they would have dinner, and the son would stay with the mother,
and in the morning he would pick him up. So they did get along
very well, although they weren't married.

"So, when they arrested Moson and took him off to jail, they
called his ex-wife and said, 'You can come and bail him out.' And
immediately she said, 'Oh, my God,' and she left her work to bail
him out. Well, his son—since she had been notified that he
couldn't come to my school anymore—was at the Montessori
school in Culver City, where he had attended before Moson
started working for me. And while the wife had come to bail him
out of jail, the police went to Culver City to kidnap his son from
school. They snatched him. And they told the school owner that
they had been sent there by the boy's mother because she was detained, and that they were going to bring him to her. They kept her
in questioning for quite some time, and they said, 'You know, your
husband's been molesting your son,' and she said, 'You're crazy!
We've had our difficulties, and we're not married, but you're nuts!
He's a wonderful father. He's a great person. There's no way!' And
they said to her, 'Well, you're trying to cover up for him. You're
going to lose custody of your kid.' That's what they said! Unless she
would acknowledge that he was molesting their son, and allow the
son to be taken for a medical exam, and psychological exam, they
were going to take him away.

"So what they did is they took her son away, and they examined
him and—thank God—he didn't have anything—not even minute
things. Maybe he hadn't been constipated, thank God! He was a
very stable little boy. You know, there are some kids that will fold

under that kind of pressure and questioning, but not this one. He is very strong, very together little kid. So what they did, when they found nothing . . . they put him in a foster home. For five days the parents didn't know where the son was. They couldn't communicate with him. They were hysterical. They had a really close relationship with the son. They weren't the kind of parents that just leave him with anybody. They were really good parents. And they couldn't find out where he was, but they knew that the police had taken him away. The police said they had put him in a foster home for his own protection.

"So Moson was released from jail on five thousand dollars bail. He was destroyed! He knew he could never work in the school again. Criminal charges were never filed, to this day. So I guess he's just going to have to wait out the statute of limitations. Now, just in the last two or three weeks, the Department of Social Services is threatening to take his son away. And Moson could never be alone with his son. He had to be in someone else's presence. But now they've lifted that. He has complete custody of his son. And yet, they closed the school down. Charges were never filed. They closed the pre-school portion of my Rolling Hills School. They have no jurisdiction over my elementary school portion. They closed the pre-school.

"And then the Department of Social Services, because I was fighting it, they offered to settle with me. Before we even went to trial for an administrative hearing. That's the catch—they can hold an administrative hearing without there even being any charges. So, before we went to court, the Department of Social Services contacted my attorney and said, 'What will it take to settle with your client?' And he said, 'Well, don't jeopardize her license and you've got a deal.' And they said, 'Well that's all take and no give.' And he said, 'Well I don't know what you want.' And they said, 'Sell the school, and stay away from it.' And they would give me time to sell it to somebody else. Without any evidence that I'd ever done anything. And I said, 'No way.'

"And by this time I had received nine lawsuits, by parents. The profit motive. In a pre-school you have to have a million dollars liability insurance per child. And they know that. So anyway, I wouldn't settle with the Department of Social Services. I said, 'Look, I'm either guilty or I'm not guilty. And I'm not guilty. And

I'm not going to sell, and I'm not going to make someone else director of the school. I intend to go back to work on Monday.' And they said, 'Fine, we'll see you in court.' So we went to court and we had the full-blown hearing. And one child testified that she had been molested. For months she had said that she wasn't, but after going and going and going so many times for questioning, she couldn't handle the pressure any more, and she said what they wanted her to say. She said that she was molested, but she said that she was molested out on the grassy area right in front of the school, and that we were all too busy and that we didn't notice! Right in front of all the classrooms. And she said the teachers saw this but were all too busy and didn't notice or do anything about it, while she was being raped, vaginally. Well, the doctor gets on the stand and says that she's been sodomized at least eight to ten times. This is Dr. Carol Berkowitz. She's from Harbor General, the home of Dr. Summit. She says all of the kids have been molested, every single one of them that she examines. Everyone in the world has been molested.

"So the child, under cross-examination . . . my attorney said, 'Do you know this lady?' and she said, 'Yes,' and she was giggling and waving to me. She had always liked me. And she said I was a nice lady. And my attorney said, 'Moson didn't really put anything in your vagina, like you said, did he?' And she said, 'No.' And he said, 'I bet a lot of people told you to say that, didn't they?' and she said, 'Yes,' and he said, 'And I'll bet they even brought you presents, didn't they?' and she said, 'Yeah!' and she grinned and giggled, because they gave her a doll, and stuff like that.

"And then the Judge, Judge Rosalyn Chapman, she ruled that the child had been molested! The doctor said she was sodomized, the child said she was raped vaginally, the whole thing was just incredible! So we filed an appeal. We're going to go back to court. But it's so costly it's really not worth doing. We're just doing it because you just can't let them get away with doing a thing like that.

"And then you know what happened when we refused to settle with the Department of Social Services? The attorney for the Department of Social Services said to my attorney, 'We're going after Krikorian's throat.' That was Ron Pearson. He said he was going for my throat. And shortly after that they filed papers to close my Torrance school down. And you can't just close a school down unless you have a real strong reason, so they said that my director of my Torrance school, John—he's been teaching there for twelve years—outstanding reputation and an incredible following—he had been the director of my school at Torrance, and they made an allegation against him! Of course, he's the only male at my Torrance school. He was never arrested. He was never charged. And he's been ordered by the judge never to set foot in my school. Because the state took us to court and tried to get us closed down. And a Superior Court judge overruled it, and gave us a preliminary injunction keeping the state from closing us down. And so the state took us to the appellate court. And the appellate court said no, we're not going to take this case. You've been ordered by the Superior Court judge to leave it alone.

"So my Torrance school is still operating and has an incredible waiting list of people still wanting to get in. We finished the administrative hearing a few weeks ago, and we will be getting the results of that in December. But the judge's finding has been ordered sealed by the Superior Court judge.

"The state wanted to have closed circuit television for the kids, but according to the California law, you have to have proof that the child is terrified of the defendant. But there was never any evidence that any child was afraid of me. They didn't want any children to testify in front of me because they knew the children would be less inclined to tell these wild stories in front of me. They didn't want them to testify in front of me, and Judge Lopez said, 'Okay I will allow the child to testify on closed circuit television.' And my attorney said, 'Wait a minute! You can't just arbitrarily say that! They don't meet any of the criteria in the closed circuit law.' The judge said, 'I can be as creative as I want. I can make up any new law that I want.' In an administrative hearing they have that kind of freedom. So we took a writ of mandate over to Superior Court, and the judge decided that he would not rule on it at that point. He said, 'I'm not going to rule on this matter now. What I want the judge to do is go on and finish hearing the case, and order his decision sealed, and it will be sent to me, at which time we will have a hearing on December tenth for the legality of the closed circuit T.V.' And if the judge rules us guilty, we are to lose our license. They've never even charged me with any criminal acts. They're just destroying me administratively.

"I intend to file civil actions, and yet it's very difficult, when we've had a hearing and we were found guilty. I first have to file my appeal, which we have, and then I have to win that appeal. And if I don't, we just have to file another appeal. We just have to keep going. You can't let them get away with that kind of outrage. But in the last year and a half I've spent over a hundred twenty-five thousand dollars on attorneys' fees. How far can you go? I just cannot believe that people don't see what's happening. People keep saying, 'Yeah, but what about the medical evidence?' They keep saying that. The strongest medical evidence they have is that the doctor says, 'This child has been molested.' But the symptoms they have are exactly the same as you would see if the child has been riding a bike or a trike. And it is nothing unusual for young children to masturbate too. I mean, they're very preoccupied with that when they're little. They're very curious. And so, there are so many things that it could be. And that's their strongest evidence. Out of twelve hundred cases—I'm talking about all the preschools, not just mine, but McMartin, Manhattan Ranch,* all of those. The strongest evidence that they have is the same as a child would have if he were constipated, or had a little rash or an itch. That's all they have.

"And yet they say, 'Oh, but we have got medical evidence.' And so the public buys it. And they say, 'Okay so they've got medical evidence. How can you deny that?' They also examine the kid after they've been told that he's been molested, and they say, 'History of molestation,' and 'Examination is consistent with molestation.' Which means nothing.

"We're going to continue fighting until the money runs out. We're going to keep fighting. You can't let them get away with that."

It is interesting to note that the children in Krikorian's administrative hearing also told of witnessing the murder of infants and the mutilation of animals. Their testimony was full of inconsistencies and contradictions. One said she was never molested. The judge threw out all testimony of one five-year-old girl because, he said, he couldn't distinguish what was fact and what was fantasy in the

*See Chapter IX

child's testimony. She had said that all the teachers and students watched the killings of infants at the school. Another child said a teacher had touched her ". . . and he said he would take my cat away."

The mother of one of the child witnesses told the court that Dr. Carol Berkowitz, head of the pediatric clinic at Harbor Medical Center, had said that she found signs that her daughter had been "fully penetrated in both [vaginal and anal] areas no less than eight to ten times," and that it was "recent . . . two to three months prior to the exam."

Krikorian's attorney, David Allen, pointed out that the child had left the school more than a year prior to the doctor's examination. In cross-examining the mother, Allen elicited the fact that she had at first told the police that a neighbor had molested her daughter.

"The girl never said anything until months of interrogation by police and the D.S.S.," Allen said. "It's an incredible example of pressure tactics used on a small child to get her to say what they wanted to hear."

IX

Ruby

"Only One Is Still Alive"

Michael Ruby was sixteen when he took a part-time job as a teacher's aide at Manhattan Ranch Pre-school in Manhattan Beach, California. He needed money for repairs on his Volkswagen. He was placed in the job by his high school job counselor, who described him as a good kid, a typical California teenager who surfed and played football. He taught at the school during the 1983–84 school year.

On July 25, 1984, he was arrested and charged with molesting two five-year-old girls and a six-year-old boy. One child said that Ruby performed sexual acts while standing on his head, and orally copulated himself. Another child stated that Ruby equipped the entire class with diving equipment and took them down a manhole, through underground tunnels to the ocean, after sodomizing him, urinating on him and threatening to kill him. There were also allegations by the children that he molested them in a haunted house.

The first complaint was made by the wife of a police officer. The woman said her son had told her that "Mr. Mike" had treated him meanly, had placed him in a trash can and had hung him from a tree. The boy asked his father to beat Ruby up and kill him. The mother reported this to the Department of Social Services. D.S.S.

sent an investigator who concluded the allegations were "unfounded."

The mother took her son to the Manhattan Beach Police Department, where she received a warmer reception. He was interviewed by Detective Patty Picker, who was also prominent in the investigation of the McMartin case. Picker stated in her report that the boy told her that Ruby had molested him in a teachers' restroom, and that he molested other children and took pictures of them. The child was sent to be interviewed by Dr. Cheryl Kent, a psychologist who had interviewed a number of children allegedly molested at the McMartin Pre-school. A physician at Martin Luther King Hospital examined the child and found no evidence of sexual abuse.

On July 10 police received a call from the mother of a five-year-old girl. She believed the child had been molested at the pre-school. The mother arranged an appointment with Dr. Kent. According to police reports the child named five teachers who molested the children and took photographs of them. Dr. Carol Berkowitz, a child abuse expert at Harbor General, examined her and reported that her anus was "abnormal" and "consistent with sexual abuse."

An arrest warrant was issued for Ruby, and a search warrant for Ruby's home, the homes and cars of seven of the school's teachers, and for the school. Detective Jane Hoag, also prominent in the McMartin case, stated, "I have formed an expert opinion that Michael David Ruby is a pedophile."

On July 25, late in the afternoon, Michael Ruby left the school on his bicycle and headed for his home. A police officer pulled him over and threw his bicycle into the trunk of the car. They read him his Miranda rights and told him he was being arrested for child molesting. "I was scared to death," Ruby said. He was taken to the police station and booked. Ruby was told that he could refuse to answer questions, but he said, "No, I want to get this straightened out." When he was told of the allegations, he said, "This is crazy!"

"There is never enough time for that," Ruby told the police. "I'm never alone with the kids," He was at the school for only two and a half hours each day. He also stated that he was a virgin and had never had sex with anyone.

Michael Ruby was driven to a juvenile detention facility. On the

way, he said, the officers insulted him and told him horror stories
about how accused child molesters are treated in jail. When he
arrived at Juvenile Hall he was told by members of the staff there
that he would be "hung up by his balls." He said there were inmates there who wanted to kill him and that, several times, he had
to run for his life.

"When they searched the school they seized all the children's
records," Carolyn Elliott told me. She was the owner of Manhattan
Ranch. "We had no emergency information. The police began calling parents of the children who attended the school, definitely trying to instigate complaints of molestation. That's their typical pattern in all these cases. They seize the records and get the addresses
and telephone numbers of the parents and they start contacting
them. In McMartin they sent a letter, but in our case they got
smarter. They telephoned everybody! They told everybody they
believed they had reason to believe the children had been molested. They told everybody they were sure Michael was guilty. Of
all the searches they made, they came up with nothing."

According to Ruby, Superior Court Judge Benjamin Aranda offered him a deal. If he would plead guilty to one count for each of
the accusing children, he would get a light sentence at California
Youth Authority. The judge told Ruby that he had sentenced five
people to prison for child molestation "and only one is still alive."

He decided to take his chances with a jury. "I couldn't say I did
something I didn't do." Ruby's bail was set at $500,000. And the
school was closed by order of D.S.S.

It is interesting to note that the police made no effort to remove
Ruby from the school at the time of the first complaint, and in fact
he continued teaching there for another three months, until the
time of his arrest. His court-appointed attorneys subjected him to
interrogations as aggressive as those of the police. He was
unshakable. He said, "There's nothing I can tell you because I
didn't do anything."

The preliminary hearing began on November 29. The seven-
year-old boy said that Ruby had sodomized him, urinated on him
and told him he would be killed if he talked. The second witness
was not called, and the prosecutor, Lisa Hart, hotly denied it was
because his lack of creditability would have undermined the case.
A five-year-old girl told the court that Ruby had raped her and

forced her to orally copulate him. When she left the stand she walked to Michael Ruby and asked him his name.

The seven children told of the alleged sex acts in a perfunctory manner, without any apparent feeling, and the tales of the manhole and the haunted house were received with skepticism by nearly everybody. Yet Ruby was bound over for trial and the judge made the children's stories the basis of additional charges. Ruby now faced a total of thirty-five counts.

"I know where the manhole is," Judge Aranda said. As for the haunted house, "The way he described it was so graphic and so definitive that to have ignored it would have been to say I didn't believe him at all." Deputy District Attorney Lisa Hart was pleased with the children's testimony. "The kids were very, very brave," she said.

The question everyone was asked was: Why were none of the other teachers named by the children charged along with Ruby. Lisa Hart said they were still under active investigation. Ruby's attorney said, "The district attorney's office realizes what it has on Michael Ruby is garbage, and what it has on any other teacher is not any better." He also said that the additional twenty counts the judge had added put the original charges in perspective "because molesting in a manhole is as absurd as molestation at the pre-school."

Ruby was ordered to stand trial June 3 before Superior Court Judge Edward A. Hinz, Jr., but before that, the prosecutor asked for a hearing on her motion to close the courtroom for the trial, allowing the public and media to view the proceedings on closed circuit television monitors, a strategy that would have the effect of making Ruby seem like a dangerous maniac. But after hearing the testimony, the judge denied the motion, saying there was not sufficient cause to hold the trial in separate rooms.

In July, the trial was postponed because the judge stated it would not be likely to conclude before his vacation. The case was transferred to the court of Judge Bob T. Hight. The same week, a letter was sent out to many families by the Sheriff's Task Force, urging them to bring their children in to be interviewed—even if they had denied being molested. "This investigation goes farther than just those who have been formally charged thus far . . ." the

letter said. Lt. Richard Willey, head of the task force, said the response to the letter was good.

Lisa Hart refiled her motion to close the courtroom and place
the media and spectators in a separate room with closed circuit television. Judge Hight denied the motion, and the trial was postponed until August eighth.

It took two weeks and a pool of 300 prospective jurors before the
attorneys agreed on a panel of 12 and 6 alternates. A mother
testified that she had taken her daughter to a pediatrician for a vag-
inal infection. The doctor reprimanded the girl for not wiping
properly and prescribed a cortisone cream. He had done the same
with another girl who also testified she was molested by Ruby.

One girl testified that Ruby did it out on the playground. Another said she felt, but didn't see, Ruby touch her. "My friends
said he did it," the girl said. Ruby's attorney asked another girl if
she remembered better now what happened to her in the kindergarten a year and a half ago than when she testified last November
in the preliminary hearing. The girl said yes. He asked if that was
because she had talked to Hart at least five times, and to officers
Picker, Hoag and Noble, to Sheriff's Task Force officer Susan
McGirt, therapist Cheryl Kent and Michelle Dugan. She said yes.
Another child was asked, Do you remember Manhattan Ranch.
She said Yes. Then: Do you remember what anyone said or did
there? She said no.

There were many contradictions in the testimony. One girl who
had said Ruby stuck a foreign object into her rectum, changed her
story and said he stuck it into her genitals. The second witness admitted she had not told Detective Hoag the truth during her initial
interview. The six-year-old girl who had said that Ruby touched
her genitals now said he only touched her "behind."

The prosecutor called Dr. Gail Goodman, a University of
Denver psychologist who described herself as the country's fore-
most expert on children's eyewitness testimony. Goodman sol-
emnly told the court: "If you ask children what happened virtually
everything they tell you will be correct." McCabe contemptuously
cross-examined Goodman and read from a *Psychology Today* article she had co-authored, which stated: "We have altered people's
memories. We can get people to tell us that red lights are green

. . . memory is easy to manipulate." Finally, he asked her if she had read about the Salem Witch Hunt, and if she knew of the role of children in the 1692 hysteria that led to the deaths of more than twenty people branded as witches. "Are you aware that it was children making the claims of witchcraft when people were tried and executed in Salem, Massachussetts?" he asked. Goodman said she believed this was caused by tainted rye bread. Asked if he would bring in an expert to refute her testimony, McCabe replied, "It wouldn't take an expert."

A Los Angeles psychiatrist, Dr. Frank Williams, testified that Michael Ruby "unequivocally and absolutely does not fit the profile of an adolescent who would molest children." He said that pedophiles are always lonely and socially isolated . . . they have next to no friends and that the friends they have are usually much younger. He also stated that they don't usually participate in sports or in social groups. "I'd say this describes about one hundred percent." Williams is director of family and child psychiatry at Cedars-Sinai Medical Center.

Perhaps the most interesting testimony was that of Dr. Carol Berkowitz, a pediatrician at County Harbor General Hospital. Berkowitz testified that she had examined one of the child witnesses and said that her findings were "consistent with sexual abuse." During cross-examination, McCabe asked the pediatrician if she ever reported findings "inconsistent with sexual abuse." Berkowitz said she never used those words "because there are no findings inconsistent with sexual abuse."

(This is extremely important because Dr. Berkowitz is saying, in effect, that there is no finding inconsistent with sexual abuse, that ANYTHING or NOTHING can be diagnosed as evidence of sexual abuse if the physician is under pressure to come up with these findings.)

Dr. Lee Coleman was called to testify as an expert witness for the defense. He said that "Leading and suggestive questions, cross-germination, repeated questioning and so forth can be used to confuse a child so that eventually they are not able in their own mind to distinguish what they actually remember from their own recollection versus what adults have suggested or outright told them happened." He blamed such techniques for starting "a nationwide wave of hysteria in which innocent people have been accused." In Los Angeles County, he said, the hysteria can be blamed on the McMartin case and Children's Institute International, where most of the McMartin children were evaluated by Kee McFarlane and others.

"Next in responsibility," he said, "is the Los Angeles County district attorney's office, which was absolutely, outrageously irresponsible to have seen the videotapes of what Kee McFarlane and her colleagues were doing and still proceed. Also very high on the list is the media. How the hell could you all have seen what C.I.I. was doing with the kids and not recognize it and educate the public? It's because the media are more interested in the Dracula-type stuff. The truth is less interesting than the bull." Coleman stated that even the medical evidence described by pediatricians in the McMartin hearing and the Ruby trial is "phony."

In an interview with the news media he said, "I'm sure they don't like what I have to say, because the prosecutors in Los Angeles are about to be exposed as being involved in one of the most outrageous hoaxes the country has ever seen." Mental health professionals and others, he said, "are training children to believe they've been molested. . . . The McMartin case, the Ruby case and the Montessori case are all a total hoax. There's not one thread of evidence that one child has been molested at any of them."

Deputy District Attorney Lisa Hart, in her closing argument, asked the jurors to look at the contradictory testimony of the children as pieces in a jigsaw puzzle. "Sometimes you can see what the picture is without all the pieces." McCabe began his argument by dismantling the testimony, piece by piece. He reminded the jury of the girl's statement that she remembered the events at the kindergarten better now than a year ago because about eleven people helped her remember. McCabe asked the jurors to consider the fact that there were no videotapes, audio recordings or even written notes from the questioning of the five girls by detectives Jane Hoag and Patty Picker. "It wouldn't be proper to say they didn't use tape because they didn't want anyone to know what they said. But because they didn't use tape, you can't see what was said."

Calling the jurors' attention to the last child to testify, the district attorney's star witness, he said the six-year-old girl was absolute proof that the children were programmed into making their accusations. "Her testimony was the big event of the trial. She

showed you how a child can make up a story. She knew what she
was supposed to say and she said it." He referred to a story the girl
had told from the witness stand—that Ruby had fondled her and
four others in a playhouse on the kindergarten playground—and
then recanted after lunch, saying it didn't happen. "She told you
something in the morning and, if the case had ended at noon, you
would have believed it. But it was complete fiction. She made up
the whole thing. That was five felony counts right there in the playhouse. And not one of them happened. . . . You know absolutely
that those children were manipulated. You saw it done."

The jury deliberated for three weeks and then announced they
were hopelessly deadlocked. Judge Hight declared a mistrial. The
charges were dropped after the prosecution told the judge that the
parents of the five child witnesses did not want their children put
through the agony of a new trial.

"I don't believe that," Carolyn Elliott told me. "The kids all told
two different stories. If they had another trial they'd have each kid
telling three different stories. They just didn't have a case."

I asked her if she would try to reopen her school, now that the
charges had been dropped. "No," she said. "I have no intention of
ever doing that again."

I talked with Lee Coleman shortly after that. "The mental health
professionals," he said, "the people who are doing this, and en-
dorse these techniques, are now entrenched in police agencies, the
justice system and the mental health establishment. It will be years
before we can root them out."

X

Sacramento Snuff

More Satanic Rituals

In 1982, Gary Arthur Dill was managing the El Torito restaurant in Carmichael, California, and, among his employees were three men, Veryl Baker, a waiter, Rolando Cuevas, a bartender, and Alan Arbuckle, a waiter. Mr. Dill was married and had four young children, the youngest of whom was a boy named Bryan, about twenty months old. His other children were Heather, about eight, Erica, about nine, and a third daughter, Jenifer, six.

In 1983, Dill and his family moved to Fresno, and while they were there, Dill decided to separate from his wife, and moved out. At this time there was no indication of any problem with the children or the family, other than the fact that Mr. Dill and his wife did not get along particularly well. Sometime after that, about December of 1983, Mrs. Dill moved to Vallejo to live with her mother for economic reasons, since she no longer had the support of Mr. Dill. Her mother was Doris Bell, known to the children as "Grandma Bell."

In December of 1983, Dill was living with Mr. Holman, another employee, who also was charged in the case. The five men charged in the case were Gary Dill, John Holman, Veryl Baker, Rolando Cuevas and Alan Arbuckle.

The next significant event was on April 22 of 1984. The children were cleaning up the house and one of them came to Mrs. Bell and said, "Erica's not helping. She's humping Bryan." Grandma Bell got together with Erica and talked to her for several hours and got from her a statement that she learned about this sort of thing from her father, and that her father had been "doing things" to her. Mrs. Bell then began questioning the other Dill children. It turned out later, in testimony, that the older children denied that any molest had occurred, that the youngest daughter, Jenifer, became the leader in the "disclosures," and the other children were browbeaten into agreeing with her. Mrs. Bell kept a journal of her questioning.

A month to six weeks after she had begun questioning the children, and had done so continuously, almost daily in long sessions as long as four hours, she reported to a social worker in Solano County that the children had been molested. That was in June, 1984. That information was relayed to the Vallejo Police Department, and then on to the Sacramento Police Department, where Officer Robert Humphrey was assigned to the case.

In June 1984, Gary Dill and John Holman were taken into custody. They were brought to Sacramento from Campbell, where they had been living, and questioned by Sergeant Humphrey of the Sheriff's Department, and were released. A decision was made, either by Sergeant Humphrey or someone in the District Attorney's office, that there was not sufficient evidence to prosecute the case. There is some evidence that they had serious doubts about Mrs. Bell's credibility.

Mrs. Bell consulted a psychologist near Vallejo, took some psychological tests, and elicited an opinion from this man that she was "capable of being credible." She had a social worker from Solano County take the children to a Dr. Corwin in Orinda and had them interviewed by the doctor on videotape. She then wrote to John Van de Kamp, the attorney general, complaining of the lack of action from the Sacramento County District Attorney's Office, and asking him to do something about it.

She also commenced an investigation of her own, looking for, among other things, the house with the basement where the alleged molestations had occurred. She found a house which, she thought, fit the description, and she found, by checking documents in the county recorder's office, that it was owned by a man with the name Virgil Dove, and she thought that Veryl might be the diminutive, or nickname, for Virgil. She believed she had found the right house.

According to her own autobiography, Mrs. Bell had been molested when she was about five years old, by a brother, and she had never found any means, inside or outside her family to resolve this dilemma. There was no one she could talk to, no one she could ask to do anything about it. She apparently had a great deal of unresolved bitterness toward men, which she had carried with her throughout her life. She had been married twice, and after the death of her second husband, accused her daughter by that second husband of having been molested by him, and had the daughter institutionalized. She had interrogated the child for months and, in spite even of this, the girl did not "admit" to having been molested until she had been in the institution for almost a year.

She had also made statements that Gary Dill "had to be punished" for what he had done to his daughter, and she attempted to have his visitation rights curtailed, as well as those of the paternal grandmother. She even made allegations that the paternal grandmother had engaged in lewd sexual activities with the children which were never charged. Apparently authorities did not consider them worth taking seriously.

In September, 1984, a family was located who had lived in the Carmichael area whose children, according to Mrs. Bell, had been involved. That family was now living in a small town in Texas, near San Marcos. A representative of the Texas Department of Human Resources went out to the children's school to interview them. They were interviewed in the principal's office. They were confronted with the story of the molestation in Sacramento, which the children denied. The worker from the Department of Human Resources called Sacramento during the interview to get more details of the alleged molestation. Defense attorneys believe that she then fed the details to the children and got them to say what she wanted to hear. She questioned the children for about two hours before their parents arrived at the school. The parents were upset and asked her to stop the questioning. The children were taken to Austin, about thirty-five miles away, where a Detective Cutler conducted a videotaped interview with them, and got one of them to admit having been involved in a molestation. The other denied it. They were put into therapy with private therapists, whom they saw at least once a week.

In August, 1984, the children in Grandma Bell's house were exhibiting some symptoms of aggressive behavior toward each other; they were apparently molesting each other, sexually, according to court testimony. Social workers had the two oldest girls declared wards of the court, in order to get them out of Grandma Bell's household. Mrs. Bell had been ordered by the social workers not to question the girls any more, but she was apparently unable to restrain herself and continued the questioning, and the girls were placed in the McCauley Neuropsychiatric Institute in San Francisco.

The children in Texas were put in therapy. The younger, who denied any molestation had occurred, continued to do so for several months during her therapy, which was aimed, almost exclusively at getting her to "disclose" something about the alleged molestation. Her sister, apparently more malleable, said something had happened, and the younger sister finally went along with her story.

The five men were arrested and charged on January tenth, 1985. Bail was set at $500,000 on each. The case was called the "Snuff Film" case because one of the children had told investigators that three children had been killed and their deaths videotaped as part of a satanic ritual. The children told of cannibalism, animal mutilations, and devil worship. There were 169 counts, enough to send each of the defendants to prison for over 300 years. One of the girls told of being forced to stab three children to death. She would have been four years old at the time the alleged murders occurred. These murders, according to the children, occurred in a basement littered with human skulls and bones. No such basement was ever found.

Following the allegations of satanism and devil worship, the sheriff's office searched for evidence of these things. They found a devil mask at Baker's house. There had been a Halloween party at the restaurant, where all the waiters wore Halloween masks and costumes, and the defendants had photographs of it. But the officers took this "evidence" seriously. They found a bathrobe that belonged to one of the men, a red and black bathrobe, and they seized it.

Later on, when the prosecutor failed to produce any evidence of killings, the judge reduced the bail to $150,000. A few weeks later, after several appearances and about 900 pages of discovery, the judge reviewed the case and reduced bail to $20,000 for Baker and $10,000 for Cuevas and Holman. The sheriff's investigation on Holman indicated that Dill did not even know him at the time of the alleged molestations, and did not meet him until approximately October, 1983. A preliminary hearing was set for August.

In April, 1985, the children from Texas were brought to look at five separate lineups. They looked at all five and did not identify anyone. Apparently they had never seen the defendants before.

In June, Mrs. Bell took the four Dill children to a Dr. Rinehart in Sacramento, who was affiliated with the University of California at Davis Medical Center, and who works with county officials on suspected child abuse. He examined the children and found some warts on Bryan's anus, and a scar, about one centimeter long, on the "peri-anal" areas of two of the girls. He diagnosed them as being: "Sexually abused, severe, by history, with consistent findings." Defense attorneys refer to this doctor, among others, as being a "professional sex abuse finder," and contend that these symptoms can be caused by any number of other things.

The mother of the children, Claudia Dill, had taken them to a gynecologist in Vallejo, and had the oldest daughter, Erika, examined for possible sexual abuse. That doctor examined her vaginally and anally, and found no scars, nor any evidence of molestation.

Rolando Cuevas had been an infantry officer in Vietnam and had been severely wounded. He had massive scarring on his chest. In the children's accounts of the alleged molestation they said they had seen all five men naked, but nobody made any mention of seeing the scars on Cuevas's chest.

Cuevas and Holman were dismissed out of the case before the preliminary hearing began. Arbuckle was dismissed out after Heather testified, and both Heather and Erika failed to testify that Arbuckle was involved in any way. That left only Dill and Baker. Baker was released on his own recognizance.

According to court transcripts of the preliminary hearing, a psychiatrist stated that the two Dill girls, Heather and Erika, were screaming obscenities at the hospital, and blaming their grandmother, Doris Bell, for making them say what they said about their father, and for making them come to the hospital. Heather stated that her father was innocent.

Another issue that surfaced in the examination of the court-appointed psychiatrist was the fact that Dill had always been known to his family and friends as Gary. Arthur was his middle name, but he never used it. The children in Texas spoke of a man named Arthur as the perpetrator. They got that name from the police. If they had actually known Dill they would almost certainly have known him as "Gary."

Later on, the psychiatrist was asked, "What are the probabilities of five men and three women who have no prior relationship, coming to work at a restaurant, engage in a summer of satan worshipping, sex abuse and murder (as alleged in the complaint), and then going their separate ways after that. . . ?"

The psychiatrist answered ". . . You're talking somewhere around one in several trillion as a probability . . ."

In August, a hearing was held in Municipal Court on the prosecution's motion to determine whether the Dill girls were eligible to testify outside the courtroom over closed-circuit television under the new McMartin Law, PC 1347. The first girl testified, in chambers, with only the judge and the lawyers present, and said that most of the allegations were false. She said that her grandmother, Mrs. Bell, had made her say these things.

After the hearing in chambers, the judge decided that she could testify in open court without closed-circuit television. She testified, hesitatingly and reluctantly, that none of the allegations was true, but that her father and Mr. Baker were involved in some minimal touching of her.

On cross-examination she gave up even that, and said that her father had not molested her, nor had Mr. Baker, and that the charges were "all lies."

The next child who testified was her sister, Heather, who is nine years old. She testified in the judge's chambers that none of it was true, that nobody had been molested.

"Heather is a very strong kid," defense attorney Tom Roehr said. "A real scrapper. She never went along with the grandmother much. She never went along with the people at the hospital. She resisted all the way. And what the people at the hospital did to her is incredible! They have something they call 'matting' there. They put the kid down on a rest mat, and they fold it over the kid, so that the kid is restrained and can't move. And they keep the kid there for an hour or more, and somebody stays there to make sure the kid can't get out. Heather revolted against everything they tried to do to her. And, of course, these 'professionals' interpret that as a sign she's been terribly abused. They've got their own explanation for everything.

"Anyway, she came in and told the judge that none of it happened, that it was all a lie, and that her grandmother had put her up to saying it. But it was almost like torturing her, at the hospital! It's incredible to me that they're getting away with it.

"The judge decided she could testify in open court but the prosecutor decided he wasn't going to call her, so she just sat there in the hospital for a couple of weeks, until we could call her."

The next witness was Dana Gregg, one of the girls from Texas, who testified that the whole story was true, and that she had been coerced to stab a child to death when she was only four years old. She talked, very matter-of-factly, with no appearance of trauma or stress, but when she came to the part where she told that she had killed someone, she broke down and wept. She had been accompanied, up to that time, by her therapist as a "support person." She asked for her mommy. The defense attorneys asked that the support person be excluded and that her mother be allowed to accompany her. The judge permitted that. After a brief recess, the girl began to testify again, sitting on her mother's lap. The prosecutor asked why she hadn't told all of this initially, and she said that she had been too frightened, when she talked to Sergeant Cutler in Austin.

On cross-examination, the defense attorneys showed her the videotape of her interview with Detective Cutler, which showed a girl who was not in the slightest degree frightened, and was actually rather playful. There were also a number of audio tapes of her interviews in which it appeared that the therapist was leading her. On one occasion, when she was telling about the children being killed, she said there were two victims. The therapist asked her, pointedly, "Was it two? Or was it three?" And the girl changed her story and said, "Three." Later on, the therapist asked about the gender of the children who were killed and she said, "Two boys and a girl." And it was supposed to be two girls and a boy. And at that point, the therapist cut the session short and turned off the tape recorder, and it seemed apparent to everyone that the therapist was leading the child.

"The next witness we put on was Heather," defense attorney Tom Roehr told me. "She came back to court and testified, as she did earlier, that no one had been molested, no one had been murdered, and that none of this had happened.

"And we put Grandma Bell on as a defense witness. And we talked about this journal in which she had kept notes on how she had questioned the children. She acknowledged that she had made them sit for three or four hours, almost daily, and be questioned. She didn't appear to see anything wrong with that. Her psychiatric background was interesting. Everybody in the family had a therapist. She was obsessed with molestation."

In her court testimony, Mrs. Bell recounted her interrogation of the children and said, ". . . my theory was that the next secret had to do with cannibalism." She said she asked one of the girls: "I think I know what your next secret is. I think they made you eat part of one of those kids."

The judge reacted with incredulity: "I don't understand this at all . . . I mean, it would be bad enough to have the murder occur . . . I can't imagine having to come up with something worse. I can't understand, Mrs. Bell, where in the world you would have gotten that."

Heather was brought in a car from San Francisco in the morning to testify. She had crayons and paper in the car, and she made a little card with the words "Take it easy," and she colored it blue and pink. She asked the judge if she could give her father a present. The prosecution had been telling the court that these children were so frightened of Dill that they couldn't testify in open court, and needed the protection of PC 1347. The judge said, "Okay," and expected her to hand something to the bailiff, which the bailiff would then give to her father. She scampered off the witness stand and walked right by her father, and started rummaging around in a paper bag. She finally found the card, and proudly took it to him and gave it to him. It was a very touching moment. Many of the people in the courtroom had tears in their eyes.

According to testimony by Dr. Friedrich, Heather's mother was, generally, a depressed and emotionally unavailable parent, and all through her early years, the one who had been "there for her" was her father. Another witness, a teacher, said it was her father who always came to pick up the girl from school, and she said that when the girl saw her father, her face would brighten up, and she had a big smile, and was obviously very happy to see her father.

"And that was very important evidence," Roehr said, "Because the prosecutor had led us to believe that, during all that time, her father was brutally and sadistically abusing her, killing animals in front of her. And it just wasn't believable any more."

FROM THE JUDGE'S RULING:

Without doubt, great harm and suffering was imposed on these children as a result of the conduct of MRS. BELL. She is a very intelligent woman. She speaks well and writes in an articulate manner. She is also severely mentally ill. The Court has carefully reviewed her conduct, both through her writings, her testimony in Court, and the children's testimony. I have concluded that, while MRS. BELL appeared from her testimony *not* to recognize the harmful nature of her actions, the results of her conduct relating to her grandchildren were very damaging.

While the testimony of MRS. BELL was forthright as to details of her interrogations, her testimony must be considered in the light of her admitted biases against the defendant DILL. MRS. BELL relentlessly pursued the prosecution of these charges. She complained to the State's Attorney General about both the District Attorney and Sacramento County Sheriff's officers because they did not place credence in the stories which she brought out of the children. The lengths to which she went to support the children's stories with her own developed evidence, such as the location of the house on M Street, are indications of MRS. BELL's commitment to the prosecution of the charges in this case. Over several months of close contact with the DILL children, MRS. BELL, who had few or no skills in dealing with persons mentally ill and who herself was severely mentally ill, interrogated the children. The testimony of both DILL children, ERIKA and HEATHER, was that the many stories of sexual abuse and other terrible occurrences were agreed to by the children because they were just tired of being badgered by their Grandmother. In the words of ERIKA:

Q. Why did you tell her that?

A. 'Cause, she kept—she kept harassing me. She kept saying, "are you sure," and stuff and I didn't want to keep going on with it, so I said yes. (page 122, lines 25-28)

* * *

Q. Did you ever tell anybody that you were ever taken to a house called Veryl's house?

A. Yes.

Q. And why did you tell somebody that?

A. Because my Grandma kept harassing me. (p. 123, lines 4-8.)

* * *

Q. How were you able to describe what Veryl's house looks like if you never had really been there?

A. I just made it up. (p. 124, lines 23, 24)

* * *

Q. Did you ever tell anybody that your dad did something bad to Cindy and Mindy?

A. Yes.

Q. Do you remember who you told that to?

A. Yes.

Q. Who was that?

A. My Grandma Doris. (p. 127, lines 13-19)

* * *

Q. Why—Erika, why did you tell your Grandma Doris about Cindy and Mindy being involved if they weren't?

A. Because she kept asking me, umm, "Were there any other children?" and I said, "No," and she kept asking and asking. (p. 133, line 6-10)

* * *

Q. Can you tell why you decided to tell your Grandma Doris that Cindy and Mindy were involved?

A. 'Cause she kept harassing me and asking me, "Are you sure? Are you sure?" (p. 133, line 28; p. 134, lines 1-3)

And then when ERIKA was asked why she named other men being involved other than her father and MR. BAKER:

Q. Erika, why did you tell all those people that those three men had done bad things to you if they had not done bad things to you?

A. Because, when my Grandma started questioning me, she started, umm, harassing me.

Q. What do you mean "harassing?"

A. She would keep asking, "Are you sure?", and kept asking and asking a lot. (p. 139, line 26; p. 140, lines 1-5)

* * *

Q. Why did you tell your Grandma that?

A. Because she kept—'cause when she asked me, umm, when she caught me in the living room and then she said, umm, "did," umm, "anyone have any cameras," and I said, "No," she kept saying, "Are you sure," and kept asking me that, and I didn't like it and I wanted to get over with it to go outside so I said, "Yes." (p. 149, line 20-26)

* * *

Q. And do you remember a family session where Grandma BELL guessed that a dog had sex with HEATHER?

A. Yes.

Q. And that was Grandma—Grandma Doris's 'suggestion,' wasn't it?

A. Yes.

Q. That wasn't true?

A. No.

Q. And do you remember a family session where Grandma Doris suggested that owls were cut up and you were made to eat them?

A. Yes.

Q. And that wasn't true, was it?

A. No.

Q. That was just Grandma Doris's suggestion, wasn't it?

A. Yes. (p. 232, lines 24-28; p. 233, lines 1-11).

Finally, during the questioning of ERIKA, the subject of how she got the names of the other persons participating in the molest came up, and I asked her if her Grandmother told her the names. Her response was: "No. I told her because I didn't know any—umm—any other people." (p. 233, line 28, and p. 234, line 1)

It is not at all unlikely that all the DILL children, when asked to come up with names of persons who molested them, would pick the names of persons they knew, and in determining who the other participating children were, would pick the names of children from the neighborhood. It is logical and sensible. Most people if asked to make up a story will necessarily draw upon their personal experience, directly or indirectly, in preparing such a statement. Testimony of HEATHER made perfectly good sense when she explained why they came up with the names of additional perpetrators.

The deterioration of ERIKA and HEATHER's mental condition (which was clearly shown in a taped interview with Dr. Corwin) occurred during the period of interrogation by MRS. BELL. Casting aside conventional techniques of therapy and mental health professionals as inadequate, MRS. BELL embarked upon a program of interrogation that can only be considered inhumane. Sadly, the children's mother, CLAUDIA DILL, stood by while this occurred and a variety of others, including health professionals and law enforcement officials, were unable to recognize or do anything about the senseless harm being done to these children. I have carefully reviewed the evidence of the conduct of MRS. BELL. She had no sensitivity toward children or their needs and seemed totally obsessed with matters sexual. When she told the Court that 3¾-year-old Brian had a sexual look on his face and interrogated HEATHER about whether the alleged molest felt good, the perversity of her mental condition was glaringly apparent and was never refuted.

Thus, ERIKA and HEATHER DILL came to this Court having gone through severe mental trauma, and they, in fact, were both suffering from post-traumatic stress disorder. What did they testify?

HEATHER indicated on direct examination that all the stories of child molestation were not true but were made up at the insistence of her Grandmother. She did not change her story when vigorously cross-examined.

The record is also very clear that she denied being molested many times when she was living with MRS. BELL and was the most difficult with respect to admitting the molestation. She also has more consistently than ERIKA denied the molestations during her period at the McAuley Institute.

In her direct testimony, ERIKA testified that only her father and MR. BAKER molested her and her siblings.

On cross-examination, she recanted and stated that her father and MR. BAKER had *not* molested her, and she said that none of the molestations of other children occurred. She again said that the statements were made to various peace officers and other investigators because her Grandmother made her say those things.

However, having admitted and then recanted being molested, ERIKA on re-direct again admitted that several other incidents involving her dad did in fact occur.

The Court must evaluate the credibility of ERIKA and HEATHER's testimony. These are intelligent children. Their explanations of the conduct of MRS. BELL were clear and understandable. They were a perfectly normal reaction of a child, particularly when one considers that the interrogating sessions went on for a period of many months, and at one point, according to MRS. BELL's own testimony, for two one-week periods, occurred daily and lasted up to four hours each. It is hard to imagine any adult—let alone a child—who could withstand such an interrogation. Fortunately, adults might be able to physically escape such an environment. Unfortunately, these children could not.

The children testified clearly and congruently as to the description of MRS. BELL's procedures. By MRS. BELL's own admission, she "conjectured," for example, cannibalism, and by her own testimony (which must be considered in the light that she was well aware of the fact that she was being accused of "brainwashing" the children) shows that indeed, that was what was happening. The children's explanation of why they told the stories to MRS. BELL *is* believable.

How does the Court decide whether to believe the in-Court statements of ERIKA that MR. DILL and MR. BAKER actually molested her?

In considering the fact she admitted and then recanted, the Court can decide one story is true and the other untrue. (*People v. Bodkin* (1961) 196 Cal.App.2d 412, 415; *People v. Maxwell* (1979) 94 Cal.App.3d 562, 575.) The first version can be accepted as the truth (in this case, the admissions of being molested).

The test is whether contradictory statements, "*under all the circumstances and facts* placed before the [the trier of fact] . . . so far impeached these witnesses as to render their testimony . . . improbable or unbelievable." (*People v. Maxwell, supra,* at p. 576-577 (Emphasis Added))

". . . absent exceptional circumstances demonstrating the witness' testimony is inherently improbable, the fact that a witness' testimony is false in part does not preclude the trier of fact from accepting as true the rest of it." *(Ibid.)*

Are ERIKA's statements in Court that she had been molested to be believed, considering all the facts and circumstances before the Court?

While ERIKA on direct examination admitted some molestations occurred, her testimony seemed tentative and lacked the strength of conviction of her other responses. ERIKA said she was afraid of her father and also testified that she felt that the persons at the McAuley Institute treated her better when she responded with the story, and overall, as her testimony continued, she gradually retreated from her testimony on direct examination.

But, the most important factor in evaluating the credibility of ERIKA's testimony is the influence of MRS. BELL's interrogation.

Clearly, many of the original molestations claimed resulted from MRS. BELL's influence. Is it possible to sort out that which was untrue and that which may be true?

When inconsistencies in ERIKA's testimony are coupled with the known influence of MRS. BELL in the extensive series of interrogations, the facts become completely blurred. This is not an ordinary case of a simple admission and recantation.

The Court concludes that ERIKA's testimony as to specific events of molestation is not reliable as to the conduct of MR. DILL or MR. BAKER. The court finds it is impossible to segregate those portions of her testimony which may be the truth and those which are not with respect to the allegations of molestation. If the Court were to accept one statement as true and reject another as untrue, *there would be no rational basis,* based on the record of this proceeding, to make such a choosing. Thus, this Court cannot believe the testimony of ERIKA DILL that the alleged charges occurred.

TESTIMONY OF DANA GREGG

DANA GREGG testified in this Court not only that certain molestations occurred to several children, but that she and two other children murdered three young children. In determining the reliability and credibility of DANA, a number of factors have been considered. First, to some degree—but it is not clear the extent of this—there were a number of possible opportunities for suggestion of facts by Sgt. Cutler, therapist MacLean, and Social Worker Robinson, among others.

But, in determining the believability of DANA's testimony, the Court does *not* make any findings as to this issue of suggestion, but rather has evaluated the testimony on all of the factors required under the law as previously stated.

DANA was barely four years old at the time of the alleged incidents. Her retelling did not occur until two and one half years after these incidents. If one was to judge such testimony by adult standards of recollection, it would be difficult to give credibility to the story, let alone when one considers the age of DANA at the time of the alleged circumstances.

The Court is mindful that unusual circumstances alone are not necessarily "inherently improbable," Witkin, *California Evidence*, 2d Ed., p. 1029.

The Court further recognizes that child molestation is not normal behavior, and in such molestation situations, abnormal conduct is the rule, not the exception. Bizarre sexual conduct can occur. Her testimony is not unbelievable just because it described highly abnormal behavior.

Many elements of DANA's story may well be based on the actual experience of DANA or other children. For example, Mrs. Gregg testified that she thought DANA did leave by a bedroom window during the daytime one time, and later the windows were nailed shut. It is quite likely that in constructing her story, DANA called upon the personal experience of leaving by a window as the means of leaving in the story she told. It is not unusual for real life experiences to form the basis of and to be woven within other matters to form the basis of stories of this type.

Yet, most of DANA GREGG's testimony is inherently implausible. To mention just a few examples, her testimony about the murders simply does not make sense. It is unlikely that three children, one of whom was barely four years old, could have murdered another child, without the child even moving or objecting. Numerous other details are equally implausible. Given the age of DANA, the circumstances of her revelations of the murders, the unlikely ancillary circumstances that she climbed out her window at night, got into a car, and was driven to another place, which has never been identified by anybody, and was present with eight other children (including two about *two years old*), plus the three murder victims, and at least five adults, including some women, without her mother knowing about it, causes this Court not to believe the testimony of DANA GREGG with respect to the murders.

There were a number of other circumstances which can only be described as fanciful, such as the trip to the cemetery, and the killing of the deer at the lake or stream. Children would not be required to dig a grave. And even taking into account the obvious inability of DANA to remember specific sizes of animals, for example, these stories are totally unlikely and are *completely uncorroborated by anything in the record.*

Contrary to the prediction of her therapist, DANA was quite comfortable in Court and did not show any reservation about testifying. The only time she showed any usual emotion was when she mentioned the killings, and just as Ms. MacLean indicated whenever this matter came up, she "teared up." In telling the rest of her story, DANA did not show any of the emotion which might be expected from such traumatic events. Rather, she testified in an animated manner. She chatted on and described the story. I got the impression she very much wanted to please the Court.

It is significant that virtually no corroborating evidence has been introduced as to DANA's testimony. None of the children alleged to have participated have backed up DANA's testimony. Most importantly, there is no physical evidence to indicate that this child has been vaginally, orally and anally penetrated as alleged. Furthermore, Mrs. Gregg's testimony as to circumstantial evidence of corroboration was unpersuasive. Only after DANA's story was told and there was some pressure on Mr. and Mr. Gregg and considerable guilt on their part, did these previously innocuous factors take on any semblance of corroboration. Finally, there are glaring inconsistencies and virtually no consistency between the testimony of ERIKA and DANA. The most significant discrepancy is ERIKA's testimony of daytime molestation and DANA of nighttime conduct. This is not a trivial detail.

Finally, and most importantly, MINDY and CINDY DILLON, both of whom were identified by DANA as being present and participating in the murders and molestation, denied that any such murders or molestation ever occurred. I found MINDY and CINDY DILLON to be credible witnesses; I carefully viewed their demeanor on the stand. Their testimony was clear. They had no motive to lie. The reasons given by the People to reject their testimony do not ring true. To disbelieve CINDY and MINDY and yet believe DANA is *not reasonable*.

After applying the applicable law and all the relevant facts, I did not believe DANA's testimony.

It is very important to recognize that the issue before the Court is not whether the alleged child victims have *ever* been molested, but whether the People have produced credible evidence to cause a reasonable person to entertain a strong suspicion that these children were molested *by these defendants* on specific occasions.

As the charges have been summarized by Mr. Lewkowitz, there is no evidence in the record against Mr. BAKER, other than that arising from the testimony of witness, ERIKA DILL. Having found no credible evidence based upon her testimony, the Court orders the charges against VERYL BAKER dismissed and the defendant discharged.

As to the charges against ARTHUR GARY DILL, they are based upon the testimony of ERIKA DILL and DANA GREGG. For reasons previously stated, there is no credible evidence as to these charges. The charges, therefore, are dismissed, the defendant discharged, and his bail exonerated.

DATED: October 25, 1985

RONALD B. ROBIE

RONALD B. ROBIE
Judge of the Municipal Court

What was different in this case was simply that Mrs. Bell had no official standing as a psychologist, social worker or law enforcement officer. Her interrogation techniques did not differ significantly from those used by "therapists," social workers and police in the other cases.

"You see this kind of thing in almost all of these cases," Roehr told me. "I'm not saying that some of them don't start from a grain of truth, but I don't think this one did, and I don't think McMartin did either. I'm quite certain that there are innocent people now in prison. What happens in some of these cases is that the therapists carry things to such extremes, and the children start to compete with each other."

"All of the larger D.A.'s offices in the country now have set up child sex abuse prosecution teams," another lawyer said. "Big bucks from the federal treasury. They're funneling all that money into this crap. And all of those millions of homeless people walking the streets."

Even after the defendants were cleared, the therapists at the Neuropsychiatric Institute still insisted they believed the allegations.

Dill was just happy to have done with it. His attorney, Ernie Winters, said that Dill had been beaten by inmates, and brutally mistreated by law enforcement officers in the two county jails where he was held.

And, of course, now that Dill has been cleared, discharged, and his bail exonerated, his children will be returned to him immediately—right?

Wrong. The Neuropsychiatric Institute intends to detain them for another year. According to testimony during the preliminary hearing, the girls tried to tell the therapists at the hospital as early as January that the stories were false, but the therapists chose not to pursue it.

Dill's co-defendant, Baker, told reporters, "It's been plain hell. I lost my job, my savings, my home, my car, and I suffered a heart attack. . . . Now maybe I can get on with my life."

Arbuckle, who had been dismissed earlier, held a press conference, and said that the law enforcement authorities looked only for evidence of guilt and ignored all evidence of his innocence. He said they also ignored "heavy evidence that the children had been tampered with. . . ."

XI

Michele

"It started in Savannah, Georgia, in February, 1984," Michele told me over cookies and coffee. "I was involved in custody litigation with my ex-husband, trying to get my children back from him. I have a set of twins. They are four and a half, not quite five years old, a boy and a girl. We had private investigators investigating him, and he got wind of this. We were accused of sexual abuse games with the children, and eleven of us, my parents who lived in New York, and two of my best friends were also accused. No criminal charges were pressed. My ex-husband just wanted to single us out, so we were the ones who went to the court proceedings in family court. And through a lot of torturous hours of court trial we managed to get visitation and supervised visits from our county, where they brought my children to my house, and I got to see them two hours, one day a week.

"And in August, 1984, the decision came down that the judge believed that the accusations were true and that, based on what the children told him in chambers, and what the psychologist testified to, they believed that we had sexually abused my four-year-old kids. They believed that there had been oral sex done to the children, not penetration. If you talk to anybody, you know that's the hardest to prove—oral sex—but it's also the hardest to *dis*prove.

"I also have a fourteen-month-old child by my present husband. They came into the house at about ten-thirty at night and strip-searched him, and examined his penis and rectum area, in my home, in my presence, with a court order saying that if I didn't permit this to happen, they could take my son out of the home right then and there. It was a child protection worker and a social worker. And they said, 'Gee, this child doesn't even have any diaper rash.'

"So afterwards, we talked with them, and they said they found nothing to give them cause to take my son out of the home. And he stayed in my home from that time until we moved to New York, on September the twentieth. We basically moved to New York to get away from all the publicity and everything in Georgia, because my parents live in New York.

"And five days after we got there, there was a call placed by a child protection worker, from Georgia, saying that we had fled the state, with the child, to escape child abuse charges. And they came in and yanked my son, physically, out of my arms, while two police officers held me down. All that was left was my son's slipper on the floor in front of me and his screams and cries, which I can never forget. He was only fourteen months old. They still have him, and that was more than a year ago. He's in a foster home. They have no grounds to keep him, because they never proved there was any sexual abuse or any other kind of abuse of him. The examination disproved it. So what they're saying, basically, is they believe the other accusations to be true, and so, automatically, if you do it to two other kids, you're going to do it to a baby. And you're presumed guilty without any proof.

"So we were asked to go to this incest treatment place, and we've done so. We've gone to two sessions, and we were told that if we don't admit to actually having sexually abused our child we might as well forget about ever seeing him again. And if we *did* say we did it—which we didn't—we might as well forget about ever seeing him again. And I told them, 'I am not going to admit to something I haven't done, because that would be a lie.' And they said, 'Then we can't help you. We can't treat you.' And I said, 'Fine, we're willing to do whatever you want, but just give us our child back.' We have, on our own, paid for a private psychiatrist who examined us for seven months. Cost us over two thousand dollars, not including court costs. And she came into court for us, saying there's no way, we didn't have the personalities to do this, we didn't have the background, nothing about us would indicate this kind of behavior, either by my husband or myself.

"They threw her testimony out, and said she was biased on our behalf. We got Dr. Ungerwager involved in our case. He came down to testify on the fact that children do lie about this kind of thing. They threw his testimony out because, they said, he didn't know us well enough, and he didn't know the case well enough to come and testify.

"My child is still a very healthy little boy. The foster mother that has him takes good care of my child. He still seems happy. I don't know how he's kept it. He's just turned three in October. I pray that I'll be able to get him back, if I don't run out of money. They tell me they're going to keep him in foster care another eighteen months, until I can prove to the court that I am a good enough parent for my child to be returned to my home. Now, I've brought in my pastor, I've brought in character references. What more do they want? They want me to admit to something I didn't do.

"But they can keep your child on the premise that they are doing it for his protection. And as long as they say that they are doing it for his protection, they can keep your child. I mean, there's a lot more. I had a lousy lawyer who had conflicts of interest. But the hardest thing is being apart, from your child. We had a case worker that said to me, 'Well, we would have worked something out with you if you would go through treatment . . .'

"My parents get to see the children every twenty-one days, and every time they see my kids the first question is, 'Where's Mommy? Why hasn't she come to see me? Is she coming next time?' And my parents have been told that if they want to continue to see their grandchildren, they are not allowed to talk about me in any way—not even mention my name—when the kids ask questions. They give no reason whatsoever for this. But my parents want to see the kids, and they're so scared by that, so they're willing to go along with it. And they're so appalled. Both my father and my father-in-law fought in the war, and they were always for the government. And now it's to the point where they're very upset about the situation.

"Getting the twins back is going to be more difficult because I didn't have enough money to file an appeal. It would have cost me $25,000. And I was naive. My lawyer told me I didn't have grounds for an appeal, and I've found out since then that I have plenty of grounds. I'm planning to start proceedings in the spring, and go back through the court system, and fight it. Because, through all of this, my ex-husband's wife had me and my husband arrested and held in jail for eight days, and that was hell in itself. One count, each, of molestation. And even though the D.A. told my attorney that they had no grounds to hold us any longer, the prosecutor still went ahead with the prosecution and let us sit in jail on a thirty-thousand-dollar bail. They had no evidence. Nothing! It's taken a toll on me. It drains your energy. Most of the crying stage is over now, but I still have bad days. I just wonder what happens to people who have even less resources than I . . . they just get ground under. Some of them go to prison. Some of them take their own life, I'm sure.

"They ripped my baby out of my arms. I mean, I was holding him, and I was asking them, 'What are you doing here?' and 'What do you want?' And all he could say was, 'Grab her!' And two police officers yanked my arms behind my back. And they grabbed my son. And he cried, and screamed, 'Mommy!' Because he was a little guy. He didn't know what was going on. And then, all there was left was his bedroom slipper on the floor. That was all that was left. And when I asked the policeman, 'Who was the man that took my son?' they said, 'Go to headquarters, and maybe they can tell you.' And when I went to headquarters, all they would say was, It was a child protection worker, doing his job, and I was to call them in the morning. And I told them, 'My child has been kidnapped, and if you can't give me any more information than that, he's been kidnapped.'

"They left the papers in the mailbox the following day, telling me they were taking my son . . . What does that do to a kid . . . how can he have any sense of family, or security?"

XII

Bingley

What we have covered in this book is only a beginning; we could fill a nine-hundred-page volume with child abuse cases from California alone. In Bakersfield, law enforcement officials boasted that they were arresting as many as one hundred people per month on molestation charges. Some were grandmothers!

But there is one case that made a lasting impression; It is the story of Steven and Dana Bingley and their children.

Steven Bingley was a kind of prodigy. He bought run-down homes and apartments in Pasadena, refurbished them and sold them at a profit. At twenty-four he was earning about $300,000 per year. At 32 he was semi-retired. Bingley had one conspicuous defect: He liked to shock people with obscene language and vulgar behavior. His hero was Lenny Bruce. But he had many friends and was considered a kind and generous man.

One afternoon in December, 1984, he was arrested and charged with five felony counts of molesting his three children, who were six, five and four years old. The charges stemmed from complaints by a relative pertaining to his foul language. The children were removed from his home by county authorities and taken into custody.

Bingley defended himself, first in criminal court, then in juvenile court, and finally was able to get the charges dismissed, except for one misdemeanor charge of lewd conduct, for "talking dirty" in the presence of his children. But the children were not returned to Bingley and his wife, Dana. In an independent ruling, the juvenile court found that they needed several months' counseling before they could be returned to the parents.

The shock and stress of all this was more than Steven Bingley could handle. Something snapped. This man who had been cocky and exuberant became profoundly depressed. His friends say he began taking Valium and drinking copious amounts of vodka as well. He talked of suicide. One morning, he took a nap and never awoke.

"He was not a strong man," his wife, Dana said. "He needed people to like him. . . . He used to cry at night and tell me, 'I don't think I can ever walk like a man again.' "

Still, the county social workers refuse to return Dana's children to her, even though the accused father is now dead.

An interesting fact in this case is that Bingley was arrested after a medical examination of the children revealed no evidence of molestation. The county Department of Children's Services ignored its own guidelines when it failed to interview Dana and Steve Bingley. If the investigators had interviewed the couple they would have learned that the allegations stemmed from a long-standing family feud. According to the attorneys and family friends, the authorities looked only for evidence of guilt, and very deliberately ignored all contradictory evidence. The children, who had never indicated that they were abused in any way, said they were molested only after being interviewed at great length by the social workers. On the witness stand, the five-year-old girl was asked by the prosecutor, "Did your father put his penis in your vagina?"

"Yes," she answered.

On cross-examination the defense attorney asked her, "Do you know what a vagina is?"

"No," she replied.

Friends of the family believe the children were programmed to say they were molested. Prosecutors and police hotly deny it. The prosecutor, Deputy District Attorney Jane Blissert, said, "I don't think you could plant all that in a child's head if you wanted to." Aside from that, social workers, judges, sheriff's deputies and psychologists refuse to discuss the case. But the investigators took the children, even though none of the accusers ever reported they witnessed any sexual acts involving the children. And the children never confided any such acts to teachers, neighbors, or anyone else. The original telephoned complaints against Bingley did not include sexual intercourse, sodomy or oral copulation. Yet, he was charged with five felony counts of "unlawful intercourse," sodomy and oral copulation. Dana was charged with a felony count of threatening to intimidate a witness because of an angry telephone call to her mother protesting the complaint she had made to the police. The charge was later dropped. One of the children testified that she saw her brother and sister being molested, but the brother and sister said that was not true.

Dana Bingley has filed a fifteen-million-dollar claim against the county. Her children are now living with her sister, who lives only two blocks away, but Dana is not allowed to visit them. And the children were not allowed to attend their father's funeral.

His wife said that the experience altered his personality. "He'd wake up at night shaking like a scared child. He'd cry out, 'My God, what are they doing to my babies? What are they saying to them? What are they teaching them?' "

XIII

In Conclusion

On the day we were in Bakersfield researching the Pitts case, in which some of the defendants received four-hundred-year sentences, we saw a story in that morning's *Los Angeles Times* about a man who had murdered his sister and was let off with probation and no jail time. A few weeks before that we read of another case in which a murderer was released after only a few months in custody and committed murder again.

The sexual molestation of children is reprehensible and ought to be deterred.

But what does it say about us when we send a person to prison for four hundred years for allegedly touching a child yet let murderers walk the streets—particularly when the accused child molester is convicted on flimsy evidence or *no* evidence?

It says that we are deranged.

And what does it say about us when we are willing to destroy another person's life and family on false allegations of child abuse and consign him to prison—for the sake of scoring points toward a promotion, a pay raise, or a federal grant?

It says we are morally bankrupt.

We certainly feel that a child has the right to grow up without being molested by adults, and the protection of the young should be one of our most important priorities.

But what has America become if police and social workers can forcibly enter your home and take your children away, without due process, without even probable cause, supported by nothing more than an anonymous telephone call?

And what have we become if we let them get away with it?

Worse than that, Child Protective Service workers are permitted not only to seize children and remove them from their parents, but also to detain them indefinitely, depriving them of vital familial ties and nurture, training them to fear and accuse their parents in criminal proceedings resulting in long prison terms. *That's child abuse.*

When we were researching the Bakersfield cases, a reporter said to us, "This reminds me of the Yanichars. Do you know about the Yanichars? Back in the sixteenth century, Austria was constantly at war with the Turks, and the Turks would invade Austria, and they kidnapped infants from Austria and took them away, and put them in camps and trained them to be ruthless killers, and then brought them back to destroy their own families. These cops and Child Protective Service workers are doing the same thing. They're kidnaping babies and training them to destroy their families. When you write your book you should call it 'The Yanichars.' "

We set out to unravel the mystery, and this is what we got: very little evidence of child molestation and a great deal of extremely corrupt behavior by police, prosecutors and "mental health professionals," resulting in the devastation of innocent people's lives and families. There has indeed been child abuse—perpetrated by representatives of the government and police, who kidnapped children, made them orphans, deprived them of vital family ties and trained them to falsely accuse their parents of high crimes.

We feel that those who knowingly make false and malicious allegations of child abuse out to be held accountable for what they have done—and that goes for police, prosecutors and social workers as well as malicious parents involved in custody fights. To send an innocent person to prison on false allegations is a crime at least as serious as touching a child's buttocks.

Another issue this story raises is that we should immediately reevaluate the Welfare State hierarchy and its "social workers." At present, twenty-two cents out of every dollar allocated to welfare goes to the needy recipient, and the rest goes to support a bureaucracy of people whose task is to see that they do not get a penny more than they're entitled to—a bureaucracy we might be better off without. The issue is the violation of the family by the State—against which we have little or no recourse.

Knowing what we now know about these cases, we cannot but wonder how many innocent people are arrested, convicted and sent to prison in other kinds of cases by bad cops, corrupt prosecutors, stupid judges and juries. There certainly must be thousands. We think it's time to subject our criminal "justice" system to a very thoroughgoing scrutiny. We need better cops, better prosecutors, better judges. We do not expect to get St. Francis of Assisi for county sheriff, but we think we are entitled to a reasonable level of integrity in our public officials.

We believe that every molestation case in which there has been a conviction should be reopened and reviewed. There is convincing evidence that innocent people have been imprisoned, that naive juries and judges were unable to believe that defendants would be charged and brought to trial if no crime had occurred. And defense attorneys have not been allowed to bring all of the pertinent facts before juries.

Why so many obviously absurd allegations have been so vigorously prosecuted is an interesting question. Why are people willing to destroy others' lives for the sake of a pay raise and a step up the ladder of career advancement? Some do it because they are psychopaths. Some do it because they know their superiors require blind obedience rather than common sense and compassion. Mostly, they do it because they are scared. Money is hard to get, and there are millions who are living below the poverty line in crippling squalor and despair. People will do almost anything to keep their jobs. It's hard to imagine anything worse than being on the bottom, without money or any prospect of earning it.

When we discussed with other journalists the role of prosecutors in false accusations of molestation, many of them said, "They were just doing their jobs." We hasten to remind them that Heinrich Himmler said exactly the same thing. We all want to advance our careers and our security, but can we excuse those who do it at the cost of demolishing an innocent person's life? Are we willing to let him sit in a prison cell for the rest of his days so that a prosecutor can score points toward job security?

Chadwick Hansen, in his book, *Witchcraft in Salem*, states that when we look only for evidence of guilt and ignore all contradictory evidence, these are the elements of a witch hunt. We don't think anybody has ever made a more succinct definition of the witch-hunt phenomenon. The current cases, certainly, meet all the requirements of a witch hunt. Police, prosecuting attorneys, social workers and judges, in almost every case, have deliberately ignored all exculpatory evidence. In Bakersfield and Jordan, as well as Sacramento and Los Angeles, children were kidnapped and taken away from their families, deprived of loved ones, orphaned without any substantial evidence of abuse, and the state has stubbornly refused to return them to their parents. Cases in other states seem to follow exactly the same pattern. In the McMartin case, a seventy-eight-year-old woman, paralyzed with arthritis has been compelled to sit for two years in a preliminary hearing on charges of molestation that are too ridiculous to even discuss, while children tell of being taken up in hot air balloons.

The child abuse witch hunt raises another question pertaining to where our ethical priorities lie. In the Middle Ages, lying and fraud were considered to be major sins, while lust was relegated to a much lesser importance, because lying and fraud make chaos of all the vital relationships within the family and the community (as they have done in Jordan, Bakersfield and everywhere the child abuse witch hunt has spread). Bearing false witness against a neighbor seems to have become acceptable, something we now are able to do with casual ease and indifference, while lust has become the great disgrace, the accusation so defamatory that it becomes almost impossible to defend against. We think these priorities ought to be reexamined.

Witch hunts are built on blackmail, on accusations so ruinous that the accused, win or lose, is irrevocably branded, because the refutation never really catches up with the allegations. Torquemada and the witch hunters of Salem used the accusation of liaison with the devil. Joe McCarthy used the charge of treason. The child abuse hunters of the eighties found the ultimate weapon, an accusation so crippling that it annihilates the defendant's credibility, and his ability to vindicate himself. That cops and others would use this weapon against innocent people—as they have done—in order to advance their careers, is a measure of their cruelty, and their depravity. It's time for a sweeping examination of our law enforcement agencies, and what kind of people we are allowing to become police officers.

The child abuse witch hunt was possible because we didn't learn anything from Joe McCarthy and his thought police in the nineteen fifties. The McCarthy era was possible because we learned nothing from Adolf Hitler. And Adolf Hitler was able to take power because we learned nothing from Robespierre, Torquemada and the witch hunters of the 1690's. We don't seem to learn anything from our history.

There are some important lessons to be learned from this experience, not the least of which is the importance of not being stupid enough to believe everything we are told. Another thing we need to understand is that when government officials and police engage in criminal behavior, it is our responsibility to remove them from their jobs and hold them to answer for what they have done. If we are not willing to do that, we will deserve the police state that inevitably follows as a result of our apathy and submission. For years, the government and media have been telling us that "respect for authority" and submission to those who hold official power are indispensable virtues. A more important principle we need to understand is that government officials and police work for *us*, are paid by us, and must be made to answer to us. We cannot give people power and then turn our backs and trust that they will do the right thing. Sometimes they will not do the right thing. Nobody wants to be the first to step forward and arrest a cop, or a district attorney. Cops have lethal weapons and a license to kill. Politicians have the resources and the capability to destroy those who threaten their power. It takes organization and education.

But it can be done, and it doesn't take ninety percent of the population, or even twenty percent. It takes only a few strong people who possess intelligence and determination, and want to live in a decent, civilized environment.

Freedom is not free. The price is participation.

Bibliography and References

Arax, M. "Father Accused of Molestation Loses His Children and His Life." *Los Angeles Times*, June 1, 1985.

Armstrong, L. *Kiss Daddy Goodnight*. New York: Hawthorn Books, 1978.

Coleman, L. "False Allegations of Child Sexual Abuse: Have the Experts Been Caught With Their Pants Down?" 32-page paper available from the author, Berkeley, California. 1985.

Coleman, L. *The Reign of Error*. Boston: Beacon Press, 1984.

Cory, D. and Masters, R.E.L. *Violation of Taboo: Incest in the Great Literature of the Past and Present*. New York: Julian Press, 1963.

Ellis, A. *The Origins and Development of the Incest Taboo*. Secaucus, NJ: Lyle Stuart Inc., 1963.

Hansen, C. *Witchcraft at Salem*. New York: George Braziller, 1969.

Humphrey, H., "Report on the Scott County Investigations." Hubert H. Humphrey, Minnesota Attorney General's Office, 1985.

Masson, J. *The Assault on Truth*. New York: Farrar, Straus Giroux, 1984.

287

Nelson, B. J. *Making an Issue of Child Abuse.* University of Chicago, 1983.

Rigert, J., Peterson, D. and Marcotty, J. "The Scott County Case—How It Grew, Why it Died." *Minneapolis Star & Tribune,* May 26, 1985, p. 1A.

Rush, F. *The Best Kept Secret.* Englewood Cliffs, NJ: Prentice-Hall, 1980.

Sgroi, S., Sarnacki, P. F. and Canfield, B. L., *Validation of Child Sexual Abuse. Handbook of Clinical Intervention in Child Sexual Abuse,* S. Sgroi, ed., Lexington, MA: Lexington Books, D.C. Heath & Co., 1982.

Summit, R. "The Child Sexual Abuse Accommodation Syndrome." *Child Abuse and Neglect,* v. 7, pp. 177-193.

Appendix A

The Federal Child Abuse Act*

CHAPTER 67—CHILD ABUSE PREVENTION AND TREATMENT AND ADOPTION REFORM

SUBCHAPTER I—CHILD ABUSE PREVENTION AND TREATMENT

---

*As amended October 9, 1984. Citations, historical notes, library references, codifications, and notes of decisions not included.

SUBCHAPTER II—ADOPTION OPPORTUNITIES

SUBCHAPTER III—STATE FUNDING MECHANISMS

SUBCHAPTER I—CHILD ABUSE PREVENTION AND TREATMENT

§ 5101. National Center on Child Abuse and Neglect

(a) Establishment

The Secretary of Health and Human Services (hereinafter referred to in this subchapter as the "Secretary") shall establish an office to be known as the National Center on Child Abuse and Neglect (hereinafter referred to in this subchapter as the "Center").

(b) Functions

The Secretary, through the Center, shall—

(1) Annual research summary

compile, analyze, publish, and disseminate a summary annually of recently conducted and currently conducted research on child abuse and neglect;

(2) Information clearinghouse

develop and maintain an information clearinghouse on all programs, including private programs, showing promise of success, for the prevention, identification, and treatment of child abuse and neglect;

(3) Training materials for personnel

compile, publish, and disseminate training materials for personnel who are engaged or intend to engage in the prevention, identification, and treatment of child abuse and neglect;

(4) Technical assistance

provide technical assistance (directly or through grant or contract) to public and nonprofit private agencies and organizations to assist them in planning, improving, developing, and carrying out programs and activities relating to the prevention, identification, and treatment of child abuse and neglect;

(5) Research into causes, prevention, identification, and treatment

conduct research into the causes of child abuse and neglect, and into the prevention, identification, and treatment thereof;

(6) Study

study and investigate the national incidence of child abuse and neglect and make findings about any relationship between nonpayment of child support and between various other factors and child abuse and neglect, and the extent to which incidents of child abuse and neglect are increasing in number and severity, and, within two years after Oct. 9, 1984, submit such findings to the appropriate Committees of the Congress together with such recommendations for administrative and legislative changes as are appropriate; and

(7) Reports

in consultation with the Advisory Board on Child Abuse and Neglect, annually prepare reports on efforts during the preceding two-year period to bring about coordination of the goals, objectives, and activities of agencies and organizations which have responsibilities for programs and activities related to child abuse and neglect, and, not later than March 1, 1985, and March 1 of each second year thereafter, submit such a report to the appropriate Committees of the Congress. The Secretary shall establish research priorities for making grants or contracts under clause (5) of this subsection and, not less than sixty days before establishing such priorities, shall publish in the Federal Register for public comment a statement of such proposed priorities.

(c) Grant and contract authority; duration and review of research grants

The functions of the Secretary under subsection (b) of this section may be carried out either directly or by way of grant or contract. Grants may be made under subsection (b)(5) of this section for periods of not more than three years. Any such grant shall be reviewed at least annually by the Secretary, utilizing peer review mechanisms to assure the quality and progress of research conducted under such grant.

(d) Staff and resource availability to Center

The Secretary shall make available to the Center such staff and resources as are necessary for the Center to carry out effectively its functions under this subchapter.

(e) Use of funds

No funds appropriated under this subchapter for any grant or contract may be used for any purpose other than that for which such funds were specifically authorized.

§ 5102. Definitions

For purposes of this subchapter—(1) the term "child abuse and neglect" means the physical or mental injury, sexual abuse or exploitation, negligent treatment, or maltreatment of a child under the age of eighteen, or the age specified by the child protection law of the State in question, by a person (including any employee of a residential facility or any staff person providng out-of-home care) who is responsible for the child's welfare under circumstances which indicate that the child's health or welfare is harmed or threatened thereby, as determined in accordance with regulations prescribed by the Secretary;

(2)(A) the term "sexual abuse" includes—

(i) the employment, use, persuasion, inducement, enticement, or coercion of any child to engage in, or having a child assist any other person to engage in, any sexually explicit conduct (or any simulation of such conduct) for the purpose of producing any visual depiction of such conduct, or

(ii) the rape, molestation, prostitution, or other such form of sexual exploitation of children, or incent with children,

under circumstances which indicate that the child's health or welfare is harmed or threatened thereby, as determined in accordance with regulations prescribed by the Secretary; and

(B) for the purpose of this clause, the term "child" or "children" means any individual who has not or individuals who have not attained the age of eighteen.

(3) the term "withholding of medically indicated treatment" means the failure to respond to the infant's life-threatening conditions by providing treatment (including appropriate nutrition, hydration, and medication) which, in the treating physician's or physicians' reasonable medical judgment, will be most likely to be effective in ameliorating or correcting all such conditions, except that the term does not include the failure to provide treatment (other than appropriate nutrition, hydration, or medication) to an infant when, in the treating physician's or physicians' reasonable medical judgment, (A) the infant is chronically and irreversibly comatose; (B) the provision of such treatment would (i) merely prolong dying, (ii) not be effective in ameliorating or correcting all of the infant's life-threatening conditions, or (iii) otherwise be futile in terms of the survival of the infant; or (C) the provision of such treatment would be virtually futile in terms of the survival of the infant and the treatment itself under such circumstances would be inhumane.

§ 5103. Demonstration or service programs and projects

(a) Grants and contracts; scope of activities

The Secretary, through the Center, is authorized to make grants to, and enter into contracts with, public agencies or nonprofit private organizations (or combinations thereof) for demonstration or service programs and projects designed to prevent, identify, and treat child abuse and neglect. Grants or contracts under this subsection may be—

(1) for training programs for professional and paraprofessional personnel in the fields of medicine, law, education, social work, and other relevant fields who are engaged in, or intend to work in, the field of the prevention, identification, and treatment of child abuse and neglect; and training programs for children, and for persons re-

sponsible for the welfare of children, in methods of protecting children from child abuse and neglect;

(2) for the establishment and maintenance of centers, serving defined geographic areas, staffed by multidisciplinary teams of personnel trained in the prevention, identification, and treatment of child abuse and neglect cases, to provide a broad range of services related to child abuse and neglect, including direct support and supervision of satellite centers and attention homes, as well as providing advice and consultation to individuals, agencies, and organizations which request such services;

(3) for furnishing services of teams of professional and paraprofessional personnel who are trained in the prevention, identification, and treatment of child abuse and neglect cases, on a consulting basis to small communities where such services are not available; and

(4) for such other innovative programs and projects, including programs and projects for parent self-help, and for prevention and treatment of drug-related child abuse and neglect, that show promise of successfully preventing or treating cases of child abuse and neglect as the Secretary may approve.

(b) Grants to States; qualifications for assistance; reduction of awards; certain requirements

(1) The Secretary, through the Center, is authorized to make grants to the States for the purpose of assisting the States in developing, strengthening, and carrying out child abuse and neglect prevention and treatment programs.

(2) In order for a State to qualify for assistance under this subsection, such State shall—

(A) have in effect a State child abuse and neglect law which shall include provisions for immunity for persons reporting instances of child abuse and neglect from prosecution, under any State or local law, arising out of such reporting;

(B) provide for the reporting of known and suspected instances of child abuse and neglect;

(C) provide that upon receipt of a report of known or suspected instances of child abuse or neglect an investigation shall be initiated promptly to substantiate the accuracy of the report, and, upon a finding of abuse or neglect, immediate steps shall be taken to protect the health and welfare of the abused or neglected child, as well as that of any other child under the same care who may be in danger of abuse or neglect;

(D) demonstrate that there are in effect throughout the State, in connection with the enforcement of child abuse and neglect laws and with the reporting of suspected instances of child abuse and neglect, such administrative procedures, such personnel trained in child abuse and neglect prevention and treatment, such training procedures, such institutional and other facilities (public and private), and such related multidisciplinary programs and services as may be necessary or appropriate to assure that the State will deal effectively with child abuse and neglect cases in the State;

(E) provide for methods to preserve the confidentiality of all records in order to protect the rights of the child, and the child's parents or guardians;

(F) provide for the cooperation of law enforcement officials, courts of competent jurisdiction, and appropriate State agencies providing human services;

(G) provide that in every case involving an abused or neglected child which results in a judicial proceeding a guardian ad litem shall be appointed to represent the child in such proceedings;

(H) provide that the aggregate of support for programs or projects related to child abuse and neglect assisted by State funds shall not be reduced below the level provided during fiscal year 1973, and set forth policies and procedures designed to assure that Federal funds made available under this subchapter for any fiscal year will be so used as to supplement and, to the extent practicable, increase the level of State funds which would, in the absence of Federal funds, be available for such programs and projects;

(I) provide for dissemination of information to the general public with respect to the problem of child abuse and neglect and the facilities and prevention and treatment methods available to combat instances of child abuse and neglect;

(J) to the extent feasible, insure that parental organizations combating child abuse and neglect receive preferential treatment.

(K) within one year after Oct. 9, 1984, have in place for the purpose of responding to the reporting of medical neglect (including instances of withholding of medically indicated treatment from disabled infants with life-threatening conditions), procedures or programs,or both (within the State child protective services system), to provide for (i) coordination and consultation with individuals designated by and within appropriate health-care facilities, (ii) prompt notification by individuals designated by and within appropriate health-care facilities of cases of suspected medical neglect (including instances of withholding of medically indicated treatment from disabled infants with life-threatening conditions), and (iii) authority, under State law, for the State child protective service system to pursue any legal remedies, including the authority to initiate legal proceedings in a court of competent jurisdiction, as may be necessary to prevent the withholding of medically indicated treatment from disabled infants with life-threatening conditions.

If a State has failed to obligate funds awarded under this subsection within eighteen months after the date of award, the next award under this subsection made after the expiration of such period shall be reduced by an amount equal to the amount of such unobligated funds unless the Secretary determines that extraordinary reasons justify the failure to so obligate.

(3)(A) Subject to subparagraph (B) of this paragraph, any State which on Oct. 9, 1984 does not qualify for assistance under this subsection may be granted a waiver of any requirement under paragraph (2) of this subsection—

(i) for a period of not more than one year, if the Secretary makes a finding that such State is making a good-faith effort to comply with any such requirement, and for a second one-year period if the Secretary makes a finding that such State is making substantial progress to achieve such compliance; or

(ii) for a nonrenewable period of not more than two years in the case of a State the legislature of which meets only biennially, if the Secretary makes a finding that such State is making a good-faith effort to comply with any such requirement.

(B) No waiver under subparagraph (A) may apply to any requirement under paragraph (2)(K) of this subsection.

(4) Programs or projects related to child abuse and neglect assisted under part B of title IV of the Social Security Act [42 U.S.C.A. § 620, et seq.] shall comply with the requirements set forth in clauses (B), (C), (E), (F), and (K) of paragraph (2).

(c) Additional grants to States; purpose; training and technical assistance; information and resource clearinghouses; use of funds.

(A) the procedures or programs required under clause (K) of subsection (b)(2) of this section;

(B) information and education programs or training programs for the purpose of improving the provision of services to disabled infants with life-threatening conditions for (i) professional and paraprofessional personnel concerned with the welfare of disabled infants with life-threatening conditions, including personnel employed in child protective services programs and health-care facilities, and (ii) the parents of such infants; and

(C) programs to help in obtaining or coordinating necessary services, including existing social and health services and financial assistance for families with disabled infants with life-threatening conditions, and those services necessary to facilitate adoptive placement of such infants who have been relinquished for adoption.

(2)(A) The Secretary shall provide, directly or through grants or contracts with public or private nonprofit organizations, for (i) training and technical assistance programs to assist States in developing, establishing, and operating or implementing programs and procedures meeting the requirements of clause (K) of subsection (b)(2) of this section; and (ii) the establishment and operation of national and regional information and resource clearinghouses for the purpose of providing the most current and complete information regarding medical treatment procedures and resources and community resources for the provision of services and treatment for disabled infants with life-threatening conditions (including compiling, maintaining, updating, and disseminating regional directories of community services and resources (including the names and phone numbers of State and local medical organizations) to assist parents, families, and physicians and seeking to coordinate the availability of appropriate regional education resources for health-care personnel).

(B) Not more than $1,000,000 of the funds appropriated for any fiscal year under section 5104 of this title may be used to carry out this paragraph.

(C) Not later than 210 days after Oct. 9, 1984, the Secretary shall have the capability of providing and begin to provide the training and technical assistance described in subparagraph (A) of this paragraph.

(d) Prohibition of assistance for construction of facilities; lease or rental and alteration or repair of facilities

Assistance provided pursuant to this section shall not be available for construction of facilities; however, the Secretary is authorized to supply such assistance for the lease or rental of facilities where adequate facilities are not otherwise available, and for repair or minor remodeling or alteration of existing facilities.

(e) Criteria for equitable distribution of assistance

The Secretary shall establish criteria designed to achieve equitable distribution of assistance under this section among the States, among geographic areas of the Nation, and among rural and urban areas. To the extent possible, citizens of each State shall receive assistance from at least one project under this section.

(f) Definition

For the purpose of this section, the term "State" includes each of the several States, the District of Columbia, the Commonwealth of Puerto Rico, American Samoa, the Virgin Islands, Guam and the Trust Territories of the Pacific.

(g) Availability of assistance for prevention of child abuse and neglect

The Secretary, in consultation with the Advisory Board on Child Abuse and Neglect, shall ensure that a proportionate share of assistance under this subchapter is available for activities related to the prevention of child abuse and neglect.

§ 5104. Authorization of appropriations and funding requirements for child abuse and neglect and sexual abuse programs or projects

There are hereby authorized to be appropriated for the purposes of this subchapter $15,000,000 for the fiscal year ending June 30, 1974, $20,000,000 for the fiscal year ending June 30, 1975, $25,000,000 for the fiscal year ending June 30, 1976, and for the succeeding fiscal year, $25,000,000 for the fiscal year ending September 30, 1978, $27,500,000 for the fiscal year ending September 30, 1979, and $30,000,000 each for the fiscal years ending September 30, 1980, and September 30, 1981, respectively. There are hereby further authorized to be appropriated for the purposes of this subchapter $33,500,000 for fiscal year 1984, $40,000,000 for fiscal year 1985, $41,500,000 for fiscal year 1986, and $43,100,000 for fiscal year 1987. Of the funds appropriated for any fiscal year under this section except as provided in the succeeding sentence, (A) not less than $9,000,000 shall be available in each fiscal year to carry out section 5103(b) of this title (relating to State grants), (B) not less than $11,000,000 shall be available in each fiscal year to carry out sections 5103(a) (relating to demonstration or service projects), 5101(b)(1) and 5101(b)(3) (relating to information dissemination), 5101(b)(5) (relating to research), and 5103(c)(2) (relating to training, technical assistance, and information dissemination) of this title, giving special consideration to continued funding of child abuse and neglect programs or projects (previously funded by the Department of Health and Human Services) of national or regional scope and demonstrated effectiveness, (C) $5,000,000 shall be available in each such year for grants and contracts under section 5103(a) of this title, for identification, treatment, and prevention of sexual abuse, and (D) $5,000,000 shall be available in each such year for the purpose of making additional grants to the States to carry out the provisions of section 5103(c)(1) of this title. With respect to any fiscal year in which the total amount appropriated under this section is less than $30,000,000, funds shall first be available as provided in clauses (A) and (B) in the preceding sentence and of the remainder one-half shall be available as provided for in clause (C) and one-half as provided for in clause (D) in the preceding sentence.

§ 5105. Advisory Board on Child Abuse and Neglect

(a) Appointment; membership; representation from Federal agencies and general public; functions

The Secretary shall, within sixty days after January 31, 1974, appoint an Advisory Board on Child Abuse and Neglect (hereinafter referred to as the "Advisory Board"), which shall be composed of representatives from Federal agencies with responsibility for programs and activities related to child abuse and neglect, and not less than three members from the general public with experience or expertise in the field of child abuse and neglect. The Advisory Board shall assist the Secretary in coordinating programs and activities related to child abuse and neglect planned, administered, or assisted under this subchapter with such programs and activities planned, administered, or assisted by the Federal agencies whose representatives are members of the Advisory Board. The Advisory Board shall also assist the Secretary in the development of Federal standards for child abuse and neglect prevention and treatment programs and projects. The Advisory Board may be available, at the Secretary's request, to assist the Secretary in coordinating adoption-related activities of the Federal Government.

(b) Compensation; travel expenses and per diem

Members of the Advisory Board, other than those regularly employed by the Federal Government, while serving on business of the Advisory

Board, shall be entitled to receive compensation at a rate not in excess of the daily equivalent payable to a GS-18 employee under section 5332 of Title 5, including traveltime; and, while so serving away from their homes or regular places of business, they may be allowed travel expenses (including per diem in lieu of subsistence) as authorized by section 5703 of such title for persons in the Government service employed intermittently.

§ 5106. Coordination of Federal programs; regulations; arrangements

The Secretary shall promulgate regulations and make such arrangements as may be necessary or appropriate to ensure that there is effective coordination among programs related to child abuse and neglect under this subchapter and other such programs which are assisted by Federal funds.

§ 5107. Discretionary programs; authorization of appropriations

(a)(1) The Secretary of Health and Human Services, either directly, through grants to States and public and private, nonprofit organizations and agencies, or through jointly financed cooperative arrangements with States, public agencies, and other agencies and organizations, is authorized to provide for activities of national significance related to child abuse prevention and treatment and adoption reform, including operation of a national center to collect and disseminate information regarding child abuse and neglect, and operation of a national adoption information exchange system to facilitate the adoptive placement of children.

(2) The Secretary, in carrying out the provisions of this subsection, shall provide for the continued operation of the National Center on Child Abuse and Neglect in accordance with section 5101(a) of this title for each of the fiscal years 1982 and 1983.

(3) If the Secretary determines, in fiscal year 1982 or 1983, to carry out any of the activities described in section 5101(b) of this title, the Secretary shall carry out such activities through the National Center on Child Abuse and Neglect.

(b) There is authorized to be appropriated to carry out this section $12,000,000 for each of the fiscal years 1982 and 1983. Of the amounts appropriated under this subsection for any fiscal year, not less than $2,000,000 shall be available to carry out title II of the Child Abuse Prevention and Treatment and Adoption Reform Act of 1978 [42 U.S.C.A. § 5111 et seq.].

SUBCHAPTER II—ADOPTION OPPORTUNITIES

§ 5111. Congressional findings and declaration of purpose

The Congress hereby finds that the welfare of thousands of children in institutions and foster homes and disabled infants with life-threatening conditions may be in serious jeopardy and that some such children are in need of placement in permanent, adoptive homes; that many thousands of children remain in institutions or foster homes solely because of legal and other barriers to their placement in permanent, adoptive homes; that the majority of such children are of school age, handicapped, or both; that adoption may be the best alternative for assuring the healthy development of such children; that there are qualified persons seeking to adopt such children who are unable to do so because of barriers to their placement; and that, in order both to enhance the stability and love of the child's home environment and to avoid wasteful expenditures of public funds, such children should not have medically indicated treatment withheld from them, nor be maintained in foster care or institutions when adoption is appropriate and families for them can be found. It is, therefore, the purpose of this subchapter to facilitate the elimination of barriers to adoption and to provide permanent and loving home environments for children who would benefit by adoption, particularly children with special needs, including disabled infants with life-threatening conditions, by—

> (1) promoting the establishment of model adoption legislation and procedures in the States and territories of the United States in order to eliminate jurisdictional and legal obstacles to adoption; and

> (2) providing a mechanism for the Department of Health and Human Services to—

>> (A) promote quality standards for adoption services, pre-placement, post-placement, and post-legal adoption counseling, and standards to protect the rights of children in need of adoption;

>> (B) coordinate with other Federal departments and agencies, including the Bureau of the Census, to provide for a national adoption and foster care information data-gathering and analysis system; and

>> (C) maintain a national adoption exchange to bring together children who would benefit by adoption and qualified prospective adoptive parents who are seeking such children.

§ 5112. Model adoption legislation and procedures

(a) Issuance and publication of proposals based on recommendations of panel; comments by interested individuals, etc., and consultation; issuance and publication of final version; prohibition against conflict with interstate compacts

Not later than eighteen months after April 24, 1978, the Secretary of Health and Human Services (hereinafter referred to as the "Secretary") shall issue, based on the recommendations of the panel described in subsection (b) of this section, proposed model adoption legislation and procedures and publish such proposal in the Federal Register for comment. After soliciting and giving due consideration to the comments of interested individuals, groups, and organizations and consulting further with such panel, the Secretary shall issue and publish model adoption legislation and procedures which shall not conflict with the provisions of any interstate compact in operation pursuant to which States are making, supervising, or regulating placements of children.

(b) Panel; appointment, membership, functions, etc.

(1) Not later than ninety days after April 24, 1978, the Secretary shall appoint a panel (hereinafter referred to as the "panel") to be composed of not less than eleven nor more than seventeen members generally representative of public and voluntary organizations, agencies, and persons interested and with expertise and experience in facilitating the achievement of the purposes of this subchapter (including, but not limited to, national, State, and local child welfare organizations, including those representative of minorities, and adoptive parent organizations). The panel shall (A) review current conditions, practices, and laws relating to adoption, with special reference to their effect on facilitating or impeding the location of suitable adoptive homes for children who would benefit by adoption and the completion of suitable adoptions for such children; and (B) not later than twelve months after the date on which the members of the panel have been appointed, propose to the Secretary model (including adoption assistance agreement) legislation and procedures relating to adoption designed to facilitate adoption by families of all economic levels.

(2) The panel shall be terminated thirty days after the Secretary publishes the final model legislation and procedures pursuant to subsection (a) of this section.

(3) Members of the panel, other than those regularly employed by the Federal Government, while serving on business of the panel shall be enti-

tled to receive compensation at a rate not in excess of the daily equivalent of the rate payable to a GS-18 employee under section 5322[1] of title 5, including traveltime; and, while so serving away from their homes or regular places of business, they may be allowed travel expenses (including per diem in lieu of subsistence) as authorized by section 5703 of such title for persons in the Government service employed intermittently.

(c) Comprehensive adoption assistance legislation; encouragement and facilitation; establishment of model provisions; coordination with national, State and local organizations; improvement of State legislation

The Secretary shall take such steps as he or she deems necessary to encourage and facilitate the enactment in each State of comprehensive adoption assistance legislation and the establishment in each State of the model legislation and procedures published pursuant to subsection (a) of this section. The Secretary shall coordinate efforts to improve State legislation with national, State, and local child and family services organizations, including organizations representative of minorities and adoptive families.

(d) Review of legislation and procedures; facilitation of adoption opportunites for disabled infants with life-threatening conditions

The Secretary shall review all model adoption legislation and procedures published under this section and propose such changes as are considered appropriate to facilitate adoption opportunities for disabled infants with life-threatening conditions.

§ 5113. Informaton and service functions by appropriate administrative arrangement; establishment in Department of Health and Human Services; implementation authorities

(a) The Secretary shall establish in the Department of Health and Human Services an appropriate administrative arrangement to provide a centralized focus for planning and coordinating of all departmental activities affecting adoption and foster care and for carrying out the provisions of this subchapter. The Secretary shall make available such consultant services and personnel, together with appropriate administrative expenses, as are necessary for carrying out such purposes, including services to facilitate the adoption of children with special needs and particularly of disabled infants with life-threatening conditions and services to couples considering adoption of children with special needs.

(b) In connection with carrying out the provisions of this subchapter, the Secretary shall—

(1) Provide (after consultaton with other appropriate Federal departments and agencies, including the Bureau of the Census and appropriate State and local agencies) for the establishment and operation of a Federal adoption and foster care data-gathering and analysis system.

(2) conduct (directly or by grant to or contract with public or private nonprofit agencies or organizations) an education and training program on adoption, and prepare, publish, and disseminate (directly or by grant to or contract with public or private nonprofit agencies and organizations) to all interested parties, public and private agencies and organizations (including, but not limited to, hospitals, health care and family planning clinics, and social services agencies), and governmental bodies, information and education and training materials regarding adoption and adoption assistance programs;

(3) notwithstanding any other provision of law, provide (directly or by grant to or contract with public or private nonprofit agencies or organizations) for (A) the operation of a national adoption information exchange system (including only such information as is necessary to facilitate the adoptive placement of children, utilizing computers and data processing methods to assist in the location of children who would benefit by adoption and in the placement in adoptive homes of children awaiting adoption); and (B) the coordination of such system with similar State and regional systems;

(4) provide (directly or by grant to or contract with public or private nonprofit agencies or organizations, including adoptive family groups and minority groups) for the provision of technical assistance in the planning, improving, developing, and carrying out of programs and activities relating to adoption;

(5) encourage involvement of corporations and small businesses in supporting adoption as a positive family-strengthening option, including the establishment of adoption benefit programs for employees who adopt children;

(6) continue to study the nature, scope, and effects of the placement of children in adoptive homes (not including the homes of stepparents or relatives of the child in question) by persons or agencies which are not licensed by or subject to regulation by any governmental entity; and

(7) consult with other appropriate Federal departments and agencies in order to promote maximum coordination of the services and benefits provided under programs carried out by such departments and agencies with those carried out by the Secretary, and provide for the coordination of such aspects of all programs within the Department of Health and Human Services relating to adoption.

§5114. Study and report of unlicensed or unregulated adoption placements

The Secretary shall provide for a study (the results of which shall be reported to the appropriate committees of the Congress not later than eighteen months after April 24, 1978) designed to determine the nature, scope, and effects of the interstate (and, to the extent feasible, intrastate) placement of children in adoptive homes (not including the homes of stepparents or relatives of the child in question) by persons or agencies which are not licensed by or subject to regulation by any governmental entity.

§ 5115. Authorization of appropriations

There are authorized to be appropriated $5,000,000 for the fiscal year ending September 30, 1978, such sums as may be necessary for the succeeding three fiscal years, and $5,000,000 for each of the fiscal years 1984, 1985, 1986, and 1987, to carry out this subchapter.

SUBCHAPTER III—STATE FUNDING MECHANISMS

§5116. Congressional findings and statement of purpose

(a) The Congress finds that—

(1) disturbing increases have occurred in recent years in the numbers of younger Americans who are abused;

(2) many children who run away from home, who fall prey to pornography and prostitution, who suffer from a dependency on alcohol and drugs, and who become juvenile offenders, have been victims of child abuse;

(3) research has shown that abuse tends to repeat itself, and many times parents who abuse their children were once victims themselves;

(4) given the increased demand for treatment and crisis intervention in child abuse and neglect cases, Federal funds distributed to

States are most often used for treatment and little is left for prevention efforts;

(5) since 1980 some States have begun to recognize the critical need for prevention efforts, and trust funds (generated by surcharges on marriage licenses, birth certificates or divorce actions, or by special checkoffs on income tax returns) are being established to allow such States to pay for child abuse and neglect prevention activities despite depressed State economies and budget cutbacks;

(6) in recognition of the increased cases of child abuse and neglect, other States have established significant funds for child abuse and neglect prevention activities through direct appropriations; and

(7) the Nation cannot afford to ignore the importance of preventing child abuse.

(b) It is the purpose of this subchapter, by providing for Federal challenge grants, to encourage States to establish and maintain trust funds or other funding mechanisms, including appropriations to support child abuse and neglect prevention activities.

§ 5116a. Definitions

As used in this subchapter—

(1) the term "Secretary" means the Secretary of Health and Human Services; and

(2) the term "State" means each of the several States, the District of Columbia and the Commonwealth of Puerto Rico.

§ 5116b. Grants authorized

(a) Authority of Secretary

The Secretary is authorized, in accordance with the provisions of this subchapter, to make grants to eligible States.

(b) Payments; fiscal years

Payments under this subchapter may be made in any fiscal year following the establishment of a funding mechanism for child abuse and neglect prevention activities.

(c) Authorization of appropriations

There is authorized to be appropriated such sums as are necessary to carry out the provisions of this subchapter for the fiscal year 1985 and for each of the four succeeding fiscal years.

§ 5116c. State eligibility

Any State is eligible for a grant under this subchapter for any fiscal year if such State has established or maintained in the previous fiscal year a trust fund or other funding mechanism, including appropriations, which is available only for child abuse and neglect prevention activities, including activities which—

(1) provide statewide educational and public informational seminars for the purpose of developing appropriate public awareness regarding the problems of child abuse and neglect;

(2) encourage professional persons and groups to recognize and deal with problems of child abuse and neglect;

(3) make information about the problems of child abuse and neglect available to the public and organizations and agencies which deal with problems of child abuse and neglect; and

(4) encourage the development of community prevention programs, including—

(A) community-based educational programs on parenting, prenatal care, perinatal bonding, child development, basic child care, care of children with special needs, coping with family stress, personal safety and sexual abuse prevention training for children, and self-care training for latchkey children; and

(B) community-based programs relating to crisis care, aid to parents, child-abuse counseling, peer support groups for abusive or potentially abusive parents and their children, lay health visitors, respite or crisis child care, and early identification of families where the potential for child abuse and neglect exists.

§ 5116d. Limitations

(a) Grant amount; definition

(1) Any grant made to any eligible State under this subchapter in any fiscal year shall be equal to the lesser of—

(A) 25 percent of the total amount made available by such State for child abuse and neglect prevention activities and collected in the previous fiscal year in a trust fund (excluding any interest income from the principal of such fund) or through any other funding mechanism, including appropriations; or

(B) an amount equal to 50 cents times the number of children residing in such State according to the most current data available to the Secretary.

(2) For purposes of clause (B) of paragraph (1), the term "children" means individuals who have not attained the age of majority, as defined by such State.

(b) Application; contents; approval; Secretary; notice of disapproval; hearing

(1) No grant may be made to any state until an application is made to the Secretary containing such information as the Secretary deems essential to carry out the purposes and provisions of this subchapter. Each application shall

(A) specify that the trust fund advisory board, or in States without a trust fund mechanism, the State liaison agency to the National Center on Child Abuse and Neglect, established by section 5101 of this title, will be responsible for administering and awarding of the Federal grants to eligible recipients carrying out activities described in section 5116c of this title;

(B) provide assurances that any assistance received under this subchapter shall not be used as a source for non-Federal funds for the matching requirements of any other provision of Federal law; and

(C) provide for keeping records and making such reasonable reports as the Secretary deems essential to carry out the purposes and provisions of this subchapter.

(2) The Secretary shall approve any application that meets the requirements of this subsection, and the Secretary shall not disapprove any such application except after reasonable notice of the Secretary's intention to disapprove and opportunity for a hearing with respect to the disapproval.

§ 5116e. Withholding

Whenever the Secretary, after reasonable notice to any State and opportunity for hearing within the State, finds that there has been a failure to comply with any provision of this subchapter, the Secretary shall notify the State that further payments will not be made under this subchapter until the Secretary is satisfied that there is no longer any such failure to comply. Until the Secretary is so satisfied, no further payments shall be made under this subchapter.

§ 5116f. Audit

The Comptroller General of the United States, and any of his duly authorized representatives, shall have access for the purpose of audit and examination to any books, documents, papers, and records of any applicant and any other entity receiving assistance under this subchapter that are pertinent to the sums received and disbursed under this subchapter.

§ 5116g. Report; Congress

The Secretary shall prepare and submit to the Congress at the end of each year a compilation and analysis of any reports submitted by eligible States under section 5116d(b)(1)(C) of this title.

Appendix B

Notice of Motion to Disqualify the District Attorney

California vs. Buckey

MUNICIPAL COURT OF THE STATE OF CALIFORNIA
FOR THE COUNTY OF LOS ANGELES

THE PEOPLE OF THE STATE OF CALIFORNIA,	Case No. A 750900
Plaintiff,	NOTICE OF AND MOTION TO DISQUALIFY DISTRICT AT-
v.	TORNEY, STATEMENT OF FACTS, AND MEMORANDUM
RAYMOND CHARLES BUCKEY, et al.,	OF POINTS AND AUTHORI- TIES CAL. PENAL CODE § 1424
Defendants.	

TO THE ATTORNEY GENERAL OF THE STATE OF
CALIFORNIA AND THE DISTRICT ATTORNEY OF THE
COUNTY OF LOS ANGELES:

PLEASE TAKE NOTICE that, on Tuesday, June 5, 1984, at 9:00
a.m., in Division 30, before an appropriate judge having jurisdiction in this matter, defendant RAYMOND CHARLES BUCKEY,
by and through his attorney of record, Daniel G. Davis, will move
to disqualify interim District Attorney, Robert H. Philibosian and
the entire office of the Los Angeles District Attorney.

This motion is being brought pursuant to California Penal Code
Section 1424, on the grounds that interim District Attorney Robert
H. Philibosian has undertaken prosecution of the instant case with
conflicts of interest rendering unlikely the defendant would receive
a fair trial in this matter. This motion will be based on its contents,
any supplemental pleadings, the entire court record, and evidence
adduced and arguments presented at hearing.

Dated: May 24, 1984   _____

            DANIEL G. DAVIS
            Attorney for Defendant
            Raymond Charles Buckey

STATEMENT OF FACTS

The following statement is provided pursuant to the specific requirements of Section 1424 of the Penal Code that a motion to disqualify a District Attorney "must set forth a statement of facts relevant to the claimed
disqualification." A declaration is not required. Nonetheless, the following statement is being submitted substantially in the spirit of a declaration, insofar as its contents are supported by good faith information and
belief. Moreover, because of the serious nature of the claims, effort has
been made to provide a succinct statement.

The scope of the disqualification sought begins, specifically, with interim District Attorney, Robert H. Philibosian, and extends to the en-
tirety of his deputy staff in the Los Angeles Office. Where mentioned, the
actions of law enforcement representatives are attributed to the District
Attorney, beginning sometime in September 1983 and extending to the
present, an approximate eight (8) month period.

From that experience, it is respectfully asserted that three (3) primary grounds emerge for disqualification of the District Attorney:

(1) Interim District Attorney, Robert H. Philibosian, has publicly exploited the McMartin Preschool case, in abuse of his powers as prosecutor and obligations to insure fair and impartial prosecution, in order to gain political name recognition and advantage.

(2) Interim District Attorney, Robert H. Philibosian, and his staff, have promulgated extrajudicial statements violative of ethical standards for prosecutors.

(3) Interim District Attorney, Robert H. Philibosian, and his staff, have implemented investigative and other prosecutorial procedures which, in themselves, have been psychologically and socially harmful to the children involved.

1. Political Exploitation of Prosecutorial Powers

Sometime after the arrest of Raymond Charles Buckey in September 1983, interim District Attorney Robert H. Philibosian retained the services of political advisors to direct him in his campaign for his presently appointed position. In response, Philibosian's political advisors undertook research and surveys, determining Philibosian was in need of better public name recognition, and that he should publicly identify himself with criminal prosecution involving child molestation or abuse charges.

Accordingly, Philibosian seized upon the McMartin Preschool case and began intensely zealous efforts to exploit the case for political publicity value. In so doing, Philibosian directly and indirectly promoted extensive media disclosure of incremental rumors, suspicions and information, developed through his office's investigation of the case. Throughout, Philibosian presented himself to the public in close association with the prosecution of the case, often choosing to seat himself at the counsel table, during the most highly publicized aspect of the case. On each such occasion, he made no statement or action within the courtroom, but merely sat in front of the attending public and television cameras. Thereafter, he would conduct an informal press conference outside the courtroom, expressing a variety of opinions, purported facts and accusations regarding the case, the defendants and evidence.

Conflict between politics and prosecution have been actual and apparent in literally all of the aspects subject to the discretion of the District Attorney, including release of criminal records, surveillance of defendants, arrest of defendants, bail recommendations, discovery of evidence, intimidation of defendants and their defense staff and prolonged failure in filing a complaint.

Early in the investigation, Raymond Buckey's prior arrest record was released to the public. Shortly after original charges were dismissed against him, he and his entire family were subjected to unnecessarily intense and harrassing surveillance. Although several defendants made explicit requests for voluntary surrender, the District Attorney instead caused surprise physical arrest substantially covered by news media, for no other purpose but to obtain political notoriety and advantage.

On March 22, 1984, all defendants were subjected to extremely high recommendations of bail. Once some of the defendants qualified for bail, however, the District Attorney then quickly moved for "no bail" conditions, to the considerable financial and emotional loss of the defendants. Similarly, after the District Attorney agreed to release of costly tapes to the defense, it reversed its position, again, to the delay and extreme financial loss of the defendants.

For a period of approximately two (2) months of April and May 1984, the District Attorney has failed and delayed in filing a complaint in this matter. As a result, judges attempting to move the case through appropriate proceedings have acted with inconsistent and uncertain jurisdiction. Consequently, virtually all the Municipal Court proceedings have become a waste of time, public facilities and funds.

Finally, less than two weeks before interim District Attorney Robert H. Philibosian enters a primary election for his position, a complaint is now being filed in this matter. Predictably, the District Attorney will dismiss the priorily existing indictment, and attempt literally to begin proceedings anew. This clear abuse of the power to dismiss charges and refile a complaint is timed to reestablish the interim District Attorney's name in the minds of the voters.

And more recently, information is surfacing that law enforcement representatives of the District Attorney have been undertaking a series of abusive procedures in connection with this case. Deputy Sheriffs in the Los Angeles County Jail, on one occasion, placed a known criminal informant into the same jail cell with Raymond Buckey, for purposes of attempting to induce or concoct adverse evidence against him. Other Deputies of the Los Angeles Sheriff's Department have undertaken to intimidate and interrogate defense investigators and the defendants themselves, under the guise of conducting investigation of unrelated matters. And most recently, District Attorney investigators have begun conducting unannounced interrogation and intimidation of potential defense witnesses or persons supportive of the defendants.

2. *Extrajudicial Statements Violative of Ethical Standards for Prosecutors.*

A thorough examination of information directly and indirectly promulgated by the District Attorney to the news media reveals an actual or apparent attempt to resolve the case by publicity in advance of trial. All information generated by secret grand jury proceedings has been revealed only by the District Attorney and, on one occasion, by a Superior Court judge. The District Attorney has presented his statements of evidence in the case as proven and established. Knowing that defense counsel were ethically constrained or subject to order not to reveal the contents of grand jury proceedings, the District Attorney early took advantage in releasing one-sided parts of information adverse to the defendants.

Of particular note was the publicized allegation by the District Attorney that the McMartin Preschool was primarily dedicated to procuring young children for commercial, pornographic purposes. The District Attorney also asserted income from the school was a fraud upon the parents and children. Yet, as late as May 18, 1984, the District Attorney finally and reluctantly admitted there exists no evidence of pornographic photographs, much less, connection of the McMartin Preschool to an underground market for child pornography.

Indirectly, the District Attorney has funneled one-sided increments of information to the public, through select members of the news media and the prosecution's own witnesses. Using television newscasters and child counsellors, the District Attorney has encouraged, induced and aided in the dissemination of information that otherwise would be inadmissible in court, as irrelevant, remote or hearsay. Through the same newscasters and child counsellors, moreover, the District Attorney has publicly criticized defense counsel and tactics—in advance often even of defense attorneys entering into the case.

In so doing, the District Attorney has manipulated and exploited both the news media and child counselling services, for purposes of obtaining both political advantage in the campaign for District Attorney and hostilizing the public towards the defendants and their right to a fair and impartial trial.

3. *Prosecutorial Procedures Harmful to Children*

Since the commencement of investigation in this matter, beginning in early September 1983, and continuing through the present date, the purported child victims in this case have been subject to investigative and other preparatory procedures of the District Attorney. These procedures were designed and implemented without adequate consideration for the real psychological and social harm to all children involved. Through the news media, law enforcement and child counselors, the children examined on behalf of the District Attorney's Office have been terrorized, traumatized and hostilized against defendants in this matter.

The Manhattan Beach Police Department sent a form letter to all parents whose children then had been currently a student at the Preschool. Contrary to any respected procedure for investigating child molestation allegations, parents were directed to conduct examination and evaluation of their own children, without any training, supervision or guidance from experienced child counselling personnel.

Thereafter, all responding parents were directed to the Children's Institute International where they underwent standardized and depersonalized indoctrination and evaluation. Many parents were separated from their children and subjected to indoctrination sessions with purported counsellors, who incited them to anger, loss of independent perspective, emotional trauma, despair and sense of helplessness. The children themselves were subjected to an organization and procedure substantially based on a presumption that all Preschool students had been either witnesses or victims of molestation.

Substantially, with total disregard of the defendants' possible innocence, a three-agency machine was created to ready, rehearse and educate young children as witnesses in forthcoming criminal proceedings. The first agency involved was Children's Institute International, which readily reached conclusions of molestation, for further processing to law enforcement. The second agency consisted of the Manhattan Beach Police Department and increasingly District Attorney investigators, which functioned to convert the institute's determination of molestation into a police report in support of criminal prosecution. The final stage directly affecting the children was that still in operation today, the office of the District Attorney.

While interim District Attorney, Robert H. Philibosian, has exploited the McMartin Preschool case for political name identity, he has ignored his campaign's harmful consequences to the children. His own investigative and preparatory procedures have already subjected many parents and their children to frightful, prejudiced and hostilized indoctrination and interrogation by law enforcement and coordinating agencies. As a result, many children and their parents may well withdraw from participating in ultimate courtroom proceedings—not because of anything done by the defendants or their counsel, but because of what already the District Attorney has put them through.

Perhaps, more importantly, many children and parents who could act to exculpate the defendants have withdrawn altogether from any association with the McMartin Preschool case. The likelihood of more parents and children removing themselves from participation is all the more enhanced, if not insured, because of District Attorney Philibosian's reoccuring penchant for publicly politicizing his association with the case.

Dated: May 24, 1984   Respectfully submitted,

DANIEL G. DAVIS
Attorney for Defendant
Raymond Charles Buckey

MEMORANDUM OF POINTS AND AUTHORITIES

1. The Courts have both statutory and inherent judicial power to disqualify the District Attorney, in order to assure fairness to the accused and sustain public confidence in the integrity and impartiality of the criminal justice system.

People v. Conner, 34 Cal.3d 141, 146 (1983).

2. A motion to recuse the District Attorney should be granted whenever a conflict of interest exists that would render it unlikely that a defendant would receive a fair trial.

CAL. PENAL CODE, Section 1424.

3. The term "conflict" within the meaning of Section 1424 exists whenever it is reasonably apparent the District Attorney has not fairly and impartially exercised its discretionary powers in the prosecution of the case.

People v. Conner, 34 Cal.3d 141, 148 (1983); *People v. Superior Court (Greer)*, 19 Cal.3d 255, 268–69 (1977).

4. The District Attorney is obligated by his position of public power to avoid, as much as possible, the appearance of impropriety or conflict of interest, in the exercise of his official duties.

People v. Rhodes, 12 Cal.3d 180, 185 (1974); American Bar Association Standards Relating to the Prosecution Function, Std. 1.2.

5. The District Attorney must remain free from personal involvement appearing to bias his judgment by factors extraneous to his objective and impartial handling of a case. Otherwise, he should be disqualified from the affected case in order to insure

(1) the integrity of the fact-finding process,

(2) the fairness or appearance of fairness of court proceedings,

(3) the orderly and efficient administration of justice, and

(4) public trust and confidence in the judicial system.

People v. Municipal Court (Henry), 98 Cal.App.3d 690, 693 (1979).

6. Even the mere appearance that a District Attorney is using his influence and position to further the success of his public career operates to weaken the public's confidence in the system of criminal justice.

See People v. Rhodes, 12 Cal.3d 180, 186 (1974).

7. The District Attorney is obligated not only to prosecute but also to seek justice. He is a representative not of an ordinary party to a controversy, but of the government itself, whose obligation to prosecute impartially is as compelling as its obligation to govern at all. Accordingly, in criminal prosecutions, the District Attorney's primary interest is not that he win a case, but that justice be done. For a District Attorney, the normal advocate's interest in the result of the case must be subordinate to the demands of prosecutorial impartiality.

People v. Conner, Cal.3d 141, 148 (1983); *People v. Municipal Court (Byars),* 77 Cal.App.3d 294, 300 (1978).

8. The prosecutor should not exploit his office by means of personal publicity connected with the case before trial, during trial and thereafter.

American Bar Association Project on the Standards for Criminal Justie: Standards Relating to the Prosecution Function, Std. 1.3.

9. The prosecutor should not release certain types of information, and should be aware of the dangers of prejudice in making pretrial disclosure of the anticipated testimony of prospective witnesses and opinions concerning evidence or argument in the case, whether or not it is anticipated such evidence or argument will be used at trial.

National District Attorney's Association, National Prosecution Standards, Std. 26.2b.

10. The prosecution shall familiarize local police agencies with the state, court, constitutional and case law concerning fair trial and free press, and shall encourage them to adopt policies which will protect both the rights of the individual and the ability of the state to proceed in criminal prosecution.

National District Attorney's Association, National Prosecution Standards, Std. 26.3.

11. The lawyer should try his cases in court and not in the newspaper or through other news media. He should not publish, cause to be published, or aid or abet in any way, directly or indirectly, the publication of any newspaper or other documentary medium, or by radio, television or other device, of material concerning a case on trial or pending, or anticipated litigation, calculated or which might reasonably be expected to interfere in any matter, or to any degree, with a fair trial in the courts or otherwise prejudice the due administration of justice. If extreme circumstances of a particular case require a statement to the public, it should not be made anonymously and reference to the facts should not go beyond quotation from the records and papers on file in court or other official documents. No statement should be made which indicates intended proof or

what witnesses will be called, or which amounts to comment or argument on the merits of the case.

Code of Trial Conduct, American College of Trial Lawyers, Std. 24: Publicity Pending Litigation (DR7-107).

12. A photocopy of Rule 3.6 regarding trial publicity of the Model Rules of Professional Conduct, adopted by the American Bar Association, is attached to this memorandum for further consideration.

13. The District Attorney and law enforcement representatives are first and primarily responsible for protecting the needs of involved children in molestation prosecutions from unnecessary psychological harm. CAL. PENAL CODE, Section 288(c).

Dated: May 24, 1984   Respectfully submitted,

_____

DANIEL G. DAVIS
Attorney for Defendant
Raymond Charles Buckey